The American Leadership Tradition

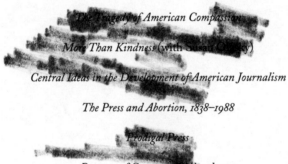

Marvin Olasky

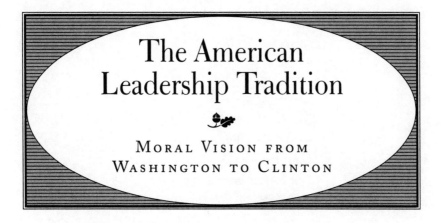

The American
Leadership Tradition

MORAL VISION FROM
WASHINGTON TO CLINTON

THE FREE PRESS

THE FREE PRESS
A Division of Simon & Schuster Inc.
1230 Avenue of the Americas
New York, NY 10020

Copyright © 1999 by Directed Reporting, Inc.
THE FREE PRESS *and colophon are trademarks of Simon & Schuster Inc.*

Designed by Jenny Dossin
Manufactured in the United States of America

1 3 5 7 9 10 8 6 4 2

Library of Congress Cataloging-in-Publication Data

Olasky, Marvin N.
   The American leadership tradition : moral vision from
Washington to Clinton
   p. cm.
   Includes bibliographical references and index.
   1. Presidents—United States—Sexual behavior.   2. States-
men—United States—Sexual behavior.   3. Presidents—United
States—Professional ethics.   4. Statesmen—United States—
Professional ethics.   5. United States—Politics and Govern-
ment—Moral and ethical aspects.   I. Title.
E176.1.043 1999   98-43422
973'.09—dc21   CIP

ISBN 0-684-83449-9

For Pete, David, Daniel, and Benjamin

Contents

Foreword

If you have picked up this book not an already dedicated Olaskyite, and thus prepared to read every page, if you are thumbing through these pages to see if you should invest yourself in the text, let me settle the question straight off.

Of the tens of thousands of books published each year, all but a few are written to do no more than entertain. The vast majority are soon forgotten, though some do become fad sensations like *The One Minute Manager* (the title says it all), or the various 6, 8, 10, or 12 steps to eternal bliss. But most serve their greatest purpose perhaps helping vacationers to while away their time at the beach.

But now and again, a book comes along that sets forth a great idea and that in turn changes the way people think about fundamental questions. Such books can shape societies and steer the current of history. This was surely the case when Jonathan Edwards's *Narrative of Surprising Conversions* fueled a massive revival on both sides of the Atlantic in the colonial era, or when Adam Smith's *Wealth of Nations* changed the way the modern world thought about economics. Or one could look to the darker side and suggest Marx's *Manifesto*. Some books change the course of great debates.

It is perhaps not too great a stretch to suggest that a generation or two hence, historians will look back at this era and put Marvin Olasky among the pantheon of seminal thinkers who have changed the way people and societies think. For it was Marvin Olasky's masterful work *The Tragedy of American Compassion* that profoundly influenced the great welfare debate of the eighties and nineties. Olasky the historian put the issue in such clear historical focus that the claims of modern politicians were exposed for what they are, flawed utopianism. No one was cited more frequently than Olasky in the debates that raged in the Capitol, resulting in even liberals vowing to end "welfare as we know it." And that's just what the political establishment did. It was a historic turning point, the first time the push for big government truly stalled, and that push has happily been in retreat ever since. The momentum was reversed. That is no small accomplishment. Olasky deserves much of the credit for it, and anyone who can do that is someone worth listening to.

And you should listen now because Olasky has tackled a subject in this book of immense importance in the libertarian nineties, a decade that has redefined tolerance to mean the suppression of all moral discourse and the acceptance of any private behavior without regard to its public consequences. "What people do in private is no one's business but theirs," so goes the popular refrain. We're told that private morality—or immorality—has no effect on public policy; and the consistent high ratings of President Clinton during the heat of charges of sexual misconduct in office suggest that most Americans share this view.

The temptation is great to buckle under to this hue and cry. After all, the nation is at peace, the economy continues to beam, and the world has gained a new respect for America. So what if what our leaders do in private disgusts or dismays us? What business is it of ours? Isn't it overall job performance that counts, as President Clinton never tires of reminding us?

Now Marvin Olasky challenges that notion as he challenged the welfare myth, with a serious work of historical scholarship. He shows, among other things, the many links between private morality and public policy. His research should persuade even the most self-indulgent and permissive among us that it does matter for the common weal and even for the national security whether or not high public officials lie as a matter of course or convenience; whether they are faithful to their wives or prone to sexual adventurism; whether their god is power, money, or self rather than the God of the Bible and our American fore-bears. Here is indisputable evidence of the role of private morality in civic leadership. Olasky's book should lay to rest once and for all the view that argues the separation of the two.

This will not be a welcome book for many, for it lays to rest the claim that one's moral conduct is a strictly private matter. As a people, Americans are connected by the same moral threads; and when influ-ential and outspoken members of society decide to begin unraveling the web in order to gain a little more "freedom" for themselves to "swing," they jeopardize the safety and prosperity of us all, as the author repeatedly shows. The proponents of modern moral nihilism will surely take this book seriously, for they know that when these issues are measured up against the clear lessons of history, their cause is doomed.

And those who believe in unchanging standards of moral conduct, standards that must be applied by all alike, and who see in those stan-dards a reflection of the God of Scripture and the Judeo-Christian tra-dition, should use Olasky's book as an apologetic for the case for a more principled leadership for America—in every arena of society—and for the world.

In the pages that follow, you will thrill over the inspiring models of moral leadership in our nation's history; and even more important, you will be equipped to offer answers to Americans groping in the moral fog of the nineties.

One can only pray that Olasky's work as a historian, which helped reverse the momentum of the march of big government, will be simi-larly used to halt the slide into moral despair.

CHARLES COLSON

Acknowledgments

Throughout the research, writing, and editing of this book, my wife, Susan, has been both sounding board and sound advisor. She has been kind in this way through twenty-two years of marriage and through many books that could have produced great tension. Long-term unions, like books, can be divided into friction and nonfriction; Susan writes nonfriction.

The four children to whom this book is dedicated have helped a middle-aged history writer to think about not only providing a legacy but telling a story. Their history-related schoolwork has moved from silhouette-cutting in elementary school to reputation-ripping in college, but what they often have not received in their classes is a sense of living, breathing (sometimes huffing and puffing) individuals thrust into conflict. I want to give them that.

I am grateful to the Progress & Freedom Foundation, the Capital Research Center, and particularly to friends Howard and Roberta Ahmanson of Fieldstead & Company. My thanks also go to Free Press editors Bruce Nichols and Albert DePetrillo, who pushed my storytelling mind to wrap up the loose ends, and to copy editor Charlotte Gross.

Introduction

Last week, as I was putting the final touches on this book, the talk shows were full of sad mutterings and indignant sputterings: "Private activities don't matter." "They all do it." "America down the drain." "We should have paid attention."

Although callers did not couch these statements in theoretical terms, each opinion represented a way of looking at history generally, and more specifically a way of looking at the lives of leaders.

The first statement, "Private activities don't matter," is probably the dominant view among both Washington journalists and the general public: A president's religious views or sexual practices have no relation to his public policy decisions. That separation of private and public has the merit of helping us refrain from gossip, but it also deprives us of important information. This book's study of men like Lincoln and Wilson shoots a hole through the compartmentalization theory. *The American Leadership Tradition* shows the links between religious beliefs and policy decisions, and also the links between lying about adultery and lying about other matters.

The second statement, "They all do it," is the cynical view: Even if there is a spillover from private to public, it is useless to look for a clean leader because all are dirty. If true, we might as well stop the periodic attempts to throw the bums out because new bums will replace them. This examination of leaders like Washington and Cleveland, however, shows that the theory of immoral equivalence is not true. Some statesmen have been libertines, but others have stood personally and philosophically for both liberty and virtue—and the choice of leaders makes an enormous difference.

The third statement, "America down the drain," is the lament of disappointed idealists. We have seen civic decline in America over the past several decades, but *The American Leadership Tradition* shows that the good old days had heroes like Jackson but also rogues like Henry Clay. Nor are recent presidencies pure tales of disintegration: John F. Kennedy worshipped sex and ignored God, but he functioned well amid some crises. There are always surprises and comebacks, and there is always hope.

The last statement, "We should have paid attention," is the lament of disillusioned liberals. Chris Matthews expressed this poignantly on CNBC when he said, "We, 49 percent of us at least, bought this box of cereal called Bill Clinton. Inside some of us expected to find, perhaps, one of those little plastic toys slipped in between the box and the wax paper. Instead, we opened the box one winter day this year to find not a harmless novelty item, but a spider, an eight-legged hairy bug crawling in what we expected to be a hearty January breakfast. We now have to live with it, including those of us who were so hungry for leadership in this aging century that we heard it and discounted back when we had the choice . . . that telltale scratching in the box."

This book is for conservatives and liberals, for citizens thinking through their votes and journalists like Chris Matthews thinking through their responsibility. Except for the last chapter, it is not about Bill Clinton, but about ways to listen more closely for that telltale scratching in the box, ways for both Democrats and Republicans, as they look toward presidential races of the year 2000 and beyond, to develop some reliable early warning systems.

Although the scandal headlines of 1998 make this book seem topical, it actually had its genesis in anticipation of an anniversary: Fifty years ago Richard Hofstadter fired a shot heard round the historians' world. His book *The American Political Tradition, and the Men Who*

Made It, published in 1948, became a standard text for a generation of college history courses, and won a general readership as well. Hofstadter's secular, liberal approach and writing skill produced a book that has been one of the most influential and widely read historical volumes of the past half century, but he did not discuss the way leaders wrestled with spiritual or personal problems.

Hofstadter did not provide an early warning system. His rock was economics, and on that rock he built his analysis, as did most of his colleagues. "My generation," he wrote, "was raised in the conviction that the basic motive power in political behavior is the economic interest of groups." At one point in *The American Political Tradition,* just in passing, Hofstadter did a drive-by shooting of those who emphasized moral basics—they have a "crude" theology and a "childish conception of religion"—but that segment of America seemed hardly relevant to public affairs issues in 1948.

What was important in 1948 was avoiding another depression: The first paragraph of Hofstadter's introduction to *The American Political Tradition* emphasized his book's usefulness in dealing with the "keen feeling of insecurity" that stuck to many Americans after "unstable booms and the abysmal depression." Hofstadter wrote that most of his colleagues assumed that "another severe economic slump" would arise out of an erratic private enterprise system, and he naturally emphasized ways in which political leaders had moved to tame the capitalist beast.

A half century later Americans have a "keen feeling of insecurity" at least as great as that of 1948, but the causes are different. That severe economic slump never arrived, but statistics of illegitimacy, abortion, and divorce, as well as a much-discussed coarsening of American culture generally, suggest a severe ethical slump. Fifty years ago Hofstadter was motivated to see whether and how leading American political figures worshipped Mammon. Now, it is more relevant to see whether and how key leaders worshipped God, whether and how they were able to keep their lusts under control, and what effect their beliefs and personal lives had on the public policies and political positions they adopted.

The proposition of this book is that assessing religious beliefs and sexual morality is crucial to understanding motivations and actions of

American leaders, and that even excellent writing like Hofstadter's lacks something essential when it emphasizes political rhetoric and ignores both soul and body. Religion and sex seem like a strange combination, except among those few ancient faiths that made worship and adultery identical through the use of shrine prostitutes. One goal of biblical religion, however, has been to bind (Latin, *religare*) its adherents to long-term thinking, to help them overcome impulses toward immediate gratification, of which sex may be the strongest.

The Bible repeatedly attacks adultery, not because it is necessarily the greatest sin, but because it shows a breaking of vows that regularly leads to other ruptures. People, of course, are not always of a piece. A statesman with a good marriage might not be able to run a good government. A statesman who worships sex rather than God is not always more likely to seek immediate gratification in public policy areas as well. But it is unusual for lifelong recklessness and lifelong discipline to be combined in one leader, and when they appear to be, shouldn't we watch for Jekyll to turn into Hyde? As Edmund Burke wrote, "great men are the landmarks and guideposts of the state." And when guideposts misdirect, citizens who follow their leaders begin to wallow.

The thirteen individuals profiled in the pages that follow provide landmarks. Most of them were selected by Hofstadter fifty years ago: He chose "figures of singular human interest who were excellent representatives of main currents in American political sentiment." Each of us wrote about the major presidents, and also found Henry Clay (an early Bill Clinton) impossible to resist. Hofstadter added John C. Calhoun and Wendell Phillips from the nineteenth century, but I wrote about Booker T. Washington and John D. Rockefeller, each representative in different ways of an era that de-emphasized politics. Hofstadter profiled Herbert Hoover, I looked at Kennedy and Clinton. Like Hofstadter, I have not used footnotes, but a complete bibliography lists references.

The American Leadership Tradition is intended to be provocative; the research has increased my esteem for several of those often classified as "great," but it has also forced me to refuse to polish the brass on some other statues. This book is also intended to be succinct; each of the thirteen leaders profiled within has merited volumes of biography, but I have tried to convey briefly a sense of American cultural movement by providing evocative detail and then organizing the information into two main acts separated by an interlude.

The first five chapters profile statesmen from the American Revolution through the Civil War: George Washington and the successor who partly imitated him but had different values, Thomas Jefferson; Andrew Jackson and his competitor who could never make it to the White House, Henry Clay; and Abraham Lincoln, who in many ways synthesized the divided heritage of Washington, Jefferson, Jackson, and Clay. A post–Civil War interlude examines leadership outside government by profiling Booker T. Washington and John D. Rockefeller, representative leaders from a period when newspapers often treated news from the capital as insignificant.

We then move to Act Two, five chapters on leaders from the 1880s through the 1960s: Grover Cleveland, Theodore Roosevelt, Woodrow Wilson, Franklin D. Roosevelt, and John F. Kennedy. Here the movement is less thesis and antithesis and more a clear path toward defining deviancy down: Cleveland and Theodore Roosevelt developed firm ethical standards as they grew older, Wilson and Franklin Roosevelt looser ones, and Kennedy virtually none at all on a personal level. The book closes with a chapter on the helter-skelter tendencies of recent years, perhaps exemplified by Bill Clinton.

Throughout, the emphasis is on storytelling, not sermonizing, but I have kept in mind what Theodore Roosevelt said in his 1912 address as president of the American Historical Association: "The greatest historian should also be a great moralist. It is no proof of impartiality to treat wickedness and goodness on the same level." A lesser historian can attempt the same. If we look out and refuse to see any shadows, our eyes are fooling us, and we can expect at least six more weeks of winter.

Act One

(1789–1865)

CHAPTER I

George Washington

One guest on a Geraldo Rivera talk show concerning Clinton scandals argued for the "everyone does it" position by claiming that George Washington was the father of his country's immorality. Washington, she joked, probably left splinters from his false teeth in someone's thigh, but no one was looking to report such matters then. Not true, but at least such a comment gets us away from thinking of Washington the monument, frozen-faced in Gilbert Stuart paintings. It's good to remember that, despite the "I cannot tell a lie" legends, few of young Washington's neighbors saw him as a candidate for storybook sainthood. His life was a struggle to become a man of one piece, with private and public lives in harmony.

Born in 1732, Washington was homeschooled largely by his father and his older half brother, Lawrence. Like other children he copied into an exercise book maxims of behavior: "Spit not into the fire, nor set your feet upon the fire, especially if there be meat before it. Cleanse not your teeth with the tablecloth, napkin, fork, or knife." But that was easy; adolescence was hard. When Washington was sixteen some of his friends called him the "stallion of the Potomac," and his mentor, Lord Fairfax, warned the young ladies of Virginia, "George Washington is beginning to feel the sap rising, being in the spring of life, and is getting ready to be the prey of your sex, wherefore may the Lord help him."

The sap was rising, but Washington over the next decade prayed regularly for self-control. When Washington was sixteen he wrote a sonnet to one young lady, Frances Alexander, which read in part,

> *Why should my poor restless heart*
> *Stand to oppose thy might and power*
> *At last surrender to cupid's feathered dart. . . .*

But when she did not surrender, he desisted. Washington's self-control impressed Lord Fairfax, who concluded, "He is very grave for one of his age, and reserved in his intercourse, not a great talker at any time. His mind appears to me to act slowly, but, on the whole, to reach just conclusions, and he has an ardent wish to see the right of questions."

Not until later did "George Washington slept here" signs become customary along the eastern seaboard, and no one today knows whether Washington remained virginal. Those he courted, however, considered him a gentleman, although not a sufficiently highborn one to warrant engagement. At twenty Washington proposed marriage to a Virginia beauty, Betsy Fauntleroy, and was rejected. Later he courted Mary Eliza Philipse, whom he called "deep-bosomed," and was rejected. He also admired passionately Sally Fairfax, a young woman married to his friend George William Fairfax. It appears that she also longed for him, but both respected her wedding ring sufficiently to hold off.

Washington first gained fame at age twenty-three, as an aide to General Edward Braddock in 1755 during the French and Indian War. That year Braddock's 1,500 British soldiers were attacked by Indians and quickly descended into panic. Braddock was mortally wounded and every other mounted British regular officer also was hit. Washington, with two horses shot from under him, and four bullet holes in his clothing, remained uninjured. Able to lead the withdrawal of stunned survivors, he received wide commendation for his steadiness under fire. Washington was caustic about British soldiers who did not act honorably: "The dastardly behavior of those they call regulars exposed all others that were inclined to do their duty to almost certain death . . . they broke and ran as sheep pursued by dogs."

When Washington returned from war, he momentarily broke and ran one emotional step too far. He wrote to Mrs. Fairfax that she had drawn him, "or rather I have drawn myself, into an honest confession of a single fact": that she was "the object of my Love." If Washington's story were fiction, some nineteenth-century British novelist would have had Mr. Fairfax die in a shipwreck at this point. But in fact, he lived on, and Washington stopped his errant courtship, quickly after it began, by marrying the recently widowed Martha Custis. Never again is there a record of him coming close to not only thinking but also acting in a way he knew to be dishonorable.

Martha Custis (five feet tall and plump) may have met George Washington (six feet two and muscular, with size 13 shoes) at a dance or party during the eight years she was married to Daniel Parke Custis. She and George Washington had heard of each other for years, but their first substantial meeting occurred on March 16, 1758, when she was eight months a widow and he was worried about going too far with Sally Fairfax. He proposed to her nine days later and they married ten months later, then lived happily together for forty-one years until death did them part. Martha had a four-year-old son and two-year-old daughter from her previous marriage, and soon Washington's orders for goods from London included items such as "six little books for children beginning to read" and "one fashionably dressed baby [doll]."

The wealthy widow carried with her six thousand acres and a hundred slaves, but she also brought a warm femininity that complemented well Washington's rough spots. Her ability to make guests feel welcome was important to Washington, who liked to be hospitable but was not particularly convivial. Between 1768 and 1775 the Washingtons at Mount Vernon entertained about two thousand guests. During the Revolutionary War, Martha Washington frequently joined her husband and became not only a hostess for officers but also a mother to lonely soldiers. In 1797, Washington wrote to a friend one afternoon, "Unless someone pops in unexpectedly, Mrs. Washington and myself will do what I believe has not been done within the last 20 years by us, that is to set down to dinner by ourselves."

They had no children together. They did have lots of dogs, with names like Drunkard, Sweetlips, and Truelove. George Washington may have been sterile, and therefore ready to be the father of a republican country and not a hereditary monarchy. Other men who did not have offspring (even when the likely physical cause lay within themselves) traded in wives for those they thought could do better. Washington did not. Nor did Washington follow the British practice of taking mistresses when his middle-aged wife sagged in places and grew plumper in others. Even during the Revolution, with what today we would call groupies readily available to a commanding presence, Washington wore around his neck a miniature portrait of his wife. He wrote to her, "I retain an unalterable affection for you which neither time nor distance can change."

TRUSTING IN PROVIDENCE

Martha Washington was hospitable to visitors and even more enthusiastically hospitable to God's working in her. After breakfast, "every day of her adult life," according to a grandson, Martha went to her bedroom to read from the Bible and pray for an hour. Her husband was not so constant. Judging by the references he made, Washington knew the Bible, and he also carried out church duties as a vestryman from 1762 onwards, with the responsibility of handling parish collections. But he was reluctant to talk publicly about Christ and erratic about taking Communion in church, and that has led to historians' speculation that he was a deist, believing that God had created the world but was no longer active in it.

Washington's reasons for at times refraining from the Lord's Supper are still a mystery. However, his talk and reports were full of discussion of Providence—the belief that God is powerfully active in the world, and that everything from the destiny of nations to the flight of sparrows, or bullets, is under God's sovereign control. That comfort in and calm about Providence gave Washington the sense of security that calmed contentious legislators and soldiers. His willingness to think of the long term grew as he learned to say yes to whatever God willed.

This was particularly evident during the Revolutionary War, when defeats were frequent and victory rare. In 1776, Washington stated, "No man has a more perfect reliance on the all-wise and powerful dispensations of the Supreme Being than I have." Bucking up his co-combatants, he declared in 1777, "A superintending Providence is ordering everything for the best. . . . in due time all will end well." When developments were dark in 1778, he wrote, "Providence has heretofore taken us up when all other means and hope seemed to be departing from us; in this I will confide." In 1779, as the war wore on, he bucked up himself: "I look upon every dispensation of Providence as designed to answer some valuable purpose, and I hope I shall always possess a sufficient degree of fortitude to bear without murmuring any stroke which may happen. . . ."

Similar quotations from throughout the war are readily available. But Washington always believed that as help came from God, gratitude expressed in obedience was due Him. Since God demanded that those engaged in immorality change their ways, private matters had public consequences: "Purity of morals [is] the only sure foundation of public happiness in any country." When Washington frustrated the British, they tried to strike back by saying he was a moral hypocrite who enjoyed the "wonderful charms" of his female slaves. They supplied no evidence, and Washington responded by denouncing the "low dirty tricks" of the British.

A Moral Army

Washington's sense of God in charge carried over to his thoughts about building a winning army. His hope was to upgrade the American militias to British efficiency while retaining a much higher moral standard. At a time when army camps were homes for blasphemy,

Washington decried the "foolish and wicked practice, of profane cursing and swearing." He insisted, "We can have little hopes of the blessing of Heaven on our arms, if we insult it by our impiety and folly." He demanded the appointment of regimental chaplains and commanded his soldiers to "attend carefully upon religious exercises. The blessing and protection of Heaven are at all times necessary but especially so in times of public distress and danger."

Disunited as the new states were in many ways, they stood together in supporting Washington's endeavors to contain vice. For example, the Virginia convention that turned the original colony into an independent state also concluded in 1776 that a commanding officer should "take such steps as to him appear most proper for preventing profane swearing, all manner of gaming, as well as every other vice and immorality among officers and soldiers under his command." Some observers said Washington would lose men by insisting on tough standards, but he understood that the opposite was true. The task of British officers was to make their men compliant. The task of American officers was to show volunteers that the patriotic effort was virtually a holy cause. Only the totally committed could be relied on.

In practice, godly discipline won victories. After defeats in 1776 in and around New York City, Washington became an entrepreneurial general: learning the enemy's vices, looking for an opening, using surprise. Washington had his men cross the Delaware River on Christmas Eve during a storm which the British thought would stop the best soldiers, let alone defeated Americans who were supposedly slouching off in dejection. Meanwhile, Johann Rall, commander of the mercenary Hessian forces encamped at Trenton, saw no reason to fortify his garrison or emphasize outposts. When a Tory farmer delivered a note to Rall saying the American army was about to attack him, Rall was intent on his card game and merely slipped the note into his pocket. The next morning Rall's men were routed.

Washington's dogged generalship, in comparison with British commanders' sloth, again made a difference eight days after the Battle of Trenton, when Lord Charles Cornwallis's army pinned Washington's forces against the Delaware River. Cornwallis liked his relaxation and is reputed to have said, "We've got the old fox safe now. We'll go over and bag him in the morning." During the night the American army slipped around the British left flank and was able to rout a British regiment at Princeton.

Fish rotted from the head. The main British army at that point was commanded by General Sir William Howe, based in New York. He showed no interest in moving to attack, in part because he was absorbed in adultery with his mistress, Elizabeth Loring, the wife of a British commissary officer who sought promotion. In the words of one American general, "Howe shut his eyes, fought his battles, drank his bottle, had his little whore. . . ." Worried American Tories even circulated a song:

> *Awake, arouse, Sir Billy,*
> *There's forage on the plain.*
> *Ah, leave your little filly,*
> *And open the campaign.*

But Howe waited.

And, taking the chain of command all the way back to London, the failure of many links becomes evident. John Montagu, Earl of Sandwich and First Lord of the Admiralty, was in charge of the naval war against American rebels. He was known for leaving his office to hit the gambling halls for twenty-four-hour stretches; servants brought him a hunk of meat stuck between two slices of bread, and the word "sandwich" was born.

Montagu was a key member of a social club known as the Mad Monks of Medmenham. Medmenham was a semi-ruined abbey that a leading British politician, Sir Francis Dashwood, had purchased in the early 1750s and refurbished in pornographic splendor. Montagu loved Medmenham's "garden of lust," which featured shrubbery pruned to resemble a woman's private parts. He loved the stained glass windows that contained indecent pictures of the Twelve Apostles, the chapel ceiling with a huge pornographic fresco, the library said to contain the country's largest collection of pornographic books, and the London prostitutes who came to the abbey and dressed as nuns.

The other key British leader of the war effort, George Sackville (also known as Lord Germain), had different tastes. He was secretary of state in charge of the land war, much to the chagrin of generals who remembered that Sackville was court-martialed from the British army fighting in Germany in 1759. The official charge was cowardly refusal to advance during a battle, but the court-martial followed charges of sodomy as well.

Despite such a résumé, but with the help of other semi-closeted homosexuals, Sackville schemed his way to a political comeback. One London poet wrote about Sackville's

> *lips that oft in blandishment obscene*
> *Hath been employed.*

Army officers called him the "buggering hero." During the American Revolution, Sackville appointed two reputed homosexuals to key positions, as well as some financially corrupt individuals, in return for payoffs.

BRITISH DEPRAVITY AND STRATEGIC DEPRIVATION

Americans owed their victory at Saratoga, the biggest rebel triumph of the war's first six years, to Sackville's sexual preoccupations. The British plan for 1777 was to send one army south from Canada and Howe's forces north from New York City, with a meeting up the Hudson River that would supposedly cut off New England from the other colonies. But Secretary of State Sackville faltered because of his desire to get into bed with a lover: He hurried off to a country weekend after signing the dispatches to be sent to Canada but not those to New York, and they never were sent. The eventual result: American forces swarmed against the British army that marched south from Canada and soon found itself facing failing supplies, no hope of help, and—surrender.

During the four years after Saratoga the poorly supplied American army had little good news and many bad months. At Valley Forge during the harsh winter of 1777–78 few soldiers had coats, half were without blankets, more than a third were without shoes, and some lacked other essentials for health amidst winter. One in every four soldiers who wintered at Valley Forge died there. The winter of 1779–80 in Morristown, New Jersey, was even worse. At one point hungry men surrounded by snow had rations only one-eighth of the normal amount. Finances also were a problem. Rarely during the war were Washington's men paid on time or in full. In January 1781 some Pennsylvania and New Jersey troops mutinied and deserted.

Yet Washington would not give up. When he furloughed militia soldiers to go home to harvest crops, enough came back to hold the British at bay year after year. Washington, it turned out, was the ideal leader for an army of volunteers. He had perseverance and an integrity that made him so popular among his soldiers that some who wanted to leave stayed on so as to avoid disappointing him. And when others were depressed, Washington buoyed them with his faith that God would make the Revolution "ultimately" succeed.

"Ultimately" often seemed like an eternity as the war wore on. But as the most critical period of the war approached, the private lives of British leaders continued to affect military performance. Compare Washington's passion for victory with the passions of Montagu, the First Lord of the Admiralty. Montagu was infatuated with his live-in lover, Martha Ray, but so was a young ensign, James Hackman. When Martha Ray refused to elope with Hackman he shot her in the face as she emerged from the theater. Montagu, informed of her death as the British were beginning the campaign that ended in their defeat at Yorktown, flung himself on his bed and cried, "Leave me alone, I could have borne anything but this!"

Montagu's womanizing also affected his relations with officials who reported to him. He made one mediocre officer, James Gambier, who had pimped for him and threatened blackmail, a rear admiral. Some talented officers resigned because, as Captain John Leveson-Gower put it, Montagu "never had any decency." According to the *Dictionary of National Biography*, "many officers of character and ability ... refused to accept a command while he remained at the admiralty." While Montagu was paying attention to sexual rather than military affairs, those who were not dissipated stopped participating.

Secretary of State Sackville's reputation for sexual and financial lust also deprived the British war effort of significant support. In 1779, Sackville was accused of pocketing state money. Both the war effort and the man leading it became increasingly unpopular in England; in the words of a contemporary opponent, "The most odious of tasks was assigned to the most odious of instruments." Sackville was supposed to work closely with Montagu in coordinating the army and navy, so they oozed cordiality in public but privately spread the idea that each defeat was the other's fault.

Contempt for Montagu became open as the war wore on. Charles Churchill described him best in Act Three of his play *The Duellist:* Montagu was

> *Too infamous to have a friend,*
> *Too bad for bad men to commend.*

He was frequently portrayed as mixing Admiralty business with personal interest. One satirist had Montagu say "enchanting devil" while watching a young woman leave his office, and then immediately turn his attention back to the bribes he needed to sustain his sugar daddy habits: "I must now to business; and try to raise a sum, by advancing some worthless scoundrel over the head of a hundred men of merit."

One such scoundrel, Sir George Rodney, an adulterer, gambler, and debtor, had the task in 1781 of providing naval support for General Charles Cornwallis, who was marching through the Carolinas and Virginia. Instead, Rodney concentrated on building his own fortune and his own adulterous résumé in the West Indies. Cornwallis himself received his job because he was Sackville's "special favourite." The British commanding general in New York, Sir Henry Clinton, who could have helped out, disliked Cornwallis because Sackville had made it clear that the overall command would go to Cornwallis as soon as he had gained a military victory in the South.

Clinton did not want to help Cornwallis achieve that promotion. Clinton also was occupied (like his predecessor, General Howe) with a pretty mistress whose husband pimped her to the commander in exchange for promotion, and did not move out of New York with reinforcements until it was too late. One of his last acts upon leaving the city, however, was to give a copy of his will to his mistress. The corruption was thorough and extended into the ranks. British soldiers fought when they could not avoid it, but otherwise dedicated themselves to gambling, drinking, and cavorting with camp prostitutes.

Cornwallis, surrounded by American and French forces, surrendered his troops on October 19, 1781, after reporting that his supplies were depleted. American soldiers found in the British camp 144 cannon and mortars, thousands of big gun cartridges and 120 barrels of powder, 800 muskets and 266,000 musket cartridges, 73,000 pounds of flour, 60,000 pounds of bread, 75,000 pounds of pork, 30,000 bushels of peas, 1,250 gallons of liquor, and enough other military materials and foodstuffs to hold on for many more weeks. Clearly, the British at Yorktown did not have the will to win, and gave in as soon as they could semi-honorably do so.

Again, the difference between Britain's leaders and George Washington, and between Britain's forced fighters and America's volunteers—including some foreign volunteers like the Marquis de Lafayette—was evident. Many Americans thanked Washington for establishing a virtuous army, and God for granting it victory. Immediately after the British surrender George Washington noted the "surprizing and particular interposition of Providence in our favour," and ordered that "divine service shall be performed tomorrow in the different brigades and divisions."

BECOMING A HAPPY NATION

The war was not settled officially until 1783, two years after Yorktown, but Washington's task was essentially completed. One nod from him, and Washington's army (with support from many civilians) would have made him King George I of America. Washington refused, emphasizing instead the value of statesmen following in the steps of "the Characteristicks of the Divine Author of our blessed Religion." Otherwise, Washington observed, "we can never hope to be a Happy Nation." Washington held that an American was in a desperate way if he could look in a mirror and not see a man of honor.

Washington always loved land—to explore it, to own it, to farm it. But the extent of the country that emerged from war was too great for even a well-traveled Virginian to grasp. Citizens of one state had little contact with those from another because travel was not only frequently painful but also lengthy. Four miles per hour was the average speed for a stagecoach between Maine and Maryland, if it did not break down. Travelers generally had to bounce over roads alternately furrowed and muddy. Stagecoaches typically were filled by persons and enough baggage to leave legs cramped and travelers sweating profusely in mid-summer heat or offering each other teeth-chattering serenades during freezing winter weather. Others rode very ungently down streams that could quickly bring whitewater rapids.

Movies about that period tend to show neat homes and well-manicured lawns, but America in reality was a poor nation. Ornithologist Alexander Wilson, who traveled the country at the end of the century watching birds but also people, noted that New England displayed "wretched orchards; scarcely one grain-field in twenty miles; the taverns along the road dirty, and filled with loungers bawling about lawsuits and politics." Wilson, an equal-opportunity critic, described North Carolina as a place where "the taverns are the most desolate and beggarly imaginable; bare, bleak, and dirty walls, one or two old broken chairs and a bench form all the furniture. . . . The house itself is raised upon props four or five feet, and the space below is left open for the hogs, with whose charming vocal performance the wearied traveler is serenaded the whole night long."

Wilson liked birds better than people, but a French observer who was fond of the United States, the Duc de Liancourt, was surprised to see Americans scrupulous in some respects but not in others: "The people of the country are as astonished that one should object to sleeping two or three in the same bed and in dirty sheets, or to drink from the same dirty glass after half a score of others, as to see one neglect to wash one's hands and face of a morning." Foreign travelers were also surprised to see both churchgoing and rough-and-tumble fighting common in much of the country. Gouging, kicking, and even biting ears or other body parts were acceptable behavior in fights on which spectators laid large wagers.

None of that bothered Washington, but one pursuit did: the ownership of slaves. During the Revolution, Washington urged that slaves be enlisted with the offer of freedom if the Americans won. In Philadelphia early in 1779, with war offensives becalmed, he thought through his own situation and almost decided to extricate himself from the plantation economy by selling the Mount Vernon slaves and using the money for investment. In the end he stayed pat. He still hoped to return to the comforts of home after the war and realized that a lack of free farm labor would make operating Mount Vernon without slave labor impossible.

Thereafter, it seems that at least every seven years Washington contemplated the switch from slaveowner to employer. In 1786 he said that he was filled with "regret" about the institution of slavery and his role in it. He said "no man living wishes more sincerely than I do to see the abolition of it." Again Washington wondered how to extricate himself personally. Morally, he objected to selling slaves, yet he was unwilling to take the huge economic loss involved in freeing them. Washington's internal tension influenced his views on America's future: Concluding that the slave system was both inefficient and wrong, he split from agrarians like Thomas Jefferson and looked favorably on the growth of manufacturing and cities. Washington's admiration for a business economy grew alongside his moral uneasiness about the basis of the South's plantation economy.

THE WASHINGTON PRESIDENCY

Washington knew that Americans were satisfied to be part of a loosely federated United States in which the government would take responsibility for foreign policy, while leaving domestic affairs almost entirely to state governments. He knew that anyone who ignored the realities of distance and travel that left states separated, and tried to set up a strong central government, would receive bruises like those incurred during a rough-and-tumble.

Nevertheless, when Washington received news of the Massachusetts uprising led by Daniel Shays in 1786 and 1787, he began to think that some form of government stronger than the Articles of Confederation might be needed. Washington's friend (and former general) Henry Knox told him that the Shaysites demanded the cancellation of all debts and believed "that the property of the United States . . . ought to be the common property of all." Washington argued that the insurgency had to be stopped, or else "what security has a man for life, liberty, or property?" The Massachusetts government raised a strong militia and crushed the rebellion early in 1787, but a recognition of trouble moved Washington to support the call for a constitutional convention.*

The Constitution that emerged from the famous meeting barely received passage, with federalists gaining close wins in several key states only because everyone knew that Washington would be the first president. His support for a new arrangement influenced not only adoption of the Constitution but also the document itself. As one Georgian wrote, the Constitutional Convention would not have given the executive branch powers so extensive "had not many of the members cast their ideas towards General Washington as President; and shaped their Ideas of the Powers to be given to a President, by their opinions of his Virtue."

Washington received a unanimous vote from the electoral college in 1789 and rode northward to the temporary capital, New York City, amid triumphal processions that could readily turn a politician's head. Trenton was typical: Dozens of girls dressed in white, and older women as well, lined both sides of the road as Washington approached. "Welcome, mighty Chief!" they sang in a chorus composed for the occasion, and happily laid to rest afterwards:

Welcome to this grateful shore!
Virgins fair, and Matrons grave,
Those thy conquering arms did save,
Build for thee triumphant bowers
Strew, ye fair, his way with flowers.

Ships and salutes welcomed Washington to New York and made such an impression that he described in his diary "the decorations of the ships, the roar of cannon, and the loud acclamations of the people."

How Washington reacted to such applause defined him as a statesman. He wrote that the acclamation "filled my mind with sensations as

---

*For analysis of the reasons, see Chapter Seven of my book *Fighting for Liberty and Virtue: Political and Cultural Wars in Eighteenth-Century America* (Wheaton, IL: Crossway, 1995; Washington, DC: Regnery Gateway, 1996).

painful . . . as they are pleasing" because he knew how fickle a populace could be. He wrote that he could readily imagine "the reverse of the scene, which may be the case after all my labors. . . ." Washington believed he could be entrusted with power because he was not under his own authority but God's. Americans knew that he expressed his trust in God and had not violated the trust of his wife, so they trusted him with power. But he worshipped neither the power nor the popularity, and so was willing to lose both if need be.

Washington's personal life shaped the Constitution, and Washington began shaping the presidency even as he was sworn in. He added to the presidential oath of office words that were not part of it: "So help me God." Every president since then has done the same. But not every president has spent a third of his inaugural address in a discussion of God's Providence and in "fervent supplications to that Almighty Being who rules over the universe." And few presidents have had the presence of Washington, who possessed, in the words of one observer, Benjamin Latrobe, "something uncommonly commanding and majestic in his walk, his address, his figure, and his countenance."

Yet Washington, as his term of office began, was far from an almighty president. The government struggled to come together in New York, a city in 1790 that boasted 33,000 inhabitants without a sound water supply or sanitation, and with little in the way of paved roads or police. Paths in Manhattan meandered and so did Congress; jealousies and fears among politicians entering Congress from north and south were great, and it often seemed that only confidence in Washington held things together. So much was his leadership prized, and so much was it understood that the safety of the young republic depended upon the self-restraint of those in power, that political leaders of all stripes panicked when the president early in his first term was taken ill with pneumonia and seemed to be dying. Thomas Jefferson wrote to a friend, "You cannot conceive of the public alarm on this occasion. It proves how much depends on his life."

The constant flattery of Washington was enough to turn almost anyone's head. The *New Hampshire Recorder* in 1790 offered this somewhat heretical ode:

Behold the matchless Washington
His glory hath eclips'd the sun;
The lustre of his rays so bright,
'Tis always day, there's no more night.
The greatest sage upon the globe,
Well may he wear the imperial robe. . . .
And when he drops this earthly crown.
He's one in Heaven's high renown;
He's deify'd, exalt him high,
He's next unto the Trinity.
My language fails to tell his worth,
Unless in Heav'n he is the fourth.

At the height of such adulation Washington began attending Sabbath worship services regularly. He missed only one during the first twelve weeks of 1790, and on that day the weather was terrible. Washington was showing Americans who worshipped him a better object of worship.

The most vital domestic issue in Washington's first term concerned the extent of federal power. Debate on the religious freedom segment of the First Amendment was typical. James Madison proposed sweeping wording: "The civil rights of none shall be abridged on account of religious belief or worship. . . ." But congressmen wanted assurance that state and local support of religion, and public displays of belief, would not be banned. Washington argued that "of all the dispositions and habits which lead to political prosperity, religion and morality are indispensable supports," and he did not want anyone to use the Constitution to cut into those supports. The amendment's eventual wording was specific: "Congress shall make no law. . . ." Communities, states, and citizens were able to continue to encourage religious expression.

Avoiding Foreign Entanglements

With domestic basics settled, foreign policy issues became key. Secretary of State Jefferson and many others wanted to bring the United States into an alliance with revolutionary France. The alliance seemed natural. Both countries had done away with their kings—the French by cutting off Louis XVI's head—and become republics. Both countries had a free and rambunctious press. (Many French journalists, not making a distinction between liberty and license, had quickly turned to the production of pornography.) France had come to the aid of the United States after the Battle of Saratoga in 1777, and only the French navy made Yorktown possible. Many Americans wanted to say immediately, "Lafayette, we are here."

Washington disagreed because he understood quickly that the French Revolution as it developed was far different from the American. (When the French left seized power in the early 1790s, Lafayette barely escaped with his life.) Washington refused to tie the United States to a France falling into "the highest paroxysm of disorder." He accurately predicted "a crisis of sad confusion," with French political leaders "ready to tear each other to pieces." To keep the United States out of the war between England and France that broke out in 1793, he issued a Neutrality Proclamation that encouraged Americans to trade with both sides but ally themselves with neither.

Washington also emphasized military defense. In his annual address to Congress for 1793, he stressed, "If we desire to avoid insult, we must be able to repel it." Washington's supporters in Congress beat back attempts to scuttle plans for an American navy. Congress appropriated funds for eight frigates, and Washington's officials saw that the money was spent quickly and efficiently. "If we desire to secure peace," Washington insisted, "it must be known that we are at all times ready for war." He also emphasized the need for an army college to ensure the United States "an adequate stock of military knowledge."

Washington's willingness to make war infuriated those who thought it bliss to be alive in the days of a French Revolution that could do no wrong. Suddenly, parts of the populace turned on Washington. Thomas Paine called him "the patron of fraud" and "a hypocrite," and then moved on to adjectives like "treacherous." Benjamin Franklin Bache, Franklin's grandson, called Washington "the source of all the misfortunes of our country." The *New York Journal* made up charges that Washington was a man of "gambling, reveling, horseracing and horse whipping." Had Washington's enemies found any evidence of presidential sexual relations outside marriage, they might have howled him out of office, and America's future would have been far different—but there was none. Nevertheless, as attacks rained on what had been his presidential parade, Washington yearned to retire. "I would rather be in my grave than in this place," he once declared. "I would rather live out my days on the farm than be emperor of the world."

Meanwhile, Washington's thoughts about farming inevitably brought him back to the question of slavery. In 1793, Washington wrote to a British agricultural reformer that he would like to free his slaves and rent out most of Mount Vernon to skilled English tenant farmers, who would then hire the ex-slaves. That tenant plan had the advantage also of not leaving his ex-slaves "set adrift" and possibly starving, but Washington never carried through on it. A Polish visitor in 1798 observed that "Washington treats his slaves far more humanely than do his fellow citizens of Virginia." Finally, Washington wrote a will by which all of the slaves he owned (Martha owned some personally) would be freed following his death.

After Washington left the presidency in 1797, he was able to ride through his plantation daily and express satisfaction with the opportunity to be "again seated under my Vine and Fig tree." However, correspondence with political friends showed an uneasiness about the direction of the country and some personal yearning as well. Thomas Jefferson had become openly critical of Washington for refusing to embrace French ideals and supposedly supporting "monarchical and aristocratic" ways. In a denunciation that was printed in newspapers across the country and popularly assumed to refer to Washington, Jefferson attacked "apostates who have gone over to these [federalist] heresies, men who were Samsons in the field and Solomons in council, but who have had their heads shorn by the harlot of England." Washington probably could have injured Jefferson's presidential hopes severely by striking back publicly, but he held his fire.

Washington tried to renew contact with Sally Fairfax, recipient of his love letter four decades earlier. She and her husband had moved to England just before the Revolution, but in 1798 Washington wrote to Mrs. Fairfax and asked that she return to Virginia. He noted that over the years since her leaving "so many important events have occurred and such changes in man and things have taken place." Yet, "none of which events however nor all of them together have been able to eradicate from my mind the recollection of those happy moments, the happiest of my life which I have enjoyed in your company." Mrs. Fairfax preserved Washington's letter, but there is no record of a reply. She never did return. And Washington, despite some unrequited longing, never broke from a conclusion he had reached from comparing his life with that of some unmarried associates: "domestic felicity" was superior to "giddy rounds of promiscuous pleasure."

Publicly, Washington continued to emphasize the thoughts of his farewell address in 1796: "Of all the dispositions and habits which lead to political prosperity, religion and morality are indispensable supports." The fear of the Lord is the beginning of sound public policy, he declared: "Where is the security for property, for reputation, for life, if the sense of religious obligation desert the oaths, which are the instruments of investigation in Courts of Justice?" Political works without faith were dead, Washington insisted, for there was no evidence "that morality can be maintained without religion."

In December 1799 the sixty-seven-year-old Washington suddenly came down with what was probably either diphtheria or a virulent streptococcus infection. Doctors who followed the practice of the time—removing half a pint of blood from Washington, and then repeating the operation four times—merely weakened him. Given the state of medical knowledge then, none of the other likely treatments of that era would have worked either. With hand-wringing physicians surrounding him, and Martha sitting near the foot of his bed, Washington kept attempting to shift his body into a position that would allow him to breathe less painfully. His secretary, Tobias Lear, repeatedly helped to turn him, and Washington repeatedly said that he hoped he was not being too much trouble. Lear replied that he was eager to help, and Washington murmured, "Well, it is a debt we must pay to each other, and I hope when you want aid of this kind, you will find it."

Washington then tried a sitting position, as the doctors applied poultices of wheat bran to his legs. "I die hard, but I am not afraid to go," Washington said. "My breath cannot last long." He told the doctors, "I feel myself going. I thank you for your attention. You had better not take any more trouble about me. . . ." Then a fear struck him: He had read several newspaper reports of men thought to be dead who were buried while still alive. Gasping after each phrase, Washington told Lear, "I am just going. Have me decently buried, and do not let my body be put into the vault in less than three days after I am dead. Do you understand me?" When Lear said, "Yes, sir," Washington gave his last words: "'Tis well."

Soon, a printed cotton kerchief sold in shops presented a deathbed scene and described Washington as having died "like a Christian and a Hero, calm and collected, without a groan and without a sigh." The kerchief writer listed Washington's "VIRTUES . . . Self command and Self denial, moderate in Prosperity, undaunted amid Danger, unbroken by adversity . . . unperverted by great and general applause." Samuel Adams made a prediction concerning Washington's relationship to future presidents: "Perhaps the next and the next may inherit his Virtues, [but] the Time will come" when the worst takes over.

That time was long in coming because Washington remained the country's gold standard for over a century, and Americans expected their presidents to be sober, upright, and proper both in their private and public dealings. Washington had been able to control his impulses and to show that he saw himself as under God's control; Americans came to demand at least that appearance in their leaders. Much is masked concerning Washington's interior. It seems that he acted in such a virtuous way primarily because he loved God, but his characteristic self-restraint in expression leaves an opening for those who say he primarily loved his reputation. Whatever the reason, the public result was magnificent: George Washington was not only the father of our country but also the father of high expectations concerning the presidency, expectations that each of his successors for many years tried to meet.

CHAPTER 2

Thomas Jefferson

Historical research is always full of surprises. Before I studied the founding of the Republic, my tendency was to think that Washington probably had something to hide since he discoursed little about his personal life. Concerning Jefferson, on the other hand, I wanted to believe that a man who penned such noble words in the Declaration of Independence lived up to them in his life. But Jefferson had a private life and set of beliefs not consistent with the public image he liked to present; a wordsmith adept at manipulating language, he did not always realize the complexities of action. Jefferson's study of Washington's public posture kept him from making public mistakes during much of his political career, but his arrogance eventually led to unrealistic policies that almost destroyed the young United States.

JEFFERSON'S THEOLOGICAL FURY

Thomas Jefferson was born in 1743, the oldest son of a rich and kindly father. Peter Jefferson died when Thomas was fourteen, and the grieving boy, inheritor of thirty slaves and over 2,500 acres of land, was sent to live with and study under an arrogant, mean clergyman, James Maury. Hell had no fury like a Jefferson become fatherless and thrust into a corrupt Anglican Church at a crucial time in his intellectual development. Thomas came to identify Christianity with the church at its worst, in the person of Maury. When Jefferson studied at William and Mary College and read on his own thereafter, he found a substitute for the Bible: Enlightenment philosophy and political theory, with its emphasis on rational decision-making by the best and the brightest.

Jefferson made sweet public statements about Christianity, but his private letters, especially as an older man, were tart. He called Matthew, Mark, Luke, and John "groveling authors" who displayed "vulgar ignorance" and transmitted "superstitions, fanaticisms, and fabrications." He called all the apostles a "band of dupes and impostors," and labeled Paul the "first corrupter of the doctrines of Jesus." He wrote that belief in the Trinity was proof that "man, once surrendering his reason, has no remaining guard against absurdities the most monstrous." Among Christians, Jefferson complained, "gullibility which they call faith takes the helm from the hands of reason and the mind becomes a wreck."

Jefferson's rebellion against Christian theology was intense even during his presidency, when he wrote his famous line about the "separation of church and state." At that time he was spending many evenings alone in the dingy President's House. Night after night, next to a small lamp, with darkness all around him, he sliced from the Bible with a pen knife all the theistic passages that showed God doing miracles, responding to prayer, or being a thoughtful father to His people. Miracles? Out. Christ's conception and resurrection? Out.

Jefferson at times seemed obsessed. He even became absorbed in trying to determine the authentic Jesus by thinking about the "style and spirit" of New Testament words. He had no training in assessing texts. He had no training in dealing with ancient manuscripts. Nevertheless, Jefferson was ready to decree the principles that he believed Christ should have enunciated. He then told others that he had discovered "the genuine precepts of Jesus himself" and could thus be "a real Christian." He continued to hide from the public, however, his full dislike for many biblical precepts, and for many of the Christians who voted for him.

Jefferson early on had some embarrassing experience with one biblical injunction: "Do not covet your neighbor's wife." He fell in love with Betsey Walker, the wife of a friend and neighbor, and apparently slept with her. That affair was covered up for four decades, until an elderly Mrs. Walker revealed all to the *New York Evening Post* in 1805. The *Post* described how Jefferson "stole to the chamber of his absent friend at dead of night." Jefferson then confessed privately in a note to Secretary of the Navy Robert Smith, "I plead guilty . . . when young and single I offered love to a handsome lady."

In 1772, Jefferson married Martha Wayles Skelton. They loved each other and had four daughters. But Martha died in 1782, and Jefferson never remarried. An overseer at Monticello, Edmund Bacon, said that on her deathbed Martha told Thomas that "she could not die happy if she thought her four children were ever to have a stepmother brought in over them. Holding her hand in his, Mr. Jefferson promised her solemnly that he would never marry again. And he never did."

That story arose during an era in which dying mothers were more likely to ask surviving husbands to remarry so that the children would receive maternal care. Yet, evidence for the pledge is that Jefferson—a handsome, smart, powerful, and wealthy man who had increased his estate to over 130 slaves and thousands of acres—never did remarry. Instead, he left the door wide open to temptation, and it came in major ways at least twice.

One affair began in 1786 when Jefferson spent many days and evenings in Paris with Maria Cosway, a blonde, blue-eyed, twenty-seven-year-old beauty. Mrs. Cosway was unhappily married to

Richard Cosway, a bisexual artist who painted pornographic pictures on snuffboxes for British aristocrats. She yearned for a rescuer. Although no one has left an unambiguous record of what went on between Mrs. Cosway and Jefferson, even one of Jefferson's adulatory biographers, Dumas Malone, notes that he "fell deeply in love" and may have engaged in "illicit love-making." Certainly, the religious beliefs that help men to say no to illicit sex had only a tenuous grip on Jefferson in the 1780s, and probably no hold at all as time went by. Jefferson once listed the biblical commandments he thought worth observing. He wrote down injunctions against theft, murder, and false witness, but left out adultery.

Two months after Jefferson and Mrs. Cosway met, he was undecided about continuing the affair and wrote her a twelve-page letter titled "My Head and My Heart." In it Jefferson has his head telling his heart, "you were imprudently engaging your affections under circumstances that might cost you a great deal of pain." The heart, however, tells the head to stow the philosophy, because "the solid pleasure of one generous spasm of the heart" outweighs "frigid speculations."

Jefferson weighed the possibility of political embarrassment and venereal disease against generous and pleasurable spasms. He and Mrs. Cosway continued to see each other on and off through 1787 and 1788. Then, she had guilt feelings and he showed renewed caution as the Constitution was adopted and it looked as if he would be called back into domestic political service. Prudence placed a tourniquet on passion. Jefferson and Mrs. Cosway had talked about traveling around the United States together, with Mr. Cosway staying in Europe, but James Madison sent Jefferson a cautionary letter describing the reception Americans gave to the new French minister to the United States and his mistress. The "illicit connection," Madison wrote, reduced the minister's political effectiveness, since adultery was "offensive to American manners."

UNION OF SEX AND SLAVERY

In 1789 it appears that Maria Cosway was replaced in Jefferson's thought, and apparent action, by Sally Hemings, a sixteen-year-old slave who was serving him in Paris and was described as "mighty near white," "very handsome," with "long straight hair down her back." Known at Monticello as "Dashing Sally," she was one-fourth black. Her mother's mother had been a plantation owner's mistress. So had her mother—and her father was also the father of Jefferson's deceased wife, Martha.

The charge that Jefferson had a slave mistress first became prominent in 1802, in newspaper reports by journalist James Callender. Jefferson had subsidized Callender's exposés of political enemies, but the writer turned on his master when the newly elected president did not give him a cushy administration position. Callender snooped around Monticello, interviewed Jefferson's neighbors, and reported that Jefferson "keeps, and for many years has kept, as his concubine, one of his slaves. Her name is Sally. The name of her eldest son is Tom."

Callender had an ax to grind, but other journalists came up with the same information. A report in the *Frederick-Town Herald,* reprinted in the *Richmond Recorder* late in 1802, commented on Callender's charge and added the results of an independent investigation: "Other information assures us that Mr. Jefferson's Sally and their children are real persons, and that the woman herself has a room to herself at Monticello. . . . Her intimacy with her master is well known."

The report also noted that Sally's son Tom "bears a strong likeness to Mr. Jefferson." The story concluded, "although the subject is a delicate one, we cannot see why we are to affect any great squeamishness against speaking plainly of what we consider as an undoubted fact interesting to the public." Other journalists over the years had a similar sense. Frances Trollope's travel book, *Domestic Manners of the Americans,* noted in 1832 Jefferson's "children by Quadroon slaves." Additional inquirers found that Monticello slaves and ex-slaves referred to Sally Hemings as Jefferson's "concubine."

Although Jefferson never acknowledged the relationship, at least one of his friends did. John Hartwell Cocke, who worked with Jefferson closely in the founding of the University of Virginia, wrote of the tendency of many unmarried plantation owners to keep a slave woman "as a substitute for a wife." Cocke wrote that in Virginia such a "practice prevails as much as anywhere—probably more—as Mr. Jefferson's example can be pleaded for its defense."

Some historians have denied that the relationship could have existed because it was out of character for Jefferson to have sex with a slave. But that is regarding either Jefferson as superhuman or slaves as subhuman. Those who say that Jefferson would not have taken unfair advantage of another person have to deal with the way he bought and sold human beings, gave them as wedding presents, and made ten-year-old slave boys work in a nail factory for twelve hours a day.

Physical evidence suggests that Jefferson was involved with his deceased wife's half sister for many years. Appearances can be deceiving, but one of Jefferson's legitimate grandchildren reported that Sally Hemings "had children which resembled Mr. Jefferson so closely that it was plain that they had his blood in their veins." Once, a visitor dining at Monticello with Jefferson was startled to raise his eyes to the slave standing behind him and see so close a father-son resemblance. Circumstantial evidence suggests the connection as well. All seven of the Hemings children were conceived either in Paris or at Monticello when Jefferson was at home. When he was away for long periods, she did not conceive.

There is also the evidence of freedom, which Jefferson, despite his rhetoric, did not give his numerous slaves—except for those who appear to have been his children. One of Sally Hemings's sons, Madison, reported that Jefferson had pledged to her that all of their children would be free at age twenty-one. That is what happened, officially or through winks and nods. According to Ellen Coolidge, Jefferson's granddaughter, the Hemings children "were white enough to pass for white," so four of them "walked away and staid away—their whereabouts was perfectly known but they were left to themselves."

The relationship held some political danger, but Jefferson owned Sally; she was under his control. By the time the story emerged nationally, Jefferson already was a popular president. He and his supporters at that point were able to ignore ballads such as the one printed in Boston and Philadelphia newspapers and designed for singing to the tune of "Yankee Doodle":

> *Of all the damsels on the green,*
> *On mountain, or in valley,*

> *A lass so luscious ne'er was seen,*
> *As Monticellian Sally.*

Furthermore, Jefferson insisted upon discretion and treated Sally well. Jefferson's carefully kept expense records in Paris show that in a period of seven months he spent 216 francs on Sally's clothes, at a time when gloves could be bought for two francs. Nor is there any reason to think that Sally Hemings was not attracted to Jefferson. In any event, a relationship with him would give her the position of highest status that a slave could have.

The founding fathers were used to floundering political careers when adultery became public. Judging from the contemporary testimony and evidence, Jefferson practiced the politically safest sex he could, outside marriage. Publicly, both before and during his presidency, he restricted himself to elegant Platonic flirtations. Women gazed at the red-freckled face of tall and handsome Thomas and yearned to tousle his red hair turning gray. The letters of Mrs. Margaret Bayard Smith were typical. She oozed that when Jefferson, "with a manner and voice almost femininely soft and gentle . . . entered into conversation on the commonplace topics of the day . . . there was something in his manner, his countenance and voice that at once unlocked [my] heart."

WHEELS WITHIN WHEELS

Had voters known Jefferson's real thoughts concerning Christianity or his real actions concerning sex, he would not have gone far politically. Both in sex and in religion, then, Jefferson developed a pattern of hiding his real beliefs and practices.

The Declaration of Independence is a case in point. Delegates to the Continental Convention knew of Jefferson's hatred for the corrupt Anglican Church. They did not know that his anti-Anglicanism was part of a dislike for Christianity generally that would eventually become a hatred. Delegates knew what they wanted to say, but they needed Jefferson's "happy talent for composition," as John Adams described it. Jefferson came through wonderfully, rapidly writing an elegant declaration with resonating expressions like "endowed by their Creator with certain unalienable Rights" and "the Laws of Nature and of Nature's God." In the exuberance of the moment no one stopped to ask who Jefferson thought the Creator was, or to ask whether the expression "Nature's God" almost made it seem that nature had created God and now owned Him.

The Declaration of Independence made Jefferson's reputation, even though he was more stylist than originator. Patriots called him "the pen of the revolution." (Washington was its sword, Patrick Henry its voice.) Jefferson then showed his priorities by resigning from Congress and returning to Virginia to lead the drive to disestablish the Anglican Church. He succeeded in pushing clergymen such as the hated Maury off the public payroll, and half a century later, thinking back about his successes, considered that one of his finest.

The public perception of Jefferson was that he opposed Anglicanism but not Christianity. Unlike his friend Thomas Paine, Jefferson was careful not to indicate otherwise publicly. He rode his reputation as Declaration of Independence–writer to election and reelection as governor of Virginia in 1779 and 1780. Jefferson's administration was disastrous, however. A British invasion of Virginia found the state so ill prepared for defense that Governor Jefferson had to flee from Monticello.

Portrayed as a coward, he sat out the political and military action of the remainder of the war. Martha's death in 1782 left Jefferson thinking that his entire life had gone sour. He announced his retirement from public life. But partly because he was an Enlightenment-friendly intellectual who could get along well with liberal French philosophes, and partly as a mercy assignment to awaken Jefferson from a psychological coma, Congress in 1784 sent him to Paris as U.S. minister to France.

During Jefferson's five years there, his emotions and intellect were frequently at war, and not only concerning Mrs. Cosway. Jefferson's heart relished the sheltered ease of the French aristocracy before the Revolution: "Here it seems a man might pass a life without encountering a single rudeness." But Jefferson's head rejected that life, for he could not help observing that most Frenchmen were "ground to powder by their form of government."

PLAYING IT BOTH WAYS

Jefferson's reputation as a document writer, and his rapport with the initial leaders of the French Revolution, led Washington to make him the nation's first secretary of state. Jefferson served from 1789 through December 1793, remaining committed to the revolutionary governments of France until George Washington ordered neutrality in the new wars commencing between France and England. Jefferson continued to maintain distinct public and private faces, however. During a cabinet meeting Jefferson indicated his approval of the Neutrality Proclamation that Washington had put forward, but in private correspondence he pretended to have stood with revolutionary France and voted against it. He told his friends that the proclamation was Alexander Hamilton's doing and part of a British plot.

Jefferson's desire to please Washington while supporting France led him to act at times in other two-faced ways. He gave French officials information about internal cabinet debates, so that French ambassador Edmond Genet could tell Paris how "Secretary of the Treasury Hamilton, attached to the British interest, exerted the greatest influence on the mind of the President, and it was only with the greatest difficulty that he [Jefferson] counteracted their efforts." Washington opposed a plan by Genet to pay American freebooters to take over Louisiana, then under Spanish control, with the goal of an independent country under French supervision. Jefferson told Kentucky leaders that the plan had his blessing.

From 1794 on Jefferson was out of office but clearly running for president. He wanted to do so with blessings from Washington and campaign management by Madison. At first he sent to Madison information gained in private talks with Washington that would "enable you to shape your plan." He was careful in his plotting, even to the point of having an associate carry to Madison letters which "could never have been hazarded by post." But in July 1796, Washington finally realized that Jefferson had been scheming against him for years, and he ended their relationship. Jefferson would have to run for president on his own, against Washington's handpicked successor, John Adams.

Jefferson finished second to Adams in 1796. He spent the next four years masterminding strategy, while Madison worked the snuff-filled rooms. Jefferson wrote frequent letters to colleagues and disciples, with specific instructions about committing both time and money to influencing public opinion through newspapers. He instructed Madison to "set aside a portion of every post day to write what may be proper for the public." He pressed editors loyal to him to attack the Federalists and keep pushing hard. Jefferson's journalistic approach proved right when Adams and his congressional allies became so enraged at press attacks that they overreached, passing a Sedition Act that deprived Jeffersonians of freedom of speech and the press. Jefferson wisely made that the key issue in his victorious presidential campaign of 1800.

That election struggle resonated with religious claims and counter-claims. Yale president Timothy Dwight thought that Jeffersonians were "blockheads and knaves" intent on severing "the ties of marriage with all its felicities." Jeffersonians countered with a question addressed to Alexander Hamilton, who had lost his chance for the presidency when caught in adultery, but was still politically active: "What shall we say of a faction that has at its head a confessed and professed adulterer?" Jefferson's own fornications had not yet been made public.

Jefferson ran on issues—press freedom, frugality in the central government, and containment of centralized power-grasping—that resonated with American voters. He summarized well the essential campaign themes in one August letter: "The true theory of our Constitution is surely the wisest and best, that the States are independent as to everything within themselves, and united as to everything respecting foreign nations. Let the general government be reduced to foreign concerns only . . . and our general government may be reduced to a very simple organization and a very inexpensive one,—a few plain duties to be performed by a few servants."

Jefferson's opponents did not believe him. One sharp attack on Jefferson came in September in a pamphlet written by the Reverend John Mason of New York entitled *The Voice of Warning to Christians, on the Ensuing Election of a President of the United States.* Mason accepted no compromises in his ministry—during one sermon, when a blood vessel burst in his nose and blood spurted out, he continued preaching—

and his pamphlet was equally tough. Jefferson, Mason wrote, appeared angelic, but in truth denied the Bible, justified atheism, and considered blacks to be subhuman. Mason summed up Jefferson's beliefs and character in one word: "infidel."

Mason and others predicted a Jefferson administration that would be like the French Revolution. A Boston newspaper screamed that Jefferson's election would place "the seal of death . . . on our holy religion" and lead to the installation of "some infamous prostitute, under the title of the Goddess of Reason . . . in the sanctuaries now devoted to the Most High." Assuming that the new president's personal views would dominate his political moves, Jefferson's opponents predicted that he would use federal authority to hinder churches in large and small ways.

Dire Fears Unfulfilled

Jefferson, however, was discerning enough politically not to do what his Christian opponents said he would do, and confident theologically as well: People were rational, Christianity was irrational, so it would naturally die out as people gained education. In that confidence and a desire for reelection, he was willing to be patient. As Alexander Hamilton described Jefferson, he was "as likely as any man I know to temporize, to calculate what will be likely to promote his own reputation and advantage."

Jefferson wooed his Christian opponents through several small but symbolic public policy actions. He authored a plan of education for District of Columbia schools and included as reading texts parts of the Bible that he did not consider dangerous. He signed treaties with the Kaskaskia, Wyandot, and Cherokee tribes that included the provision of federal money to build churches and support clergymen. He extended three times a 1787 act that designated federal lands "for the sole use of Christian Indians and the Moravian Brethren missionaries for use in civilizing the Indians and promoting Christianity."

Jefferson was also careful to frame some of his controversial initiatives in ways that would attract those concerned with spreading the gospel. When Jefferson asked his cabinet for their opinions of how the

Lewis and Clark expedition would be received by the populace, Attorney General Levi Lincoln warned that Federalists would criticize the expedition unless it was advertised as an aid to missionary efforts. Jefferson made sure to include in his final instructions the goal of learning about Indian religions so as to help "those who may endeavor to civilize & instruct them." Such cleverness led Jefferson-watchers such as Augustus Foster, secretary of the British Legation, to note Jefferson's "cynical expression of countenance."

Jefferson even showed up at services held almost every Sunday in the hall of the House of Representatives, with the chaplain or some visiting minister in charge. The diary from early in 1801 of Manasseh Cutler, a minister and member of Congress, shows that Jefferson's attendance was noted and appreciated: "Attended worship at our Hall. Meeting very thin, but the President, his two daughters and a grandson attended, although a rainy day." Other entries were, "Attended worship. . . . Jefferson at the Hall in the morning," and "Attended worship at the Capitol. . . . Mr. Jefferson and his secretary attended."

Cutler finally offered grudging respect, noting that although Jefferson's attendance was "no kind of evidence of any regard for religion," it showed that Jefferson had given up "the idea of bearing down and overturning our religious institutions." Actually, Jefferson had done nothing of the sort. Letters that he wrote to friends and supporters show that he was purposefully disarming his opponents, based on his strategic sense that if he and other freethinking republicans did not "shock or revolt our well-meaning citizens who are coming over to us in a steady stream, we shall completely consolidate the nation in a short time—excepting always the royalists and priests."

Of course, Jefferson's attendance at worship services may have arisen from not only political cleverness but also a desire for company. He described the new President's Mansion as "a great stone house, big enough for two emperors, one pope and the grand lama." What would several decades later be called the White House was often lonely during Jefferson's years, as Sally remained at Monticello. Jefferson's two married daughters served as hostesses from time to time, as did Dolley Madison, wife of Secretary of State James Madison. Private secretaries such as Meriwether Lewis responded to his professional needs.

Yet, Jefferson at times had only a pet mockingbird for intimate conversation. He headed to Monticello whenever he could, spending eight of his first twenty-two months in office at home.

The District of Columbia included the town of Georgetown west of the Capitol, with its charming brick mansions, backed by gardens, on tree-lined streets. The rest of the district, however, could boast of little more than the unfinished Capitol, a large stone structure standing on an eastern hill with a dozen crude wood boardinghouses surrounding it, and the big executive mansion, which had a half-dozen brick houses sprinkled nearby.

From one of those houses, the home of the Madisons on F Street between Thirteenth and Fourteenth, came relished invitations to officials who otherwise would have poured their evenings into social black holes. When Jefferson wanted to escape the mansion at night he headed to the Madisons', where he "spoke almost without ceasing," according to Senator William Maclay of Pennsylvania, in a "loose and rambling" manner that nevertheless "scattered information."

The Madisons offered food that even sober-sided New England reverends revered: beef that "had in the dish spices and something of the sweet herb and Garlic kind, and a rich gravy," wrote Manasseh Cutler. Party-goers at the Madisons' offered gossip about Vice President Aaron Burr, a highly promiscuous widower, and about Jefferson's brilliant young secretary, Meriwether Lewis, who was infatuated with Burr's married daughter, Theodosia. Washingtonians whispered about Minister Louis Turreau, the French ambassador, caught by a justice of the peace in the act of brutally beating his wife. They talked of Captain Zebulon Pike, who had come to the capital after discovering his peak and was on the road to sexual conquests, until it turned out that he was married.

The Reverend Cutler had wanted the capital to be a center of church life, but more popular than any house of worship during the Jefferson administration was the Washington Jockey Club, located four miles from town. The racetrack, one mile long and forty feet wide, was so popular that on race days Congress sometimes sat for only half an hour and then adjourned so that members could hurry over to watch, wager, and wag tongues. There, where people were not so packed in that conversations could be overheard readily, the talk often turned to Thomas Jefferson: What did he truly believe? What were his secrets?

AN ATTEMPT TO SEPARATE CHURCH FROM CHURCH

Jefferson directed his greatest ire against Presbyterians and Congregationalists, most of whom still stood firmly with the Reformation understanding developed by John Calvin. He constantly sought to drive a wedge between them and other Christians who were tending to move away from an emphasis on God's sovereignty and man's depravity. Jefferson called Calvinists "mere Usurpers of the Christian name, teaching a Counter-religion made up of the deliria of crazy imaginations." He equated Pennsylvania Presbyterianism with "fanaticism" and attacked "the blasphemy and absurdity of the five points of Calvin, and the impossibility of defending them." He called Presbyterians "the loudest, the most intolerant of all sects, the most tyrannical, and ambitious," and charged (without any evidence) that they were ready to burn at the stake those who disagreed.

As he won over many Baptists by displaying his benevolence toward missionaries, Jefferson took several steps to divide Christians and conquer. One opportunity came when pro-Jefferson Baptists in Danbury, Connecticut, sent him a letter protesting the continued preferences that Congregationalists received from the Connecticut state government. The Danbury Baptist Association was "sensible that the President of the United States, is not the national Legislator, & also sensible that the national government cannot destroy the Laws of each State." The association, however, wanted Jefferson to raise his voice in favor of equality for all denominations: "Our hopes are strong that the sentiments of our beloved President . . . will shine & prevail through all these States. . . ."

Jefferson responded to these political allies with a kind letter similar to those politicians write by the hundreds each year: I agree with you. My hands are tied, but I'm with you and I hope you succeed. Jefferson thanked the Danbury folks for "affectionate sentiments of esteem and approbation," and told them, "My duties dictate a faithful and zealous pursuit of the interests of my constituents." Then came the "I'm sorry" line: "I contemplate with sovereign reverence that act of the whole American people which declared that their legislature should 'make no law respecting an establishment of religion, or prohibiting the free exercise thereof,' thus building a wall of separation between church and State." In other words, Jefferson was noting, Congress—the American legislature—can make no law in this instance.

Jefferson was not at all saying that the Connecticut establishment of religion was unconstitutional. Everyone in those days knew that was perfectly proper. Everyone knew that the purpose of the First Amendment was to keep the federal government from doing anything to interfere with whatever local arrangements were made. Jefferson could merely conclude his letter with words of hope: "I shall see with sincere satisfaction the progress of those sentiments which tend to restore to man all his natural rights. . . ."

Jefferson's phrase about separation, however, became more powerful than anyone nearly two centuries ago would have suspected. A mid-twentieth-century Supreme Court, searching for some historical bulwarking, stood that phrase on its head. Instead of noting what both the Danbury Baptists and Jefferson understood and meant—that the Constitution clearly blocked any federal action, and it was up to the people of Connecticut to work out their own religious agreements—the Court enshrined Jefferson's hope that Christianity would disappear from public places, and stated that this was the intention of the authors of the First Amendment.

But that was not the only irony to emerge from Jefferson's wordplay. His letter gave Connecticut Baptists a shot in the arm, and they organized politically to remove state religious preferences. When soon afterwards the Connecticut legislature made all denominations equal, such disestablishment was a blow to Congregationalists, but it removed an issue of contention among the denominations. In that manner, Jefferson's pressure may inadvertently have aided the expansion of evangelical institutions that accompanied early-nineteenth-century Christian revival.

While John Mason's fears concerning what Jefferson might do to Christianity were overwrought, his concerns about what Jefferson would not do regarding slavery were accurate. The Jefferson Memorial displays a line from Jefferson's autobiography concerning slaves: "Nothing is more certainly written in the book of fate than that these people are to be free." The memorial leaves off the next two sentences: "Nor is it less certain that the two races, equally free, cannot live in the same government. Native habit, opinion has drawn indelible lines of distinction between them." Blacks were one day to be free—and the next day deported. Jefferson, like other leaders of his time, favored African colonization.

Comparing Jefferson with Washington on this point is instructive. Neither freed his slaves during his lifetime or publicly attacked the institution. But Washington refused to engage in the most profitable part of it, breeding and selling slaves; Jefferson did. Washington in his will freed his slaves. Jefferson did not (except for his own children, it seems). Washington is not on record as having made racist comments; Jefferson in his *Notes on the State of Virginia* went on about the preference of orangutans for black women and the many intellectual inadequacies of slaves. Washington, troubled by slavery, attempted to minimize some of its worst aspects. Jefferson, while theorizing about liberty, followed his typical practice of pursuing his own advantage.

A Disastrous Second Term

The short-term success of Jefferson's outreach to Baptists, and the care he took to avoid infuriating other Christians, was evident in the 1804 campaign. Even in Massachusetts, the center of his opposition, 1,500 people from Baptist churches and other domains filled the seats of a church building on July 4 to give thanks for the Jefferson administration.

When opponents again charged Jefferson with atheism, he replied, "I consider the doctrines of Jesus Christ as delivered by himself to contain the outlines of the sublimest system of morality that has ever been taught." The well-worded message worked, and Jefferson rolled to reelection, without having to acknowledge anything divine in the writings of apostles such as Paul, James, Peter, and John, or the passages in the Gospels that describe miracles. Jefferson was even liberating himself from much of Jesus' specific teaching: If Christ's words contained "the outline," Jefferson's own words could put meat on that skeleton.

However, Jefferson's grabbing hold of part of "the ethics of Jesus"— he liked very much Sermon on the Mount passages concerning turning the other cheek—while leaving out the part that emphasizes the biblical concept of sin led him toward pacifism in foreign policy. Jefferson and his congressional allies cut the army and navy budget from $6 million in 1799 to $1.6 million at a time when English ships, French armies, and Indian braves were all major threats. A Maryland member of Congress, when asked how the United States would defend itself in case of an attack on coastal cities, simply responded, "When the enemy comes, let them take our towns, and let us retire into the country."

With America virtually defenseless, American sailors became England's particular prey. Some had deserted from British ships and found a transatlantic home, but British captains, desperately seeking seamen to fight Napoleon, started stopping American ships and seizing all sailors suspected of desertion. Since it was hard to distinguish British subjects from Americans, thousands of New Worlders found themselves back in the holds of the old.

Even when forced British impressments ran at about a thousand a year, Jefferson did not respond. One congressional critic, John Randolph, said the administration had "the policy of yielding to anything that might come in the shape of insult and aggression." The administration did yield to many foreign requests. When Sidi Suliman Mellimelli, the ambassador from Tunis, arrived in Washington, he impressed diplomat-watchers by wearing robes of "rich scarlet and gold silks topped by a twenty-yard turban of white muslin." When he presented his credentials to Secretary of State James Madison, he had one little request to make: concubines for himself and his entourage. Madison diplomatically provided at State Department expense the services of one woman named Georgia. Madison recorded the cost, as he joked in a letter to Jefferson, under the category of "appropriations to foreign intercourse."

British demands were not satisfied so easily. Jefferson's pacifism merely deepened the likelihood of belligerence during the administration of his successor, and it very nearly did not provide peace in his time. As historian Henry Adams wrote, "England had never learned to strike soft in battle. She expected her antagonists to fight; and if they would not fight, she took them to be cowardly or mean. Jefferson and his government had shown over and over again that no provocation would make them fight; and from the moment that this attitude was understood America became fair prey." In June 1807, when the captain of the American ship *Chesapeake* refused to let men from the British frigate *Leopard* search his ship for deserters, the British attacked. War seemed imminent.

KILLING LIBERTY TO MAINTAIN IT

Here's where Jefferson's belief that he could get away with two-faced approaches, along with his pacifistic pick-and-choose reading of Scripture, led to a degree of government intrusion reminiscent of pre-Revolution British measures. Jefferson, still unwilling to prepare for war, probably drew up himself and certainly forced through Congress an Embargo Act that prohibited as of the beginning of 1808 any American exports to foreign ports, and even any foreign travel by American citizens. Jefferson was like a parent locking up a child in his room for fear of the bullies outside. Unemployment among American shipbuilders, sailors, and would-be exporters grew.

Smugglers did not give in, however, and Jefferson found it necessary to use force against American citizens to uphold the embargo established to avoid using force against foreign oppressors. As the embargo bound up the nation's feet without producing decreased kicking from either England or France, law-breaking escalated. Vermonters accustomed to trading with Canada openly defied the Embargo Act. Other Americans followed.

Since nearly all commerce among states was by coastal vessels, and since schooner captains could pretend that weather or accident had driven them to Nova Scotia or the West Indies, Jefferson had to instruct governors "to consider every vessel as suspicious which has on board any articles of domestic produce in demand at foreign markets, and most especially provisions." Buyers and sellers of wheat, instead of freely trading, were to get certificates from governors allowing them to trade. Those without certificates were to be detained.

The governor of Massachusetts predicted that a refusal to issue certificates to all applicants would lead to "mobs, riots, and convulsions," but Jefferson persisted in his policies. When an armed mob in Newburyport prevented customs officials from detaining a ship about to sail, Jefferson complained about a "rank growth of fraud and open opposition by force." When people in Louisiana wanted to bring in flour from eastern states, Jefferson became the nation's chief dietitian: "I have been averse to letting Atlantic flour go to New Orleans merely that they may have the whitest bread possible."

Americans demanded the right to trade. Jefferson was determined to stop them in order to keep some American products from heading abroad. When the governor of New York reported that residents of his state were in open insurrection, Jefferson begged him to lead troops against the insurgents in order to "crush those audacious proceedings and make the offenders feel the consequences of individuals daring to oppose a law by force."

With the choice of giving up or pressing all the harder, Jefferson pushed through Congress an Enforcement Act (signed into law on January 9, 1809) that placed the entire country under government officials who could seize suspicious cargo anytime they chose. Their authority was even greater than that of the hated British port officials prior to the Revolution. Like those officials, the new bureaucrats were freed of legal liability for wrongful seizures, and were told to count on support when needed from the army, navy, or militia.

It looked as if civil war might break out. Citizens in New England towns such as Bath and Gloucester established committees of safety and correspondence, just as they had before the Revolution. They vowed "to give immediate alarm [when] any officer of the United States" tried to enforce the embargo. Citizens of Newburyport voted not to "aid or assist in the execution of the several embargo laws," and to declare "unworthy of confidence and esteem" any who did assist. Four thousand citizens at a Boston town meeting at Faneuil Hall vowed that those trying to enforce "the arbitrary and unconstitutional provisions [of the embargo] ought to be considered as enemies to the

Constitution of the United States and of this State." Town meetings elsewhere warned that administration measures would "tend to produce . . . a dissolution of the Union."

Governors began to declare their independence. Connecticut governor Jonathan Trumbull said he would not instruct his state's militia to help federal officials charged with enforcing an embargo. The measure, he said, was "unconstitutional in many of its provisions, interfering with the State sovereignties, and subversive of the rights, privileges, and immunities of the citizens of the United States." Trumbull declared that since federal legislators had decided "to overleap their prescribed bounds of their constitutional powers," state legislatures should "interpose their protecting shield between the rights and liberties of the people and the assumed power of the general government."

Ironically, this language was very similar to what Jefferson and Madison had penned a decade before for the Virginia and Kentucky legislatures in response to John Adams. In ten years, positions had reversed. The logic of embargo was pushing Jefferson to centralize control as he had accused federalists of doing—even though he knew, merely by looking at the nation's geography, that such control was impossible. But Jefferson at the end of his term kept pushing on, until Congress gave up, voting 81–40 early in 1809 to turn its back on the president and repeal his embargo. Extremism in the defense of pacifism had not worked.

Given his unpopularity at the end of his second term, Jefferson could not have been reelected, so it was easy for him to follow George Washington's example and leave. Jefferson had taken such abuse during his last year of office that he wrote, "Never did a prisoner released from his chains feel such relief as I shall on shaking off the shackles of power."

LAST YEARS

Three years after Jefferson left office, Britain and the United States began a war so ill defined that it was called only by a year, 1812. Two years after that British troops faced American forces so inadequate that Washington was readily seized and burned. But Jeffersonian unpreparedness curiously allowed for the emergence of a national anthem: The unlikely survival of Fort McHenry inspired Francis Scott Key to write about bombs bursting in air. A new national hero also emerged, as a decidedly nonpacifist Andrew Jackson pushed American forces to an even more unlikely victory in New Orleans.

Jefferson was increasingly ignored around the country, but he continued his active letter-writing and local efforts. That the United States would become Unitarian remained his fervent wish, and in 1822 Jefferson predicted in one letter, "I confidently expect that the present generation will see Unitarianism become the general religion of the United States." He went even further in another letter later that year: "I trust that there is not a young man now living in the United States who will not die a Unitarian."

Jefferson tried to push along that prospect in several ways. He plotted to have the new University of Virginia appoint Unitarians to teach courses in moral philosophy. His original plans kept Christian teaching out, and when he was forced to compromise on that he still insisted that Sunday services not be conducted on university grounds. Jefferson favored Sunday mail delivery and opposed laws for Sabbath closings, complaining privately that such rules gave Christian ministers "opportunities of delivering their oracles to the people in mass, and of moulding their minds as wax in the hollow of their hands."

Fond feelings associated with the fiftieth anniversary of the Declaration of Independence kept Jefferson from being an unpopular man when he died on July 4, 1826, the same day as John Adams. Both of them had left their presidencies under a cloud, but they had performed important service during the Revolutionary War. Adams's reputation never made much of a comeback, but Jefferson's did over the next century, as Americans forgot his actions and remembered the Declaration of Independence.

Overall, Jefferson's career provides an important example of how even a leader who scorned any Scripture he could not control, and implemented policies contrary to biblical teaching, did not quite wreck a country with a decentralized government and a citizenry committed to preserving both liberty and virtue. Privately, Jefferson was free of many religious and sexual restraints, but he apparently practiced politically safe sex and made safer religious comments than he readily could have made. He hoped that within a generation of his death the public would be ready for his progressive theology, but he knew that was not the case during his lifetime, so he could justify some political misdirection. Jefferson loved the People but not people, and such were his ambiguities of expression that both liberals and libertarians have been able to make him a patron saint.

CHAPTER 3

Andrew Jackson

Democrats for years had Jefferson-Jackson Day dinners commemorating the early years of the nation's oldest continuing political party. The placing of the two men together was accurate in that they both made important political contributions, but flawed in that their ethical stances were so opposed. Jefferson often chose cleverness over consistency and flight rather than a fight, but Jackson was the most Bible-rooted, principled, and combative of our nineteenth-century presidents. (Ironically, many among the conventional eastern clergy opposed his candidacy.)

Andrew Jackson, born on March 15, 1767, was a combatant from childhood. His father died a few days before he was born, and Jackson learned to fight his own battles. Attending school in the Waxhaw (South Carolina) Presbyterian Church, he got into so many fights because of his temper that teachers sometimes despaired. But young Jackson also learned to read so well that at age nine he was selected to read to his illiterate neighbors Thomas Jefferson's just-approved Declaration of Independence.

Later in the Revolutionary War, when General Cornwallis's troops stormed through the South on raids such as the one that chased Jefferson from Monticello, Jackson began fighting for real. In April 1781, British raiders captured the fourteen-year-old and ordered him to clean their boots. When Jackson refused, stating his rights as a prisoner of war, the British commander saber-slashed his head and hand. Soon afterwards Jackson's mother died of smallpox. The orphan "felt utterly alone." He could have fallen into self-pity, but instead read whenever he could, found mentors, and fought his way through law books, gaining admission to the bar in 1787, at age twenty.

In 1788, Jackson received an appointment as solicitor (attorney general, we would call it today) for the territory that would soon be Tennessee. He headed to a new town, Nashville, but retained much of what he had learned in church and school. Some settlers believed that Revolutionary War success had ushered in a golden age of frontier anarchy, and Jackson could have gained some immediate, short-run popularity by overlooking laws concerning debt. Instead, he sent debtors to jail. He went on to argue that government also should pay its debts, and stay small enough to keep British-style bribery and corruption from flourishing.

Jackson's enemies later on searched this period of his life for dirt concerning adultery to fling at him. But, as Jackson told one correspondent, "I was brought up a rigid Presbyterian, to which I have always adhered." That rigidity led him to direct his fighting spirit into politics and his physical passion in the direction of one woman, Rachel Donelson, whom he married in 1791. The circumstances of that marriage, however, were often flung at him. Rachel had been abandoned by a previous husband, who wrote her that he had obtained a divorce in Kentucky. Two years after they were married, the Jacksons learned that the divorce had not occurred until after the marriage date. From then on, enemies could always make accusations: Rachel had been technically an adulteress, and Jackson had "stolen" another man's wife.

Slurs concerning his marriage did not derail Jackson's political career. Elected a delegate to the Tennessee statehood convention in 1796, he fought a popular proposal to name the new state Franklin or Washington. He argued that most of the original states had been named after British monarchs or nobles, and that a free people should set a different pattern. Jackson was delighted when delegates agreed to name their state Tennessee after the Cherokee name for "the Great Crooked River" that ran through much of the state. The word "Tennessee," he said, "has a flavor on the tongue as sweet as hot corn-cakes and honey."

Jackson also won a battle against ultra-Jeffersonians who wished to ban clergymen from political office. He argued that separation of churchmen and state was unholy folly, particularly because politics needed the saltiness of those least likely to see government as god. He won that debate as well and continued to rise politically, only to find he was poorly fitted by temperament to a life of wheeling and dealing. As a member of the U.S. House of Representatives in 1796 and the U.S. Senate in 1797, he became impatient with the pace of legislation, and others became impatient with him: "His passions are terrible," Thomas Jefferson said.

Jackson also disliked separation from Rachel during the legislative terms. He resigned from the Senate in 1798 to come back to Nashville, live with his beloved, and become a businessman, buying and selling land and racehorses and owning a general store. For fifteen years he was out of the national spotlight, but appointments came to him: justice of the state supreme court, major general in the Tennessee militia. So did duels, including one with future senator Thomas Hart Benton and his brother Jesse that left Jackson with a bullet wound beneath his left shoulder that never healed entirely.

The duels came almost invariably when someone brought up the legal details of Jackson's marriage and called Rachel a loose woman. Christians and others were increasingly condemning the tradition of the duel, but Jackson still felt bound by it when his wife's honor was at stake. Jackson's most famous duel came in 1806 when Charles Dickinson, known as the best marksman in Tennessee, was apparently asked by Jackson's political opponents to deliberately insult him and provoke a duel. Jackson was ready to fight, but the night before the duel, knowing his opponent's marksmanship, Jackson removed the buttons from his coat and sewed them back on three inches below their normal position.

When the duel commenced in a poplar forest on the banks of the Red River north of Nashville, Dickinson fired rapidly at what he thought was Jackson's heart. The bullet struck three inches below his heart, breaking two ribs and lodging in the chest cavity. Jackson steadied himself, aimed, and pulled off a fatal shot that ripped through his adversary's intestines. Doctors were never able to remove the bullet in Jackson's chest, and it led to many respiratory infections that caused incessant coughing that brought up blood.

The injury did not keep Jackson from leadership during the War of 1812, when he received the label "tough as hickory" for his ability to overcome supply difficulties and lead a volunteer force of two thousand men in a successful winter campaign against Creek Indians who had massacred 250 to 400 settlers at Fort Mims in the Mississippi Territory. Jackson's forces, almost starving, routed the Creeks in a series of battles.

The last big battle came at Horseshoe Bend, where the Creeks waited confidently behind a massive breastwork of logs 450 yards long that stretched across a river bend. Jackson's aides thought the Creeks, protected by logs in front and swirling water in back, had an impregnable position. Jackson commented, "They've penned themselves up for slaughter," and he was right: Eight hundred Creeks died, and the war was over. Jackson's merciless strategy against a savage opponent succeeded; later, when he took a hard line against Cherokee Indians who had adopted peaceful agricultural pursuits, he received justified criticism.

AGINCOURT AND AFTER

Jackson's victory against the Creeks led federal officials to give him responsibility for defense against an anticipated British invasion of New Orleans. There, over the objections of local officials, he welcomed into a scraped-together army Jean Lafitte—a part-Haitian, part-Jewish, all-trouble pirate—and his corsair followers. Lafitte's men and cannon were much needed, and Jackson also believed that God could redeem even buccaneers. During the weeks leading up to the Battle of New Orleans, while others panicked at the thought of fighting British regulars who had defeated Napoleon, Jackson prayed ardently and told others, during and after the battle, that they should fear neither life nor death because "the unerring hand of Providence" is always active amidst the "shower of Balls, bombs, and Rockets. . . ."

Jackson's theology enabled him to overcome prejudice in one other crucial way as well. He worked to raise black battalions from among the freemen of New Orleans. When a paymaster refused to pay the new recruits, Jackson told him to obey orders and "keep to yourself your opinions." Jackson spoke of the black soldiers' "intelligent minds and love of honor" and offered them assurances that they would not be exposed to "improper comparisons, or unjust sarcasm."

Jackson's preparations and British arrogance were elements in a one-sided U.S. victory matched in world history only by surprises such as Henry V's Agincourt. U.S. forces in the Persian Gulf campaign of 1991 had the advantage of superior technology and training, an advantage that British forces had in 1815, but the British attacked in close order against earthworks defended by Jackson's rifles and pirate cannon. As a popular song from a century and a half later still told the story, first "they fired their guns and the British kept coming," then "they fired some more and the British went a-running." London's best were left with seven hundred dead and twice that number wounded; American losses were seven killed, six wounded.

When news of the astounding numbers spread Jackson was a national hero, but he continued the practice he had followed for two decades of reading three chapters of the Bible daily. That immersion in Scripture had not kept Jackson from fighting duels, but it did show when Jackson wrote to Secretary of State James Monroe following the New Orleans rout. Rather than taking credit for the victory, Jackson wrote, "Heaven, to be sure, has interposed most wonderfully in our behalf, and I am filled with gratitude."

Just as the Declaration of Independence made Jefferson famous, so the Battle of New Orleans brought Jackson a nation's gratitude.

Various political factions saw him as an attractive candidate because of both his past and his imposing presence. On a horse Jackson impressed even an equestrian expert who noted, "His seat is an uncommonly good one, his hand apparently light, and his carriage easy and horsemanlike." Politicians were awed by not only Jackson's carriage but also his intensity: Tall and thin, he seemed austere, honest, and determined. One journalist said that Jackson in an assembly of a thousand men "would have been pointed out above all the others as a man 'born to command.'" When walking Jackson never strolled. He strode.

Such a man was in demand as it became evident in the early 1820s that the Monroe administration's "era of good feeling" would not last. James Monroe had been an anti-federalist during the 1787 debates about ratifying the Constitution, and his emphasis on strictly limited government swept the field in 1816 and 1820 and wiped out what remained of the Federalist Party. During his second term, however, younger leaders like John Quincy Adams and Henry Clay were pushing for a stronger central government, and the question was whether Jackson would join them or choose to emphasize small government and personal virtue.

JACKSON VERSUS THE "DAMNED RASCALS"

Jackson had to sort out not only his politics but, more important, his theology. He had grown up under Presbyterian training and had read and prayed regularly as an adult, but he had never joined a church. Jackson's reputation as a duelist made evangelists such as Peter Cartwright at first believe that he placed his own will above God's. In 1816, when Cartwright was preaching in Nashville, a local pastor, Brother Mac, pulled him aside and said excitedly, "General Jackson has come in, General Jackson has come in." Cartwright knew of Jackson, but he was so irritated at the emphasis on a celebrity sighting that he said loudly, "Who is General Jackson? If he don't get his soul converted, God will damn him. . . ."

After the service Brother Mac hurried over to Jackson to apologize for Cartwright's remarks, but Jackson later that day saw Cartwright and told him, "You are a man after my own heart. I was very much surprised at Mr. Mac, to think he would suppose that I would be offended at you. No, sir; I told him that I highly approved of your independence; that a minister of Jesus Christ ought to love everybody and fear no mortal man. I told Mr. Mac that if I had a few thousand such independent, fearless officers, as you were, and a well drilled army, I could take old England."

Cartwright became a friend who vouched for Jackson's theological firmness and told of how he was once eating dinner with Jackson when a lawyer at the table started to make fun of Cartwright's Christian beliefs. Cartwright responded patiently but "saw General Jackson's eye strike fire, as he sat by and heard the thrusts he made at the Christian religion." The conversation became more intense when the lawyer asked, "Mr. Cartwright, do you believe there is any such place as hell, as a place of torment?" Jackson stirred in his seat as Cartwright answered affirmatively and the lawyer responded, "I thank God I have too much good sense to believe any such thing."

That's when Jackson could no longer hold his tongue. Cartwright reported that Jackson said heatedly, "I thank God that there is such a place of torment as hell." The lawyer, startled by Jackson's "great vehemence," then earned his spot in the hall of fame for dumb questions by asking, "General Jackson, what do you want with such a place of torment as hell?" Jackson quickly responded, "To put such damned rascals as you are in, that oppose and vilify the Christian religion." According to Cartwright's story, the lawyer fled the room.

Jackson caused other scoffers to flee when President Monroe appointed him governor of Florida territory in 1821. At the territorial capital of Pensacola, Rachel Jackson noted in her journal, "The Sabbath [was] profanely kept; a great deal of noise and swearing [was] in the streets. . . ." A week later, after Jackson gave stern orders, Rachel reported significant change: "Great order was observed . . . the gambling houses demolished . . . cursing not to be heard."

Despite his professions and practices Jackson did not join a church. He later explained defensively that church membership was not emphasized as much in the West as in the East, and that he was too great a sinner in his younger days, with a duel-fighting temper. Yet

Jackson knew that Christianity is for sinners, not for those who consider themselves righteous. He acknowledged repeatedly that it was important for him to join, and was planning to do so in 1823, but then he once again hesitated, telling his wife, "If I were to do that now, it would be said, all over the country, that I had done it for the sake of political effect." He pledged that "once I am clear of politics I will join." That time receded into the future as his muscular administration of Florida established among many the idea that Jackson could not only win battles but also run a government.

The first step in Jackson's return to life at the national capital came when the Tennessee legislature once again chose him for the Senate. Jackson spent enough time in Washington to develop a dislike for the city's social scene: In 1824 he wrote to a friend, "I would to God I could now leave the city. . . . There is nothing done here but visiting and carding." But Jackson did hand over his card at times and attend occasional receptions. He even impressed Washington denizens for having "the peculiar, rough, independent, free and easy ways of the backwoodsman; but in the society of ladies very urbane and graceful manners." Yet Jackson felt himself in hostile territory in Washington and prayed for protection to "the God of Isaac and of Jacob. . . . In Him alone we ought to trust."

THE FIGHTER VERSUS THE WRITER

In 1824, President Monroe announced that he would maintain the tradition set by Washington of two terms and out. The presidential campaign thus opened with speculation of a John Quincy Adams–Jackson ticket:

> *John Quincy Adams,*
> *Who can write,*
> *And Andrew Jackson,*
> *Who can fight.*

But Adams wanted a larger government, Jackson a smaller one, and soon Jackson's supporters began promoting him for the top spot. In the fall election Jackson gained more electoral votes than Adams or Henry

Clay, but no one had a majority and the choice went to the House of Representatives.

The eventual result was what Jackson's followers called a "corrupt bargain": Clay threw his support to Adams, Adams was elected, Adams made Clay his secretary of state. The practice would not raise eyebrows now, but it did raise Jackson's anger then. For four years he fumed as John Quincy Adams pushed government growth. In December 1825, Adams asked Congress to set up a national system of highways and canals, a national university, a department of the interior, and so on. Government, Adams wrote, had a "sacred and indispensable" duty to work for "the progressive improvement of the condition of the governed."

Adams tried to make his case by looking to Europe and contending that since countries there were making "gigantic strides . . . in public improvements," American legislators should follow foreign examples and "not be palsied by the will of our constituents." Many advocates in recent decades have banged Americans over the head with "progressive" European examples, but in the 1820s this approach was novel and, to Jackson, disgusting. Imitate Europe, from which Americans had become independent?

Jackson became so angry over the job expansion pattern of Adams and Clay that by 1828 he was charging, "The patronage of the government for the last three years has been wielded to corrupt every thing that comes within its influence, and was capable of being corrupted." Honor and fidelity were paramount for Jackson, so it was infuriating that "The administrators of the Govt have stained our national character." The 1828 presidential election, Jackson wrote, would be "a contest between the virtue of the people and the influence of patronage."

That election turned out to be one for the gutter. One newspaper backed by Henry Clay, the *Cincinnati Gazette,* charged that "General Jackson's mother was a COMMON PROSTITUTE, brought to this country by British soldiers!" Backers of Adams also attacked Jackson for overstepping his rightful authority in setting up Sabbath regulations in Pensacola and for executing six deserters during wartime. Those charges did not seem to stick, and Jackson's followers turned the labeling of Jackson as a "killer" to his political advantage by responding, "Why don't you tell the whole truth? On the 8th of January, 1815, he murdered in the coldest kind of cold blood 1500 British soldiers for merely trying to get into New Orleans."

Jackson's supporters hit back at Adams for supposedly wearing silk underwear and, as ambassador to Russia, introducing young American women to lascivious nobles. ("He pimped for the Czar.") Adams, they charged, had installed expensive furniture in the White House and used public funds to buy a billiard table and a chess set. Adams, they said, loved Europe, while Jackson was an all-American who would toss out big chunks of the growing government bureaucracy before it could get settled.

Church members divided their votes in the election. Some staid eastern clerics condemned Jackson as a man of blood, duels, and violent oaths. Sometimes, they also threw in Jackson's face the mix-up at the start of his marriage, and ignored Jackson's ardent faithfulness to his wife during thirty-seven years of marriage. There never was a hint of any extramarital conduct, but Jackson was still under fire as a hot-blooded hell-raiser. Jackson kept his temper amid most such attacks, considering them part of the political process; he went wild only when opponents besmirched Rachel's character.

Amid all the political talk, Jackson tried to hold on to the knowledge of God's sovereignty that he had conveyed to his men as they awaited British assault. When the wife of close friend Andrew Donelson died, Jackson advised him to "submit to the will of God who holds our lives in his hand and say with humble and contrite hearts, 'The Lord's will be done on earth as it is in heaven.'" To the family of a recently deceased general, Jackson wrote, "Rely on our dear Savior. He will be father to the fatherless and husband to the widow. Trust in the mercy and goodness of Christ, and always be ready to say with heartfelt resignation, 'may the Lord's will be done.'"

The hardest challenge came when Jackson had to counsel himself to bear up under hardship. Sorrow at his own hearth could well have choked Jackson's heart when Rachel sickened upon hearing that the old charges of her infidelity were current again and died following her husband's election to the presidency but before his inauguration.

Here was a real test of Jackson's faith. Some men, not seeing God's sovereignty over ballots as well as bodies, might have crowed about their success at men's hands and raged about their loss at God's. But Jackson wrote, "We who are frequently visited by this chastening rod, have the consolation to read in the Scriptures that whomever He chasteneth He loveth, and does it for their good to make them mindful of their mortality and that this earth is not our abiding place; and afflicts us that we may prepare for a better world, a happy immortality."

Rachel had urged her husband to greater piety over the years, and it would have been unsurprising for Jackson to turn away from the rectitude she and God required, had his faith been more in her than in Christ. That was not the case: Jackson continued his pattern of Bible reading and prayer, although he did it in a way that remembered Rachel as well as God. One night when Jackson was a widower and his private secretary, Nicholas Trist, needed guidance for a letter, Trist knocked at Jackson's bedroom door, was admitted, and found Jackson partly undressed and sitting at a table, reading his nightly chapters from Scripture. Jackson had a miniature portrait of Rachel that he usually wore over his heart propped up before him.

But in 1829 there was a nation to lead, and Jackson overcame his grief. He began by firing many of the Adams officials, while trying to impress upon his own supporters that positions outside government were far more central to the functioning of society than those within. When a clergyman called on him seeking a federal appointment, Jackson asked, "Are you not a Christian minister?" The clergyman replied, "I am," to which Jackson responded, "If you discharge the duties of that office, which is better than any I can confer, you will have no time for any other."

Jackson made sure his theological base was in place; he supplemented his Bible reading with regular worship at a nearby Presbyterian church. Jefferson as president had sliced up the New Testament, but Jackson in the White House spoke and wrote of Christ and the need for prayer. To his son, Andrew, Jr., Jackson wrote, "I nightly offer up my prayers to the throne of grace for the health and safety of you all, and that we ought all to rely with confidence on the promises of our dear Redeemer, and give Him our hearts." As Jackson had noted, presidents could cynically make religious proclamations if they chose, but Jackson's letters had such intense earnestness that if he had not been sincere his letters would have been immense works of art.

BATTLE OVER THE BANK

Jackson's willingness to put aside immediate gratification and fight for long-term satisfactions came to the fore during the biggest fight of his presidency, the battle over the Second Bank of the United States. The bank was a public-private partnership, with vast, government-backed financial power in the hands of a few. It was a monopoly, the only bank chartered by the United States, and the repository for all deposits of U.S. government revenues—deposits that did not draw interest. From its headquarters building, a marble faux Greek temple in Philadelphia, the bank bought influence through bribes and favoritism in making loans.

The bank's president, Nicholas Biddle, was a suave steward much admired by European visitors to America. One British traveler, comparing Biddle to the rough-hewn types he often met, called him "the most perfect specimen of an American gentleman that I had yet seen." Biddle had also gained influence in Congress by dispensing loans and favors; as Henry Clay once told him, "You hold a large flask of oil and know well how to pour it out."

The bank's friends were powerful. Senator Daniel Webster of Massachusetts was brandy's poster boy, since without it his eloquence stayed home, but with it he was spellbinding. When asked about taking bribes from the bank, he related that when he was a child his hands were so dirty that a disgusted teacher looked at one of them and said, "Daniel, if you can find me another hand in this school that is dirtier than that, I will let you off." Daniel promptly held out the other hand, and she had to let him off. The grown-up and fleshed-out Daniel Webster held out his hand to Nicholas Biddle and dirtied it with payoffs, but he could always point to another hand that was dirtier.

That did not make him clean, however—either objectively or in Andrew Jackson's eyes. Jackson believed it was fine to build fortunes through private dealing, but wrong for those with wealth to get more by wielding governmental power as Biddle did. He knew the political danger in taking on the bank and its well-oiled supporters, but he said, "Until I can strangle this hydra of corruption, the Bank, I will not shrink from my duty."

On July 10, 1832, Jackson vetoed a bill to recharter the bank that had slid through a greased Congress. His veto message laid out the principle that "In the full enjoyment of the gifts of Heaven and the fruits of superior industry, economy, and virtue, every man is equally entitled to protection by law." He argued that government should "confine itself to equal protection, and, as Heaven does its rain, shower its favors alike on the high and the low, the rich and the poor."

The bank, he went on to argue, proceeded on a different principle: It did not help some people to become wealthy by "natural and just advantages," but lobbied "to grant titles, gratuities, and exclusive privileges, to make the rich richer and the potent more powerful." Once favors are handed out, Jackson stipulated, then those without political pull "have a right to complain of the injustice of their Government."

Jackson also emphasized the constitutional framework: "Some of the powers and privileges possessed by the existing bank are unauthorized by the Constitution, subversive of the rights of the States, and dangerous to the liberties of the people." The goal of statesmen, Jackson argued, should not be to increase their own power, but to stress "leaving individuals and States as much as possible to themselves."

Even though the Supreme Court had declared a bank constitutional, Jackson included such constitutional interpretation in his veto message. (In Jackson's view, Supreme Court decisions did not "control the Congress or the Executive when acting in their legislative capacities, but [had] such influence as the force of their reasoning may deserve.") He argued that the federal government should be "felt not in its power . . . but in its protection; not in binding the States more closely to the center, but leaving each to move unobstructed in its proper orbit."

Once Jackson vetoed the bill, the bank war truly began. Biddle called the veto message "a manifesto of anarchy" and thought it so obviously bad that he paid to have 30,000 copies printed and distributed. Jackson, meanwhile, challenged the bank by removing from its vaults federal deposits and placing them in state banks; the bank would have to call in some of its loans.

Biddle then pioneered in what federally funded bureaucrats under pressure have done ever since: make sure that ordinary folks hurt. Biddle did not call in loans to his friends or to those who could readily afford to pay back the money. Instead, he demanded funds from those who would yell the loudest and tell the world that the financial sky was falling. He told associates that he planned to produce and publicize "evidence of suffering." He said he would destroy the economy to make his point: "all the merchants may break, but the Bank of the United States shall not break."

As loans to small businesses were called, many failed. Thousands of wage earners became unemployed. Protests snowed under congressmen, many of whom turned to the White House and pleaded that the deposits be returned to Biddle. Here's where Jackson's willingness to give up immediate gratification, and his loyalty to a higher power, became crucial: In response to all protests Jackson replied, "I care nothing about clamors. I do precisely what I think is just and right."

Day after day visiting delegations of businessmen besieged him. Jackson emphasized that "brokers and gamblers" were hardest hit, "and would to God they were all swept from the land!" So intense did he become in a conversation with a group of Biddle-backers that he started speaking in the third person: "Andrew Jackson will never restore the deposits! Andrew Jackson will never recharter that monster of corruption! Sooner than live in a country where such a power prevails, I would seek asylum in the wilds of Arabia."

Bank partisans such as Henry Clay packed the gallery of the Senate with bank employees and their families, and then orated about "helpless widows . . . unclad and unfed orphans . . . let [Jackson] not drive this brave, generous, and patriotic people to madness and despair." The Senate voted 26–20 to censure Jackson. Anyone without a lifetime of fortitude would have caved, but Jackson told one and all, "Go to the monster. Go to Nicholas Biddle. I will not bow down to the golden calf."

Then Biddle squeezed credit further. Senator John Tyler of Virginia complained, "Bankruptcy to the North is almost general." The impasse went on for over a year. Jackson was seemingly alone; even his own secretary of the treasury resigned. But Jackson held firm. Once, writing a letter to a friend on a Sunday morning, he almost seemed to be wavering, but then he noted, "I must stop. The church bells are ringing and I must attend."

Eventually Biddle overreached himself by refusing a loan of $300,000 to the Commonwealth of Pennsylvania, at which point Governor George Wolf turned against the bank and denounced Biddle for "bringing indiscriminate ruin on our unoffending community." The Pennsylvania Senate sent resolutions to Congress urging a rejection of Biddle's demands. The state of New York then created its own $6 million emergency fund so that state banks would not have to go crawling to Biddle.

With the tide turning in the states, congressional leaders gained new courage. House Ways and Means Committee chairman James K. Polk pushed through his chamber resolutions against restoring deposits and rechartering the bank. In July 1834, Biddle gave up, restored normal credit, and began to plan for the bank's demise. The financial crisis disappeared. Business picked up rapidly. Jackson's willingness to say no and commitment to duty had saved the day. Several parties of celebration in Washington featured punch bowls filled with "Daniel Webster punch," which was made of Medford rum, brandy, champagne, arrack (an Asian distillation of rum), strong tea, lemon juice, and sugar.

FIDELITY: SEXUAL, CONSTITUTIONAL, AND THEOLOGICAL

Jackson fought in other ways to show that he would be as faithful to the American public and to the Constitution as he had been to Rachel over thirty-seven years. He knew from the Battle of New Orleans the ability of an entrenched force to withstand assault, so he did not want government officials to entrench themselves. Arguing for term limits of four years for appointed officials, he dismissed two thousand of the federal government's eleven thousand employees. That was about the same percentage as Jefferson had axed, but Jackson's critics complained about the "spoils system." Jackson replied by observing that when citizens became bureaucrats for extended stretches, "Office is considered a species of property, and government rather as a means of promoting individual interests than as an instrument created solely for the service of the people."

Jackson's political philosophy was straightforward enough to be summarized by the Marine Corps slogan: *semper fidelis*, "always faithful." No privileges to those with political clout. No federal discrimination among citizens, benefiting some at the expense of others. (However, discrimination against those not classed as citizens, most notably slaves, remained.) No governmental redistribution of income, whether through taxes, tariffs, or government aid to individuals, businesses, or labor groups. No federal preference for one section of the country above another, and thus no legitimate reason to break up the Union.

Underlying all this was the Bible-based presupposition that since God is God and man is man, problems emerge when government, to quote Jacksonian journalist William Leggett, "assumes the functions which belong alone to an overruling Providence, and affects to become the universal dispenser of good and evil." Statesmen should not "reduce men from a dependence on their own exertions, to a dependence on the caprices of their Government." Jackson vetoed spending measures such as Henry Clay's pet Maysville Road project, discussed in the next chapter, because he understood that acceptance of federal projects designed to aid particular regions would merely encourage congressmen to sit at the pork barrel and logroll their way to legislative longevity, to build campaigns for office instead of a country.

Jackson also believed, sometimes literally, that the White House belonged to the people. The downside of his approach became clear on March 4, 1829, at history's most famous White House reception: Jackson invited thousands of his supporters to come celebrate with him, and many who had never received lessons in etiquette did. Surging crowds broke windows, smashed china, and trampled on furniture. Supporters of John Quincy Adams nodded knowingly and predicted even worse to come. At future receptions, however, Jackson and his cabinet shook hands with self-controlled, lined-up visitors. Hostesses dressed in American calico without ruffles or ornaments (women at the Adams's parties wore French dresses) welcomed guests. Democracy, rather than mobocracy, had triumphed.

Jackson's refusal to cut off supporters from lower-class backgrounds, combined with his sympathy for women who were gossiped about as his late wife had been, led to one major cabinet battle. Peggy O'Neale, a beautiful and seductive tavern maid, had for years supplied gossips with raw material. By the time she was fifteen she had been the object of a duel, the proximate cause of a suicide, and the reason a love-stricken general collapsed. At age sixteen she was frustrated in two attempts to elope. She married an alcoholic and thief, but Major John Eaton, a Jackson friend, rescued her by posting a bond of $10,000 for her financially embarrassed husband and then arranging for him to gain a berth on the frigate *Constitution* as it began a four-year trip around the world.

Eaton, according to the gossips, then took Peggy's husband's place, unofficially. When the husband died aboard the *Constitution*—from tuberculosis officially, from drunkenness according to his shipmates, and from cutting his throat because he heard of his wife's relationship with Eaton, according to Washington gossips—Peggy O'Neale became Peggy Eaton. When Jackson made Eaton secretary of war, some wives of cabinet members refused to exchange social visits with a woman who did not seem like a lady, their husbands took their sides, and Jackson took Peggy Eaton's side. Eventually almost the entire cabinet resigned, but Jackson had shown his loyalty to a woman in distress.

Jackson had his personal favorites, and at the same time opposed any official governmental favoritism, arguing that once bad legislation is adopted, the abuses it creates became obstacles to reformation. As Leggett wrote, "Those who profit by abuses are always more clamorous for their continuance than those who are only opposing them from motives of justice or patriotism, are for their abandonment." All of Jackson's strong stands can be seen as an attempt to stop big dictators like Biddle or small ones like arrogant government clerks before they could become entrenched.

No Time for Tears

One stand that Jackson took is still especially controversial. Late in the eighteenth century the federal government entered into treaties with the Cherokee Indians that guaranteed them their lands in perpetuity. In 1802, however, Thomas Jefferson gained support in Georgia by promising that the federal government would purchase Cherokee land and transfer it to the state. The contradictory promises were not a problem while Cherokees freely sold their lands to the federal government, but in 1819 the Cherokee Nation declared that it would give up no more land. By 1827 the Cherokees, who had adopted "the white man's way" of farming, towns, schools, and churches, also had a newspaper, Elias Boudinot's *Cherokee Phoenix,* and a written constitution.

The Cherokees were not like the Creeks, against whom Jackson had wrought military revenge. Cherokees owned, in Boudinot's compilation, ten sawmills, thirty-one gristmills, sixty-two blacksmith shops, and nearly six thousand spinning wheels and plows. Sadly, some powerful Georgians coveted the Cherokees' land, despised their racial identity, and tried to push them out. The Georgia legislature in 1828 stated that Georgia, regardless of federal treaty, had dominion over Cherokee land, with all Cherokee "laws, usages, and customs" null and void. The Cherokees could not even try to hold onto their rights in court, for the new Georgia law stated that no Indian "shall be deemed a competent witness, or a party to any suits . . . to which a white man may be a party."

Jackson, faced upon assuming office with the issue of upholding state sovereignty or federal guarantees, sided with states' rights. His first annual message to Congress, in December 1829, noted that the Cherokees' "present condition, contrasted with what they once were, makes a most powerful appeal to our sympathies." But he also stated, "It is too late to inquire whether it was just to include them and their territory within the bounds of new states, whose limits they could control. That step cannot be retraced. A State cannot be dismembered by Congress or restricted in the exercise of her constitutional power."

Jackson offered the Cherokees two alternatives. One was, "submitting to the laws of the States, and receiving, like other citizens, protection in their persons and property." That was overly optimistic, since Georgia had just denied Indians protection. Furthermore, that outcome would not be desired by some Cherokees, since Jackson's expectation was that "they will ere long become merged in the mass of our population." The other alternative assumed that integration would not work: "I suggest for your consideration the propriety of setting apart an ample district west of the Mississippi." That alternative received popular support, at least in Georgia, Alabama, and Mississippi.

The Cherokees responded by sending a delegation to Washington in 1830 and publishing an appeal to the nation. A few Cherokees would voluntarily move west of the Mississippi, the delegation declared, but most "cannot endure to be deprived of our national and individual rights and subjected to a process of intolerable oppression." The delegation asked "the good people of the United States" to remember that many of "*their* fathers were compelled" to leave Europe: Pressuring Indians to head west would hardly be remembering to "Do to others as ye would that others should do to you." That appeal, sadly, did not move Jackson. In this situation, he came to believe that animosity between Indians and whites made further clashes unavoidable unless the Indians became wards of Washington, and that he would not allow.

The outcome of the impasse was one of the uglier episodes of American history. In the mid-1830s, Cherokees such as John Ridge and Elias Boudinot accepted what had become inevitable and decided to head west. Ridge found the land of eastern Oklahoma good and wrote to the recalcitrant, "The soil is diversified from the best prairie lands to the best bottom lands, in vast tracts. Never did I see a better location for settlement and better springs in the world. God has thrown His favors here with a broad cast." But when most Cherokees refused to go, the talk of "voluntary" movement ended. Soldiers rounded up 12,000 Cherokees and placed them in detention camps. Somewhere between one and four thousand Cherokees died there or on the "trail of tears" to Oklahoma. There, opponents of any agreement took revenge on Ridge and Boudinot, murdering both.

Had Jackson offered leadership in pursuit of fair treatment of the Cherokees within state law, he might possibly have pointed the way toward an integrationist option. Given the tide of antebellum thought, however, that seems most unlikely. Alternatively, had more Cherokees accepted a decent land trade and moved voluntarily, fewer tears would have flowed. Jackson stayed with his decision throughout the 1830s and was not pleased with the outcome, but during the decade, as Jackson seemed increasingly aware of his sinful nature, he never counted Cherokee removal as one of his sins.

Jackson and God

In the White House during the middle of the decade and back in Nashville from 1837 on, Jackson was beginning to fail physically. The bullet that still sat by his left lung caused periodic problems. Dysentery and malaria that he had contracted during his campaign against the Creek Indians also made ghostly appearances, and rheumatism was a regular visitor. Only his teeth did not bother him; severe toothaches had tormented him so severely that he had had all his teeth pulled in 1828.

Jackson thus had a long time to ready himself for physical decay and death. He seized moments. He hosted a Christmas party in 1835 for his six grandchildren and assorted grandnieces and grandnephews, with close to a hundred other children invited. The children starting at 4 p.m. played blindman's buff and hide-and-seek in the East Room. The Marine Corps band played a march and Jackson himself led the children into the State Dining Room, which included a pyramid of snowballs; after dinner came a massive snowball battle in the East Room. Then the president shook each child's hand and said good night. But his yearning began to be heavenwards. When a cholera epidemic swept through Washington, Jackson wrote to his daughter-in-law, "knowing that we have to die we ought to live to be prepared to die well, and then, let death come when it may, we will meet it without alarm and be ready to say, 'the Lord's will be done.'"

When death did come to Jackson in 1845, he was prepared. Physically worn out but spiritually enlivened, he told one and all during the spring of that year that they should not weep for him. On May 29 he told visitors, "Sirs, I am in the hands of a merciful God. I have full confidence in his goodness and mercy. . . . The Bible is true. I have tried to conform to its spirit as near as possible. Upon that sacred volume I rest my hope for eternal salvation, through the merits and blood of our blessed Lord and Savior, Jesus Christ." Three days later, to those who saw how badly he was hurting, Jackson said, "When I have suffered sufficiently, the Lord will then take me to Himself—but what are all my suffering compared to those of the Blessed Savior, who died upon that cursed tree for me? Mine are nothing."

On the day of his death, June 8, Jackson left a political legacy: "That book," he said, referring to the Bible, "is the Rock upon which our republic rests." Then, speaking to the family members and servants that he had called to his bedside, he left a racial legacy: "I am my God's. I belong to Him. I go but a short time before you . . . I hope and trust to meet you all in Heaven, both white and black." The first clause of Jackson's will contained a strong theological legacy: "The Bible is true. . . . I bequeath my body to the dust whence it comes, and my soul to God who gave it, hoping for a happy immortality through the atoning merits of our Lord Jesus Christ."

Jackson also bequeathed a legacy to his successors in government: Like Washington he raised the bar of presidential expectations. He understood sin—his own and others—and the need to war against it. In marrying Rachel and remaining faithful to her for thirty-seven years, he learned to control his lust; he spent a lifetime learning to control his anger. His strict constitutionalism suggests that Jackson was willing to be a man under authority, and his worship of God while president showed that he was not making an idol of governmental power. A post-Jackson president was to be not only a benign presider over state affairs, but also a vigorous defender of citizens and opponent of haughty bureaucrats.

CHAPTER 4

Henry Clay

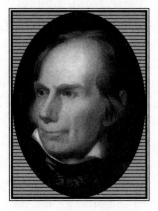

At the same time that Jackson was powerfully bonding with the American people and establishing a memory against which future presidents would be measured, a political alternative also was emerging. To some Americans of the 1830s—a time of growth in population, urbanization, prostitution, and abortion*—the future demanded not Jacksonian firmness in high office but the quickly shifting feet of Henry Clay. George Washington's presidential model was that of an upright father, but Clay attempted to move into the highest office by appearing to be a favorite uncle who did not worry about spoiling his nephews.

*For a discussion of this era, see Olasky, *Abortion Rites: A Social History of Abortion* (Wheaton, IL: Crossway, 1992; Washington, D.C.: Regnery Gateway, 1995).

Clay dominated Washington legislative pursuits for decades. From the War of 1812 through his death forty years later, Clay was first Speaker of the House, then the Senate's most influential leader, and throughout a perennial presidential candidate. He was often the person journalists predicted was most likely to succeed to the presidency, yet Americans never gave him their full confidence. Clay apparently freed himself from sexual restraints and undermined constitutional restraints, but he learned that most American voters trusted the Constitution, not him. Why Clay never made it to the presidency reveals much about the early-nineteenth-century electorate's view of character and statesmanship.

He was born in 1777 just north of Richmond, the seventh of nine children fathered by John Clay, a Baptist preacher who died in 1781. Andrew Jackson, lacking an earthly father, turned toward a heavenly one; Henry Clay turned to his own wits, and grew up without much discipline or belief that truth was important.

That scoffing attitude showed quickly in Clay's career as a lawyer. He gained his initial fame for defending creatively a woman accused of murdering her sister-in-law. The establishment of guilt was overwhelming, but Clay had his client plead temporary insanity, an uncommon ploy at that time. Furthermore, Clay said the defendant's husband, brother of the victim, had forgiven his wife, so couldn't the jury also be merciful? Clay's eloquence led the jury to impose a light sentence.

That style of eloquence was unique in his era. Most speakers took after Daniel Webster, who used grand words and grand gestures, as if he were on stage. Clay, however, spoke more intimately, as if he were in a parlor. His warm insinuations and ability to connect emotionally mesmerized audiences. (Daniel Webster would have played poorly on television, Clay brilliantly.) Historian George Bancroft thought Clay's "voice was music itself, and yet penetrating and far-reaching, enchanting the listener."

At a time when many political speakers prided themselves on making intellectual arguments, Clay went for the emotional jugular. Tears came readily to his eyes, and a handkerchief to wipe the tears came readily to his hand. When Clay spoke before Congress about the need for governmental action to help a particular constituency, his face became moist and his handkerchief wringing wet. Those who listened to Clay's "rich and tender harmony" often ended up themselves in tears. His ability to register total commitment to whatever cause he was promoting at the time swayed many.

Clay's facial expressions, however, sometimes betrayed his serious tones. At times he could not keep from smirking, even when his words indicated total seriousness. He had a hard time taking Senate debates seriously; during long orations by others he often sat in his chair licking a stick of peppermint candy. Until he became old himself, Clay bullied elderly senators, joking that "Old politicians chew on wisdom past, and totter on, in blunders to the last."

Daniel Webster once noted, "Clay with all his talents, is not a good leader, for want of temper. He is irritable, impatient, and occasionally overbearing; & he drives people off." But Clay's charm when he turned it on was immense. He was not handsome, but Clay's face was so alive that observers thought portraits never did him justice. He was "haughty and imperious," journalist Perley Poore noted, but "nevertheless so fascinating in his manner when he chose to be that he held unlimited control over nearly every member of the party."

Clay did not have such control over his family. He was married on April 11, 1799, the day before his twenty-second birthday. He stayed married for over half a century, and with his wife, Lucretia, had eleven children. Yet, as the years went by, Lucretia almost always stayed in Kentucky and Clay spent more and more time in Washington, often engaged in "frolics."

The first tour of duty, in 1806 when Clay was twenty-nine, became what the apart-from-wife Clay called a "tour of pleasure." He was not yet politically powerful enough to be exposed in major ways, and observers merely noted that he liked riding but was known for preferring "indoor pursuits." A decade later Clay briefly represented American interests in Paris, and gained the nickname Prince Hal for his drinking and wenching, but that was Paris, where the Jefferson Doctrine (foreign fornication does not count) dominated.

Once back in the United States, Clay was more discreet, but word got out. Senator William Plumer of New Hampshire commented archly on Clay's extramarital activity. Others called Clay a man who "disregards our moral relations." A pamphlet headlined, "Christian Voters! Read, Pause and Reflect! Mr. Clay's Moral Character," depicted Clay as a libertine gambler who spent too much time in "appreciation" of feminine charms. Clay's adulterous activities became so well known among Washington politicians that as late as 1868, when accusations of sexual immorality plagued Representative Thaddeus Stevens of Pennsylvania, he half defended himself by saying he was not as lewd as Henry Clay.

Nevertheless, Clay's political career survived. New Englander Benjamin French described Clay with three adjectives: heartless, selfish, and eloquent. Clay's third attribute trumped the first two in the minds of many politicians. He gambled in politics as he gambled at cards and dice, once even betting a hotel he owned. He sometimes threw away thousands of dollars at a sitting, but overall probably won more than he lost. Even Mrs. Clay, when asked by Mrs. John Quincy Adams whether she minded her husband's gambling, responded, "Oh, I don't know. He usually wins."

What Clay gambled and lost on, however, was parenting. His children, living or dying apart from their generally absent father, were all troubled in various ways. When Clay's oldest son, Theodore, gained adulthood, neighbors complained that he was "of unsound mind" and a danger to others. A sheriff's panel of twelve men agreed that Theodore was "a lunatic" whose mind was filled with "suspicions of plots and conspiracies" that led him to strike out against his imagined oppressors, including his father. The panel committed Theodore to "the Lunatic Asylum of Kentucky," and in that Lexington institution Theodore spent most of his remaining years.

Henry Clay wrote several letters to his son, but they upset him and caused "the greatest excitement," according to doctors who asked Clay to desist from all direct contact. Clay, from Washington, then made his second oldest son, Thomas Hart Clay, manager of the family's old Kentucky home in Ashland. Thomas, however, drank heavily whenever his father went away. Clay's other sons, according to journalist Harriet Martineau, had other severe problems. Theodore, she wrote, was captive to the "violence of his passions." Henry, Jr., was "so jealous and irritable in his temper that there is no living with him." The younger two, James and John, showed "no great promise of steadiness." (Clay committed his youngest son, John, to the lunatic asylum also.)

Clay also had six daughters, but through a bad run of frontier diseases two died as infants, two more in their girlhood, and the other two as young women. Clay was a good provider economically: He used his political clout to speculate successfully in land and acquire thousands of acres, numerous slaves, and many other investment properties including a hotel and part of a hemp factory. In investing his time, however, Clay chose fame and frolics rather than fatherhood. Surveying the deaths of the daughters and the problems of the sons, Martineau summarized the Clay family's "mournful domestic history" in one question: "Is it not melancholy?"

That question would have been a death sentence for other candidates because at that time severe family problems were likely to hold back politicians for reasons both compassionate and skeptical. The compassionate side suggested that leaders should tend to troubled families, not abandon them further in pursuit of higher ambitions. The skeptical side emphasized familial breakup and suggested that if a man could not govern his family well, he would be unlikely to do well by a nation either.

Curiously, neither marital infidelity nor family difficulty sank Clay. One diarist, Philip Hone, wrote that Clay was "the spoiled child of society," but with those he wanted to stroke "he is so lovely, so soothing" that they could not believe any criticism of him. Clay had excuses for all his actions and inaction, and when he was caught in a lie he was even able to play the aggrieved extremely well: "How could you suppose I mean to offend you," he would say, "there was nothing farther from my thoughts, and I am astonished that you should think so."

What also could have sunk Clay in those days was his lack of commitment to Christ. When running for office he told voters that he was "of no religious sect" but had a "profound respect for Christianity." Few believed him. Once, Clay tried to get to the right of President Jackson by asking him to set aside a national "day of fasting, humiliation and prayer" in response to a cholera epidemic. Jackson said that churches should take the initiative in such matters, lest people begin looking to government rather than God for guidance as to how to pray.

PRIVATE LIFE AND PUBLIC POLICY

Clay's initial power grabs were direct, as was his style of sexual solicitation, according to Washington gossip. Later, he was more circuitously crafty. Overall, he showed a faithfulness to the Constitution equal to the faithfulness he showed his wife.

Clay's first attempt to turn fame into fortune was straightforward. As Speaker of the House in 1816 he led House members to vote 81–67 to change the congressional pay rate from $6 per day (with the goal of getting business done quickly) to $1,500 per year. Clay, as Speaker, would receive double compensation. He said he needed it because "he had never been able to make both ends meet at the termination of Congress."

Citizens, including Clay's constituents who knew of his gambling abilities, were furious. Voters in 1816 returned to office only one-third of House members. Clay gained reelection narrowly only after promising to work for repeal of the Compensation Act. Clay did what he promised, and Congress repealed the act, but Clay from then on always put on the robe of statesmanship as he planned to generate personal or political gain through work in three public policy areas—internal improvements, protective tariffs, and politically connected national banking.

First, Clay favored federal spending for internal improvements such as roads and canals. One barrier to that, as Presidents Jefferson, Madison, and Monroe all declared, was that the Constitution did not permit it. Those presidents all said that advocates of such spending should push through a constitutional amendment. Clay could have tried to do that, but the political battle would have been hard. Instead, Clay became one of the nation's first loose constructionists; he argued that "union and peace were the great objects of the framers of this constitution, and should be kept steadily in view in the interpretation of any clause of it." Since federally funded roads and canals made for union and peace, they should be constitutional.

Clay went on to treat particular constitutional clauses as he treated Washington women of easy virtue. He argued that Congress had the power to establish post offices and post roads, and that "to establish" actually means "to make"; therefore, Congress *could* make roads. Furthermore, since Congress could regulate interstate commerce, and since states without seaports like Kentucky would not be able to participate fully in interstate commerce unless they had better roads, Congress *should* make roads. Finally, Congress in providing for the defense of the country might need military roads, so why not "make a road for ordinary purposes under the power to make a military road"?

This was government by winking: Stretch the plain meaning of words, grab more power for the good of the people. Clay's congressional colleagues were still unwilling to override the Constitution by appropriating funds for the construction of roads and canals, but he elicited a compromise: Congress appropriated funds to *improve* roads and also instructed army engineers to survey areas for potential construction.

Later, when Congress turned down Clay's plan for federal funding of a two-mile canal at Louisville, he pushed through a bill by which the Department of the Treasury bought stock in a canal company, which then built the canal and operated it. Over the years, as Clay predicted, the federal government took more control. Finally, in 1874, Washington took over the canal entirely. Clay became expert at what later would be known as the salami strategy: getting what he wanted, one slice at a time.

Clay also was adept at arguing that if the federal government did not build key roads and canals, they would not be built. This was plainly not so. The most famous American canal, the Erie, was financed and constructed by the state of New York. That canal benefited many and had a strong economic rationale. Not so with a new road Clay badly wanted, one that would replace a muddy and steeply curved road between two Kentucky towns, Lexington and Maysville, that Clay used on his travels to and from Washington.

The Maysville Road project so clearly benefited only Clay and his neighbors that even congressmen who wanted to win favor with him had trouble justifying it. Beginning in 1812, Clay pushed for Maysville Road funding during each session of Congress, to no avail. Had there been a real economic rationale for it, private investors or the Kentucky legislature would have stepped in, but neither did. Finally in 1830, Clay slipped through Congress a bill providing a subscription of $150,000 in company stock. His frustration was great when Andrew Jackson vetoed it.

Clay's second area of interest was tariffs. He orchestrated passage of the Tariff of 1824, the first major protective tariff in American history, and one which provided an average tax of 35 percent on all imported goods. That was the average, however. Clay's plantation produced many crops, including hemp, and his farmhands made finished hemp bags, in which cotton was shipped to Europe. The tariff on finished hemp doubled, and Clay was shielded from foreign competition.

Cotton plantation owners had to absorb additional costs for shipping cotton when the cost of hemp bags increased. They started calling Clay "the prince of hemp." They attacked the blatant attempt "to enrich Mr. Clay's Kentucky pets." But Clay was able to spin his self-interest into high principle by orating about what he called the American System—something for everyone. He became a master of tariff logrolling, picking up New England's support for passage of his favorite measures by shaping provisions that raised the tariff on manufactured wool to 50 percent.

Over the next decades tariff battles increasingly arose, as politicians saw the opportunity to reward friends and contributors by protecting their industries from foreign competition. Tariff battles were so politicized that Thomas Cooper in 1828 called the tariff question a "machine for manufacturing Presidents, instead of broadcloths and bed blankets." Southerners, who would have to pay more for manufactured goods, fumed about Constitution-twisting and a "tariff of abominations."

Clay tariffs were so obnoxious to the South, on grounds of both principle and principal, that John C. Calhoun and the South Carolina legislature even began to talk of "nullification." Their claim that state legislatures could declare null and void any federal acts that violated the Constitution almost led to civil war in the early 1830s. Clay, noting tough resistance, added to his reputation as "the Great Compromiser" by brokering a deal that kept the guns from going off, but lines were drawn in a way that prefigured the next generation's battles.

Amid battles over internal improvements, tariffs, and Henry Clay's third big issue—the national bank question, which we've already examined—a new political party, the Whigs, emerged. The new party was centralist, with a strong faith in the ability and desirability of a major economic role for the federal government, and a strong faith in promoting economic opportunity through centralized government action. Clay, who provided insufficient paternal care to his own family, led the way in arguing that Americans were "entitled to the protecting care of a paternal government."

ENJOYED BUT UNELECTABLE

But Clay's political paternalism was a sham, and voters knew it. Many Americans at that time enjoyed Henry Clay's antics but did not see him as the paternal influence they wanted in George Washington's seat. Clay, when running for president, always fell short, either in the nomination process or in the general election. Over the decades Clay learned what should be a politician's maxim: Live by the speech, soon overreach. He could draw voters to a political gathering by the river, but he could not make them drink. One supporter complained that Clay "could get more men to run after him to hear him speak, and fewer to vote for him than any man in America."

Clay was particularly adept at getting the denizens of the District of Columbia to run after him. Washington, which during the early nineteenth century moved from wilderness to a city with contaminated wells and open sewers, was Henry Clay's type of town, one dominated by government. What is now the Mall was then a swamp: Poor sanitation led to malaria and cholera in the summer, influenza and pneumonia in the winter. Washington's only real star was the Capitol. Terraces and well-kept lawns provided satisfaction on the outside. Inside the rotunda four John Trumbull paintings of revolutionary scenes displayed the past heroically, as Roman and Greek statuary artistically linked the present republic to ones long ago. The Capitol extended 352 feet in length but also displayed some heavenward yearning, with a tall but flat-topped dome at the building's center.

Actions inside the Capitol depended largely on strategies concocted near it, in the hotels and boardinghouses where many members of Congress lived. A few good houses stood on Capitol Hill along New

Jersey Avenue, but much of the era's inside lobbying work was done inside the shabby brick and wooden buildings where most congressmen hung their hats. Congressional sessions were far shorter than they are now, so most legislators left their families at home. Most joined "messes," boardinghouse dinner assemblages: Each mess had its own table and catering contract. Meals were often strategy sessions, with guests present only by unanimous consent.

In the early 1830s, Washington's population was up to 20,000, but streets still were unpaved and full of ruts, with cows pastured alongside. Congressmen who did not live in a Capitol Hill boardinghouse commonly used personal coaches to get around. Foreigners contrasted debates about liberty for all with the sight of speakers driven home by family slaves. Houses were so widely separated that one journalist wrote, "It looks as if it had rained naked buildings upon an open plain."

Hotels were frequent gathering places, with tables loaded down by huge decanters of whiskey, brandy, and gin. Whiskey and quinine were promoted as antidotes for Washington diseases, but for some the medicine was not salutary: Congressman Horace Binney of Pennsylvania noted that one of his colleagues, "an habitual drunkard, blew out his brains; two have died notorious drunkards, and one of them shamefully immoral. The honors are given to all, with equal eulogy and ceremonial."

To some troubled observers, Washington was beginning to be a mini-London on the Potomac, half a century after Americans had fought a war to liberate themselves not only from taxation without representation but decadent cultural influences as well. In 1829, Washington newspapers ran ads for Parisian fashions: "French dresses for balls . . . arrival from Paris of an elegant assortment of French jewelry. . . . Just received from Paris an elegant assortment of caps and pelerines direct from Mademoiselle Mintette's . . . a beautiful assortment of satin shoes."

Satin shoes decorated feet at the "salons" that leading women hosted, but the greatest elegance emerged at special parties and balls in the larger homes for which seven to nine hundred invitations commonly were extended. On the night of a big ball "the rolling of carriages sounded like continual peals of thunder," and crowds inside were often so packed in that journalist and Jackson advisor Francis Blair was reminded "of a Kentucky fight when the crowd draws the circle so close that the combatants have no room to use their limbs." Guests would stay and stay, usually not leaving until 3 a.m.

Washington during the 1830s was threatening to look so much like London that British observers praised the city. Thomas Hamilton noted in *Men and Manners in America* that "the enjoyments of social intercourse enter into the habitual calculations of every one." Harriet Martineau described Washington as a great place for those "who love dissipation . . . and those who make a study of strong minds under strong excitement." Andrew Jackson hated such dissipation, but Henry Clay loved it. He kept his wife at their Kentucky home, roamed nightly through Washington's parties, and boasted the next day of his "frolics" (the code word for adulterous sex). He made leering comments about enjoying the virgins of Virginia, and then, according to his political enemies, attempted to rape the Constitution.

He was considered for the presidency in election after election beginning in 1824, but never went all the way. Why? For a time Clay could blame his defeats on the popularity of Andrew Jackson, who beat him twice, but as he lost to lesser candidates the message became clear: A majority of American voters did not want Henry Clay as their president. John Quincy Adams explained Clay's failure by saying he was "essentially a gamester" always searching for a "killing." The *Charleston Mercury* complained of Clay's "temper, unrestrained . . . though he often wins a shrewd trick, and dips deeply into the bank, he loses in the long run."

Overall, the concern among principled leaders—that Clay could not be trusted—grew rather than diminished after each speech in which he made undiscerning listeners think he was one of them. After one such speech an observer noted, "Could he gain votes by it, he would kiss the toe of the Pope and prostrate himself before the grand lama. He is eloquent, but he lacks judgment very much."

Clay also lost out because he came from the West, thus losing credibility among easterners, yet after some years in Washington he no longer represented his native region well. Instead, he became a citizen of the capital city, relishing his political plasticity ("the Great Compromiser") and throughout most of his career considering himself superior to those who maintained outmoded ideas of "honor" or "character." Unlike Jackson, who believed in leading by brave example, Clay emphasized his ability to sway people through artful rhetoric.

Clay tried in many ways to show that he still had the common touch. He learned to play the fiddle, but suspicion about his political music-making remained. Before John Randolph of Virginia died in 1833, he said he wanted to be buried facing west so he could keep an eye on Henry Clay. But Randolph should have asked to be buried facing north, since by 1833 Clay had emphatically become a master of dissipation and duplicity, a man not of the West but of Washington.

Sometimes the frustration overwhelmed Clay. When William Henry "Tippecanoe" Harrison beat him out for the Whig nomination in 1840, Clay drank heavily, was "open and exceedingly profane," and offered "a storm of desperation and curses . . . in words befitting only a bar-room in vulgar broil." Told that he had many friends, Clay screamed, "My friends are not worth the powder and shot it would take to kill them!"

Clay kept at it. When he ran for president in 1844, the Whigs tried to inoculate him against charges of immorality by selecting as his vice-presidential running mate Theodore Frelinghuysen of New Jersey, a former senator who was president of the American Tract Society (an organization that circulated Christian literature) and well known for his piety. But Clay was unable to grab a halo by association. His fellow citizens knew him as a shameless politician who would sell out anyone or anything in an attempt to realize his ambitions. They even knew him as a man cynical enough to utter with apparent conviction a line then quoted around the country by his paid supporters: "I had rather be right than president." The saying was passed around as a joke, and it has now made its way into our history books.

Despite such propaganda the sixty-seven-year-old Clay lost to James Polk in the fall of 1844, and his presidential ambitions were over. Democrats expressed pity; John Tyler, departing the presidency, said, "We had better now leave off abusing Mr. Clay altogether. He is dead and let him rest." Running mate Frelinghuysen went deeper, writing to

Clay, "As sinners, who have rebelled against our Maker, we need a Saviour or we must perish. . . . Let us then repair to Him."

AFTER AMBITION

At about this time Clay saw that he needed repair. For decades he had invoked "the aid of the Most High" when running for higher office or about to give a gargantuan speech which might require "divine assistance" to complete. But those who knew Clay understood the hypocrisy in his words.

Clay's one perhaps-genuine religious expression in his writings until his forced retirement from presidential politics came in response to a minister in 1842 who asked of his spiritual welfare. Clay at age sixty-five wrote that he knew the issue of heaven or hell was important, but "in the active bustle of life and its varied occupations, I have perhaps too much neglected so weighty a matter. My retirement will afford me leisure for a more serious, and I hope more practical contemplation of it." During Clay's 1844 campaign he told another minister that he hoped "to attain a firm faith and confidence" in God's promises. He added, "There is nothing for which I feel so anxious. May God, in his infinite mercy, grant me what I so ardently desire!"

God did act on Clay, but through an event he did not ardently desire. The deeper issues did not come home to Clay until Henry Clay, Jr., the one son who had overcome earlier problems and was turning out right, died while fighting against Mexico at the Battle of Buena Vista in February 1847. "Oh God, how inscrutable are thy dispensations," Clay wrote. "There are some wounds so deep and so excruciatingly painful, that He only can heal them. . . . The death of my beloved son is one of them."

Clay gave speeches attacking the Mexican War; Abraham Lincoln, a newly elected Whig member of Congress in 1847, listened to his political hero declare that the pageantry and pomp of war kept young people from realizing that death, wounds, and disease were more likely outcomes for them than medals. But his son's death, and intimations of his own mortality, also pushed Clay to contemplate the eternals. On June 22, 1847, he was baptized. On July 4 he took the Lord's Supper.

Clay chose to join an Episcopal church, and cynics immediately saw base motives. One critical politician, J. B. Mower, said the conversion was a political calculation, but Clay had chosen the wrong denomination: "His joining an aristocratic church does him no good here, among the go-to-meeting portion, of Christians." But this time Clay appeared to be going beyond politics. "I shall have more leisure to dedicate my self to Him, to my religious duties, and to the proper preparation for another and a better world," he announced.

Despite his newfound religion Clay remained vain. When soprano sensation Jenny Lind, the "Swedish Nightingale," gave a concert in Washington in 1850, Clay attended, but waited to make his entrance until the overture was completed. Then, when he strode down the aisle and received an ovation greater than that accorded President Millard Fillmore, Daniel Webster, or General Winfield Scott, Clay crooned over his political triumph.

There were few such moments, however. Clay's health weakened during 1851 and 1852, as he approached age seventy-five. He coughed frequently, and some doctors diagnosed tuberculosis. Others did not, but all saw that he was failing. Clay took Communion regularly at Trinity Church in Washington and concentrated on the ministration of the gospel by Clement M. Butler, chaplain of the Senate. He talked with Congressman John C. Breckinridge about "the vanity of the world, and its insufficiency to satisfy the soul of man."

In 1852, Clay became sicker but stayed in Washington, with his wife remaining in Lexington and his living children communicating irregularly with him, if at all. He was lonely and pathetic, writing to his son James (who had suggested that Clay was overly despondent), "if you could witness my Coughing for twenty four hours, And how much I have been reduced since we parted, you would not think so."

All that kept Clay going was Christian faith, which was still new to him and not as firmly planted as years of dedication would have brought. He said he had no "apprehension of death. . . . I am ready to go whenever it is the will of God that I should be summoned hence."

He told one congressman, "I am not afraid to die, sir; I have hope, faith, and some confidence; I have an abiding trust in the merits and mediation of our Saviour." He told Senate chaplain Butler that he had "full faith in the great leading doctrines of the Gospel."

Nevertheless, scoffing cynicism had run Clay for a lifetime. In June, not feeling the full assurance that a consistent Christian life generally brings, he often seemed depressed. Still, shortly before Clay died in Washington on June 29, 1852, apart from his family with the exception of one son, he was telling people, "I trust in the atonement of the Saviour of mercy, as the ground of my acceptance and of my hope of salvation." Buried not in Washington but in Lexington on July 10, Clay was finally free from the political swamps.

Some politicians were not free of Clay, however; those who knew Clay from rhetoric rather than reality wanted to be just like him. One minor figure, Abe Lincoln of Illinois, called Clay his "beau ideal of a statesman," and used the occasion of Clay's death to orate about keeping Clay's memory alive. For most Americans, however, even though Clay may have gone through a religious conversion, the public legacy he left was one of craftiness. Unlike Jefferson, he did not have a public persona that covered over his private cravings, nor did he have a past contribution like the Declaration of Independence to fall back on when citizens were disturbed by his derelictions.

For those who hold up all early American leaders as paragons of virtue, Henry Clay's career shows that vice springs eternal. Clay's close-to-the-White House political success indicates that the legacy of George Washington was sliding several decades after the founding father's death, yet the hopes for principled integrity shown by the rise of Jackson were too strong for Clay to overcome. For a generation Clay was the most colorful figure in American politics, but voters showed they still wanted a godly fighter, not a glad-hander.

CHAPTER 5

Abraham Lincoln

Before Abraham Lincoln made his first political speech, he spent several years reading newspapers, such as the *Louisville Journal,* that promoted Henry Clay and his American System. That first speech, in Decatur, Illinois, in 1830, was a Clay echo, even to the point of stumping for government-funded improvements to the navigability of a local river. In 1844, when Clay made his last major run for the presidency, Lincoln whipped up crowds with pro-tariff speeches at Clay Clubs throughout central Illinois.

Lincoln followed Clay on not only economic issues but social and foreign policy ones as well. Like Clay, he favored schemes to transport blacks to Africa, and he opposed the Mexican War. But Lincoln, like Clay, primarily emphasized breaching the wall of separation between federal expenditure and private interests—a wall established by the Constitution, bulwarked by Madison and Monroe vetoes, and reinforced by Jackson. He was so passionate in his promotion of Clay's policies that judge and political organizer David Davis called Lincoln "the best stump speaker in the state."

After Clay's death Lincoln spoke of the great man's legacy: public policy measures that would increase American "prosperity and glory." In 1856, Lincoln received the highest compliment from one editor: He had "eloquence that would bear a comparison with Henry Clay's." In 1858, when Stephen Douglas claimed that he was adopting a Clay-like compromise position on slavery, Lincoln insisted that his Whig past showed that he was the true heir of Henry Clay. The influence continued into Lincoln's presidency. While working on his inaugural address, he had an aide fetch him a copy of Clay's speech on the Compromise of 1850. In 1862, ten years after Clay's death, Lincoln wrote about Clay's continued presence in his consciousness: "I recognize his voice speaking as it ever spake, for the Union."

But Lincoln sometimes heard other voices. He grew up with stories of George Washington and other leaders who displayed virtue both in public and private. Throughout his life Lincoln also was absorbed—sometimes in a disdaining way, sometimes searching—with the religious questions that Clay found of interest only during the last years of his life.

KEEPING GOD AT ARM'S LENGTH

Lincoln grew up with biblical teaching, which he treated in a variety of ways. First came parody. When Mr. and Mrs. Thomas Lincoln and daughter Sarah joined the Little Pigeon Baptist Church in 1823, teen-aged Abraham did not. He often listened to sermons, however, and mimicked them afterwards before a crowd of children until (as one child remembered) Lincoln's father "would come and make him quit." Lincoln continued that practice into his twenties, once giving a memorable imitation of a preacher so plagued by a small blue lizard running up his leg that the preacher took off his pants and shirt in an attempt to shoo away the reptile.

Then came critique, with electoral consequences. In 1837, after Lincoln had questioned the accuracy of the Bible and the divinity of Christ, one local politician, James Adams, called Lincoln a "deist," and therefore untrustworthy. Religious accusations plagued Lincoln again in 1843 when an opponent in the race for a congressional seat noted that Lincoln was a deist who "belonged to no church." Lincoln's law partnership with William Herndon, a frontier evangelist for transcendentalism, did not help his reputation among Christians.

Then came hypocrisy. Lincoln, as Whig nominee for Congress in 1846, ran against Peter Cartwright, that well-known Methodist circuit rider and friend of Andrew Jackson. In response to Cartwright's charge that he was an infidel, Lincoln issued a statement published in the *Illinois Gazette:* "That I am not a member of any Christian Church, is true; but I have never denied the truth of the Scriptures; and I have never spoken with intentional disrespect of religion in general, or of any denomination of Christians in particular."

Lincoln chose his words carefully. He did not say that he affirmed scriptural truth, only that he had never denied it. He did not state his respect, only that he had not been caught in disrespect. Neither statement was true about his earlier years, but Lincoln did display good manners during the 1840s. He concluded his public statement with a notice that he did not favor those with poorer etiquette: "I do not think I could, myself, be brought to support a man for office whom I knew to be an open enemy of, and scoffer at religion."

Lincoln won his legislative race and went to Washington in 1847. He heard his hero Henry Clay speak on slavery and bemoan Kentucky's failure fifty years before to adopt a program for gradual emancipation. Clay said it was not too late to try again, with a plan that would free all slaves born beyond a certain date when they reached age twenty-eight, so that "there would be very little diminution if any in the value of slave property." Lincoln agreed.

He would have liked a second term, but the Whigs stuck with their informal term limitations plan and returned him to Springfield. There Lincoln stayed until his return to national politics in the 1850s. During those years he became a successful and affluent corporate lawyer, pushing for plans, such as developing railroads, that went well with his Whiggish, Clay-like concentration on internal improvements. He seemed to ignore religious questions.

KEEPING SEX WITHIN REACH

In 1860, William Herndon, Lincoln's long-term law partner, said about the man becoming famous, "I know him better than he does himself." Herndon was not always accurate, but many of his observations have far more of the ring of truth than do romantic tales. Biographer Nathaniel Stephenson etched a Lincoln who "lacked the wanton appetites of the average sensual man," but journalist Herndon, after conducting many interviews, gave specific detail to back up his point that "Lincoln had terribly strong passions for women, could hardly keep his hands off them."

That made Lincoln sound like his hero Henry Clay, but there was another aspect to Lincoln, one pointed to in a story told by Lincoln's Springfield friend Joshua Speed and relayed by Herndon. Speed, the story goes, was involved with a pretty prostitute. Lincoln, with $3 in his pocket, asked him, "Speed, do you know where I can get *some?*" Lincoln soon was in bed with Speed's woman, but then asked her price and was shocked to find out it was $5. The woman offered him credit, but Lincoln, saying he was poor and might not be able to pay her for quite a while, got his clothes on and excused himself. The prostitute supposedly said, "Mr. Lincoln, you are the most conscientious man I ever saw."

Somehow, that story has not received as much play in schoolbooks as the one of Lincoln walking miles from the grocery store to return a minuscule overcharge. Nor have the "farmer's daughter" stories Lincoln told to ingratiate himself politically with other good old boys. One that Lincoln supposedly told on himself had him stopping at a one-room farmhouse and accepting the offer of a bed for the night that had its head at the foot of another bed occupied by the farmer's adult daughter. Lincoln was so tall that his pillow may have strayed onto the daughter's bed, and her feet ended by his head. He began to tickle them, she indicated her enjoyment, and Lincoln, according to Herndon, "then tickled a little higher up, and as he would tickle higher, the girl would shove down lower, and the higher he tickled, the lower she moved."

Herndon's stories showed Lincoln's way of winning political support by appearing not as a Washington-like father but a Clay-like brother. Yet he would be an older brother, coming into a dishonorable environment (the brothel, for instance), but then acting honorably (or at least with a desire to avoid debt); the stories emphasized tickling, not consummating. Herndon noted that Lincoln, taking after Washington, "had honor and a strong will, and these enabled him to put out the fires of his terrible passion." The battle to control passion and make honor the victor in his own internal civil war absorbed Lincoln and strengthened him for leadership in a greater war to come. "I have seen Lincoln tempted," Herndon wrote, "and I have seen him reject the approach of woman." Lincoln's political associate David Davis put it this way: "Mr. Lincoln's honor saved many a woman."

Lincoln did have serious romances prior to marriage. One, with Ann Rutledge, evidently would have ended in marriage, but she died in 1835, probably of typhoid. Lincoln was obsessed with grief for many weeks afterwards, and many years later, referring to her grave, told Herndon, "My heart lies buried there." But, after abruptly breaking one engagement with Mary Todd in 1841, Lincoln and she were married the following year. During the twenty-three years of their marriage there was no hint of adultery, even though Mary's frequently nonadultlike behavior trained Lincoln to have great patience. Mary was mercurial in temperament, and the Lincolns' immediate neighbor once told about Mrs. Lincoln in 1856 or 1857 chasing her husband down a street with a knife.

Little incidents like that aside, by the eve of the Civil War Lincoln was a homebody. Mrs. Lincoln was always intently aware of any possible slight, and could be almost insanely jealous if her husband even looked attentively at an attractive woman, but he could always outrun her. Lincoln was prepared to spend the rest of his days in Springfield as a prosperous attorney settled down with his wife.

HEADING TOWARD CIVIL WAR

For both the country and the person, what had seemed like solid ground shifted during the 1850s. New political parties—the Free-Soilers, then the Republicans—pushed aside the Whigs. Throughout the northern United States crime was increasing. Prostitution and abortion, the two closely linked, also were on the rise. Intellectual criticism of market systems was propelling the creation of communes like Brook Farm outside Boston. Other panacea-proclaiming movements—vegetarianism, "free love," no furs, graham crackers—were gaining adherents, particularly in the North. Each proponent of an "ism" claimed that if Americans did not turn his way, disaster would follow.

The sensational religious development of the decade was the rapid spread of spiritism. Those who joined what we would today call a New Age movement believed that each person/spirit had his own godstuff and should be free to pursue his own bliss. Adherents released themselves from biblical ideas of adhering to marriage. Spiritism, in short, was the first massive assault in America on the idea that God said sex should remain within marriage. Spiritists believed that there was no God as biblically understood, and thus no binding vows of faithfulness to Him or to others.

"Everyone his own god" theology carried out Andrew Jackson's democratization without his bedrock Christianity. Newspapers reported the popularity of the new faith throughout the cities of the North, much to the consternation of the Presbyterian-edited *New York Times,* which complained of a "social Antichrist overrunning the world." One New York businessman, George Templeton Strong, recorded in his diary the amazing developments: "ex-judges of the Supreme Court, Senators, clergymen, professors of physical sciences [favoring] a new Revelation, hostile to that of the Church and the Bible."

The less urbanized, more Christianized South was generally spared such developments, but it had severe problems of its own with slavery. Many Americans in the 1850s anticipated an apocalypse. Harriet Beecher Stowe's 1852 best-seller, *Uncle Tom's Cabin,* concluded, "Both North and South have been guilty before God," and only "repentance, justice, and mercy" could save the nation from God's wrath.

And yet, Mrs. Stowe and her husband, Calvin, themselves dabbled in spiritism. If God were to punish Americans for sins, which sins? Some northerners argued that the "wicked and nefarious designs of the slave oligarchy" had "filled to overflowing . . . the cup of iniquity." Some southerners, however, spoke of spiritualism, prostitution, "mendacity, perfidy, and shameless brutality" in the North's growing cities. In both North and South, many observers commented generally about pride, greed, and forgetting God.

That sense of punishment coming formed the backdrop to a curious political development, the big breakthrough of Henry Clay's ideas. The Democrats' emphasis on small government retained steady support as long as government subsidies to special interests were seen as just that. In the 1850s, however, Republican successors to the northern Whigs emphasized the way internal improvements could encourage a rapid population growth in the Great Plains states and decreased national influence for the South.

Suddenly, northern Jacksonians were listening. Opposition to western internal improvements might even suggest subservience to slave power. This combination of interests helped to build a Whig-abolitionist alliance. But Free-Soilers were suspicious of railroad lawyers like Lincoln, until his clever use of language—most notably in the 1858 "house divided" speech—made him acceptable. The Bible that Lincoln had mocked, ignored, or kissed up to suddenly became politically valuable.

Lincoln masterfully used one particular passage, from Chapter 12 of Matthew. It relates that when Jesus heals a demon-possessed man, the Pharisees say he did it by using Satanic power. Jesus responds, in the King James translation that had given Lincoln his early understanding of English-language style: "Every kingdom divided against itself is brought to desolation; and every city or house divided against itself shall not stand. And if Satan cast out Satan, he is divided against himself; how shall then his kingdom stand? . . . But if I cast out devils by the Spirit of God, then the kingdom of God is come unto you."

Lincoln grabbed that passage to imply that the South was evil and to refute the southern rejoinder that the North was worse, for if the North was also evil, it would not be opposing the evil of slavery. Furthermore, the North was capable of healing the South, not by Satanic means but by using its goodness to bring the kingdom of God southward. Lincoln was preaching a northern crusade, and preaching it so well that Congressman John Wentworth of Illinois could go around proclaiming in 1860 that John Brown had been like John the Baptist, clearing the way for Lincoln, who "will break every yoke and let the oppressed go free."

The "house divided" speech, and fervent politicking afterwards, won Lincoln the Republican presidential nomination in 1860. To overcome the old accusations of deism he included in his stump speech a line about how he could not succeed without "divine help," but it did not much matter. Some northern ministers, turning rapidly toward abolitionism, looked the other way at Lincoln's beliefs because the Republican Party was now the instrument to end slavery, perhaps through "a noble war of humanity," as abolitionist writer and preacher Moncure Conway put it.

Apocalypse now: War was a punishment for the sin of slavery, which God wanted to end, and he would continue the punishment until slavery was gone. The only way to gain God's blessing was to enter into a holy war to free the slaves, for if the nation did not abolish the peculiar institution, there would be peculiar punishments. Erastus Wright, a Springfield friend of Lincoln's, warned him that if he refused to free slaves he would painfully learn that "it is a fearful thing to contend against God."

Lincoln was not yet at that realization. His god in 1861 and 1862 was Union. William Seward had spoken about the irrepressible conflict, but once appointed secretary of state he desperately wanted to repress it. For three months after the election he offered conciliation to the South. Lincoln, however, precipitated the first shot by overruling Seward and moving to resupply Fort Sumter. The Union had to be preserved.

Apocalypse when? Early in the war Lincoln still hoped, as he told Congress in his first annual message, that the war would "not degenerate into a violent and remorseless revolutionary struggle." Senator Charles Sumner of Massachusetts in 1861, however, called for freeing the slaves and remorselessly punishing rebels. He thought Lincoln slow: "How vain to have the power of a god and not use it godlike." Abolitionist Wendell Phillips chimed in, "the bloodiest war ever waged is infinitely better than the happiest slavery which ever fattened men into obedience." In 1862, according to fiery abolitionist lecturers in the hall of the House of Representatives and at the Smithsonian, it was time to "recognize the trumpet of Judgment Day."

CRYSTALLIZED LINCOLN

Which trumpets would Lincoln hear? Something began resounding in his brain on the night of February 5, 1862, when he hosted a White House ball for five hundred "distinguished, beautiful and brilliant" men and women of "intellect, attainment, position and elegance," according to Frank Leslie's *Illustrated Weekly*. Lincoln had wanted to cancel because his son Willie had a cold and fever following a pony ride in cold rain. But the guests were coming and the band played on. Then came mourning: Willie died two weeks later, probably from typhoid fever resulting from polluted water in the White House system.

Mary Todd Lincoln's way of dealing with grief was to search out New Age mediums, including one who took the name Colchester and pretended to be the illegitimate son of an English duke. When Mrs. Lincoln heard drum-tapping noises and other sounds at a Colchester séance in a darkened room, with everyone in the room supposedly holding each others' hands, she concluded that her Willie was generating the sounds to communicate with her.

Noah Brooks, a friend of Lincoln's, took it upon himself to investigate at a subsequent séance. When the lights went out and a drumbeat sounded, he broke free from his neighbors and, "grasping in the direction of the drum-beat, grabbed a very solid and fleshy hand in which was held a bell that was being thumped on a drum-head." Someone hit him on the forehead, causing a gash, but when the lights went on spectators saw Brooks, covered with blood, holding on to Colchester, who "was glowering at the drum and bells which he still held in his hands."

Lincoln once went to a séance with Mary, but afterwards made a characteristic joke, saying he had heard several spirits presenting contradictory messages, just as his cabinet members did. Lincoln's search for meaning took a different direction. Several long talks with Phineas Gurley, pastor of the New York Avenue Presbyterian Church in Washington, helped him go through "a process of crystallization," which Gurley described as a conversion to Christ. "I have been driven many times upon my knees by the overwhelming conviction that I have nowhere else to go," Lincoln explained to Brooks. "My own wisdom, and that of all about me, seemed insufficient for that day."

Beginning in 1862, Lincoln attended Pastor Gurley's church on Sundays and sometimes on Wednesdays, at midweek prayer meetings. He also began to muse on God's nature. Lincoln's "Meditation on the Divine Will," written just after the North's second morale-sapping defeat at Bull Run, was not a politically pious missive for public consumption, but a private attempt to think through what was beyond human understanding. "The will of God prevails," Lincoln wrote. "In great contests each party claims to act in accordance with the will of God. Both may be, and one must be wrong, [for] God cannot be for and against the same thing at the same time."

Who was right? Lincoln wrote, "In the present civil war it is quite possible that God's purpose is something different from the purpose of either party. . . . I am almost ready to say this is probably true—that God wills the contest, and wills that it shall not end yet. By his mere quiet power, on the minds of the now contestants, He could have either saved or destroyed the Union without a human contest. Yet the contest began. And having begun He could give the final victory to either side any day. Yet the contest proceeds."

Was it God's will for all slaves to be freed? Lincoln noted to himself, "The Almighty gives no audible answer to that question, and his revelation—the Bible—gives none—or, at most, none but such as admits of a squabble, as to its meaning." When responding to clergymen from Chicago who asked him to carry out God's will concerning American slavery, he said, "these are not . . . the days of miracles, and I suppose it will be granted that I am not to expect a direct revelation."

While Lincoln was meditating, he still had to make specific policy decisions about slavery that embroiled him in deep controversy. When General David Hunter, in May 1862, ordered the emancipation and arming of all the slaves in his South Carolina military department, church bells in the North rang out. After Lincoln revoked that order a week later, he received warnings from governors like John Andrew of Massachusetts and groups like the Christian Citizens of Chicago. They all argued that soldiers would not have "the blessings of God" unless emancipation was their goal.

A Brooklyn Methodist minister late in 1862 called the war the "first great conflict to precede the millennium." Still, the goal often seemed to be one of keeping the millennium at arm's length if eradication of slavery meant having blacks next door. During the war northern magazines like the *Western Christian Advocate* and popular ministers like Lyman Abbott assured readers and congregations that emancipation would make life better for blacks in the South and would therefore keep them from fleeing to the North.

Whatever his private uneasiness concerning God's will, Lincoln read the Emancipation Proclamation to his cabinet five days after Confederate forces were stopped at Antietam, stating (according to Secretary of the Navy Gideon Welles), "God has declared this question in favor of the slaves." Secretary of the Treasury Salmon Chase recorded Lincoln's further explanation: "I made the promise to myself, and (hesitating a little) to my Maker," that the proclamation would follow a Union victory. Newspapers such as the *Pittsburgh Christian Advocate* rejoiced as Lincoln broke down the separation of church and army: God "will now fight for the nation as He has not yet fought for it."

The Price of Incivility

If so, it seemed just in time. As Lincoln announced the Emancipation Proclamation, Washington was a city of hospitals, over fifty temporary ones. Almost twenty more stood in and near Alexandria, across the river. Gaping wounds assaulted the eye, groaning resounded in ears, chloroform tickled the nose. Thousands of broken bodies arrived in the aftermath of battles like Second Bull Run or Antietam. Whenever Congress was not in session the Capitol itself became a hospital, with two thousand cots set up in the rotunda, legislative chambers, and hallways.

Most deaths occurred on the battlefield, but those who died in the hospitals, typically fifty per day, cost the army $4.99 per soldier (pine coffin, transport to the cemetery, and burial all included). Patients who survived, discharged long before they were fit enough to return to military duty, assembled on grounds across the Potomac in Alexandria that became known as Camp Convalescent. Over ten thousand men crowded that base at one point. During the winter many still ill slept in tents on cold ground.

The best place to recover was the museum of the Patent Office, which boasted warmth, light, clean mats on tessellated marble floors, and frequent visitation from volunteers. Once, Lincoln visited Patent Office patients just after a lady had come by to distribute tracts. He was surprised to find one recipient of a leaflet grimly laughing. "Mr. President," the soldier said. "She has given me a tract on the 'Sin of Dancing,' and both of my legs are shot off."

Other monuments to good intentions abounded outside. Before war began Congress commissioned a great dome for the Capitol, to be the symbol of national unity. In 1862 the bare ribs of the unfinished dome stood outlined against the sky. The dome was supposed to be capped by a colossal bronze statue of a female Freedom, ordered by Jefferson Davis several years earlier when he was Secretary of War. That effigy remained at ground level, on its temporary base.

South of the White House stood the beginning of what was to be a tall obelisk memorializing George Washington. Around the then-squat monument (156 feet high, flat top) stood weather-beaten sheds, and in those sheds sat ornamented blocks of stone contributed by domestic organizations and foreign potentates to honor the father of the United States. Around the blocks of the stone were slaughterhouses for the ten thousand cattle on hand to feed growing numbers of Union troops. The combined smell of the city dump, the city canal, and cattle droppings two feet deep was hellacious. Meanwhile, the son of one of George Washington's favorite generals, Lighthorse Harry Lee, was leading the main army of the rebel forces to victories in Virginia.

Lincoln contemplated the ironies. In October 1862, he told four visiting Quakers that God was permitting the war "for some wise purpose of His own, mysterious and unknown to us; and though with our limited understandings we may not be able to comprehend it, yet we cannot but believe, that He who made the world still governs it." Calling the war "a fiery trial" and himself "a humble instrument in the hands of our Heavenly Father," Lincoln said, "I have desired that all my works and acts may be according to His will, and that it might be so, I have sought his aid."

Others were more insistent that the Republican Party was doing God's will. Senator Henry Wilson of Massachusetts said the party was "created by no man" but "brought into being by Almighty God himself." An Illinois Christian leader said that a Democratic triumph in the 1862 congressional elections would force God's "chastising hand." After Republicans survived key votes, the *Western Christian Advocate* proclaimed that "the spirit of the Lord has moved upon the hearts of many. God has averted a threatened calamity. Let His name be praised." And Wendell Phillips, looking for top-down revolution throughout the South, demanded that "the whole social system . . . be taken to pieces; every bit of it."

Lincoln still hesitated to claim that demolition of the South was God's desire. His "Proclamation Appointing a National Fast Day" in 1863 asserted, "we know that, by Divine law, nations like individuals are subjected to punishments and chastisement in this world." He called the war "a punishment inflicted upon us for our presumptuous sins to the needful end of our national reformation as a whole people." Lincoln still spoke of sins of the whole people, rather than focusing on one particular sin in one particular part of the nation.

Furthermore, Lincoln's proclamation emphasized how Americans had taken for granted God's kindness: "We have forgotten the gracious Hand which preserved us in peace, and multiplied and enriched and strengthened us; and we have vainly imagined, in the deceitfulness of our hearts, that all these blessings were produced by some superior wisdom and virtue of our own." That proclamation applied the Old Testament pattern—God's faithfulness, man's forgetfulness, God's discipline—to a new people who had become "too self-sufficient to feel the necessity of redeeming and preserving grace, too proud to pray to the God that made us."

Lincoln, who had questioned prayer previously and not even affirmed it under earlier political pressure, was becoming a praying man. He told one general that as reports came in from Gettysburg during the first two days of fighting, "when everyone seemed panic-stricken," he "got down on my knees before Almighty God and prayed. . . . Soon a sweet comfort crept into my soul that God Almighty had taken the whole business into His own hands."

That sweet comfort came amid a Washington that was becoming a capital of depravity. Some sights and sounds were obvious. Infantry regiments regularly tramped the avenues with a rumbling beat. Sabers from galloping cavalry squads clanked. The dominant color scheme on the sidewalks was army blue, with a sprinkling of officers' gold braid. The movement of heavy artillery cut deep ruts into the unpaved streets. Hastily constructed storehouses filled empty spaces. But what was generally out of sight, until nightfall, was far more ominous.

What is now the Union Station area was then Swampoodle, a shantytown on the banks of Tiber Creek, the open sewer that hit Pennsylvania Avenue at Second Street, then flowed into City Canal. (The creek is now covered over.) Army camps were nearby, and hookers sold to soldiers not only their bodies but illegal whiskey bottles smuggled into the camps under long skirts. Some of the seven thousand clerks who lived in rooming houses, many far removed from families, also looked for love in all the wrong places.

Sin center, however, was the Federal Triangle area south of Pennsylvania Avenue between Sixth and Fifteenth Streets that is now home to big chunks of the Washington bureaucracy. The area was informally called Hooker's Division, after Union General Joe Hooker, who was said to have several divisions in the field and a corps of prostitutes in the army's staging area. Brothels and gambling halls dominated block after block. Those of varied tastes could choose between sites with evocative names ranging all the way from Madame Russell's Bake Oven to Gentle Annie Lyle's Place.

LINCOLN'S FAITH AND MILITARY STRATEGY

Increasingly as the war went on, the New York Avenue Presbyterian Church became Lincoln's alternative to the Bake Oven. Once, Pastor Gurley announced at Sunday morning service that "religious services would be suspended until further notice as the church was needed as a hospital." Plans already were made, and lumber to be used as flooring on top of pews was stacked outside. But Lincoln stood up (he did that often, believing that all prayers should be made standing up) and announced, "Dr. Gurley, this action was taken without my consent, and I hereby countermand the order. The churches are needed as never before for divine services."

Lincoln needed the church and the Bible. By 1864, Lincoln was even recommending Scripture reading to Joshua Speed, his fellow skeptic from Springfield days. When Speed said he was surprised to see Lincoln reading a Bible, Lincoln earnestly told him, "Take all that you can of this book upon reason, and the balance on faith, and you will live and die a happier man." When the Committee of Colored People in 1864 gave Lincoln a Bible, he responded, "But for this book we could not know right from wrong."

Bulwarked by his new communion with God, Lincoln held out initially for statesmanship rather than destruction. He told the Reverend Byron Sutherland of the First Presbyterian Church in Washington that God "has destroyed nations from the map of history for their sins," but his "hopes prevail generally above my fears for our Republic. The times are dark, the spirits of ruin are abroad in all their power, and the mercy of God alone can save us."

The theological left, however, became even more demanding as the war went on. Unitarian minister Henry Bellows told a convention of his co-religionists that God demanded not "half-way work" but the "subjugation or the extermination of all persons who wish to maintain the slave power." The South must die! That message spread. Senator Henry Wilson in 1864 proclaimed that by the coming destruction of the South, "Providence has opened up the way to that higher civilization and purer Christianity which the Republic is to attain."

Unconditional surrender of the South was essential, the Reverend Stephen Tyng declared in New York, because "Purity must go before peace," and a negotiated settlement would mean that "every death in our armies has been an unprincipled murder." The Republican Party motto became "To conquer a peace," and the drumbeat of support was incessant. From the *Christian Advocate and Journal:* "Prosecution of the war to the extinction of the rebellion." From the *Western Christian Advocate:* "We must conquer peace."

Again, as with the early proclamations concerning emancipation, Lincoln could not avoid making strategic decisions based on his religious beliefs. After all, the real question for the Union at the beginning of the war was not whether it could win. Given overwhelming advantages in men and material, and barring intervention from foreign powers, victory would come—unless God ordained otherwise—*if* the North was ready to use *any* means to attain that end.

That last clause is crucial. American generals, like their European counterparts, had two beliefs concerning the ethics of war. First, except in extraordinary circumstances, it was not proper to plan to win a battle by losing more men than your opponent did. Second, it was not right to wage war on civilians. Not until Lincoln was ready to approve the adoption of means previously considered unethical did the South's unconditional surrender come within sight.

The first change came only after long struggle. General George McClellan, taking the military code to its extreme, had refused battle unless he was certain that his forces would inflict more casualties than they would receive. Since such certainty was rarely present, he had a bad case of what Lincoln called "the slows." Lincoln ended up firing McClellan, bringing him back briefly under desperate circumstances, and then firing him again.

By December 1862, Lincoln had discovered a new strategy that he called "doing the arithmetic." The Union suffered a bloody defeat at Fredericksburg, in December 1862, but one of Lincoln's secretaries noted his reaction: "We lost 50% more men than did the enemy [the actual differential was 140 percent], and yet there is a sense in the awful arithmetic propounded by Mr. Lincoln. He says that if the same battle were to be fought over again, every day, through a week of days, with the same relative results, the army under Lee would be wiped out to its last man, the Army of the Potomac would still be a mighty host, the war would be over, the Confederacy gone." Lincoln looked for, and eventually found, generals like Ulysses Grant who would do the arithmetic. In May 1864, Grant ordered Union assaults at The Wilderness that cost 18,000 Union casualties to 10,800 for the Confederates, and at Spotsylvania Court House, with a cost of 18,000 northern soldiers in comparison to 9,000 southerners.

Early in June the arithmetic became even more severe. Grant ordered an attack at Cold Harbor that was so obviously designed for attrition that Union soldiers, before proceeding to the assault, "were calmly writing their names and home addresses on slips of paper and pinning them on the backs of their coats, so that their bodies might be recognized and their fate made known to their families at home," according to Lieutenant Colonel Horace Porter. The Confederates had 1,500 casualties that day, the Union 7,000. One of the dead northern soldiers left a blood-stained diary with a final entry: "June 3. Cold Harbor. I was killed."

RIGHTEOUS RETRIBUTION?

The other ethical change was even more radical. One publication, *Instructions for the Government of Armies of the United States in the Field (General Orders No. 100),* reiterated at the war's commencement "the distinction between the private individual belonging to a hostile country and the hostile country itself, with its men in arms." According to the orders, "the unarmed citizen is to be spared in person, property, and honor. . . . [A]ll robbery, all pillage or sacking, even after taking a place by main force, all rape, wounding, maiming, or killing of such inhabitants, are prohibited under the penalty of death, or such other severe punishment as may seem adequate for the gravity of the offense."

William Tecumseh Sherman pioneered in what had been seen as barbarism. In 1862 he wrote that articles of war making destruction of civilian property a potentially capital offense displayed "an old idea." During 1863 his forces in Mississippi sacked, pillaged, and burned down towns and plantation homes. Afterwards, Sherman bragged to

Grant, "The inhabitants are subjugated. They cry aloud for mercy. . . . They have sowed the wind and must reap the whirlwind." In the summer of 1864, Sherman pressed down on Atlanta and bombarded the city's residences with cannon that could, as he wrote in August, "pick out almost any house in town" and "make the inside of Atlanta too hot to be endured."

The conquest of Atlanta probably made the difference between Union victory and defeat. Had elections occurred in August 1864 rather than November, Democratic candidate McClellan likely would have been elected, and the war probably would have ended with negotiations and southern independence. Had the South been able to stalemate the war for three more months, Lincoln would have lost and left office in disgrace. But the conquest of Atlanta in September led many northerners (as Baptists in Ohio and Methodists in Michigan formally resolved) to see "the hand of God in the success of our arms." Abraham Lincoln was anointed. Journalist James Gilmore, interviewing Lincoln after the Atlanta victory, came away thinking that the president saw himself as God's agent "led infallibly in the right direction."

The right direction meant doing wrong by the traditional military code. Once Atlanta surrendered, Sherman ordered every resident who remained to leave the city, to the astonishment of the *Macon Telegraph*: "Modern warfare may be challenged in vain for an edict from a military satrap so utterly and inexcusably barbarous as this. To drive out a non-combatant population from their homes and effects, with nothing but the clothes upon their persons. . . . So horrible is this on helpless women and babies, that we might look for such an outrage as this to evoke a universal burst of indignation from Christendom."

Indignation never came because some Union leaders saw themselves as anointed to punish, and others regretted total war but saw it as the only way to keep the war from dragging on and on. Sherman told Atlanta officials in September, "War is cruelty and you cannot refine it; and those who brought war into our country deserve all the curses and maledictions a people can pour out." He arrested female factory workers who had made Confederate uniforms and sent them north as prisoners. In October, after his supply train was fired upon, Sherman ordered his men to "burn ten or twelve houses of known secessionists, kill a few at random, and let them know it will be repeated every time a train is fired on."

Sherman's soldiers reflected their commander's attitude on the march through Georgia, which left behind a destroyed countryside from Atlanta to the sea. One of Sherman's staff officers, Major Henry Hitchcock, noted, "It is a material element in this campaign to produce among the people of Georgia a thorough conviction of the personal misery which attends war." Another officer declared that civilians left helpless "feel now the effects of their wickedness and who can sympathize very much with them?"

Lincoln apparently did not, or not enough to instruct Sherman to follow the official rules of warfare as his army ravaged South Carolina early in 1865. Sherman informed Washington that "the whole army is burning with an insatiable desire to wreak vengeance upon South Carolina. I almost tremble at her fate, but feel that she deserves all that seems to be in store for her." The *Philadelphia Inquirer* observed that the destruction of South Carolina "is but justice, and Heaven will surely mete it out . . . the world will approve her punishment, and to the sentence of righteous retribution will say, Amen!"

Northern journalist David Conyngham noted that soldiers thought "they were doing the work of the Lord, in wantonly destroying as much property as possible." He described the night of February 17, when South Carolina's capital city, Columbia, burned: "The streets were soon crowded with helpless women and children, some in night clothes. Agonized mothers, seeking their children, all affrighted and terrified, were rushing on all sides from the raging flames and falling houses. Invalids had to be dragged from their beds, and lay exposed to the flames and smoke that swept the streets, or to the cold of open air in backyards."

Even one of Sherman's majors told his wife that he was "sickened by the frightful devastation our army was spreading on every hand. Oh! It was absolutely terrible . . . women, children and old men turned out into the mud and rain and their houses and furniture first plundered and then burned." None of this could have proceeded without at least tacit support from Lincoln. He read of the Union vengeance both in military dispatches and through coverage by the *New York*

Herald, which described devastation and noted that soldiers "throw in an occasional murder 'just to bring an old hard-fisted cuss to his senses.'"

BINDING UP THE NATION'S WOUNDS, AND LINCOLN'S

The ends justified the means to many in the North. Professor Roswell Hitchcock of Presbyterian Union Theological Seminary wrote, "The hand of God is so conspicuous to me in this struggle, that I should almost as soon expect the Almighty to turn slaveholder, as to see this war end without the extinction of its guilty cause." But was there only one guilty cause? Lincoln had been troubled about this earlier, but two weeks after the destruction of Columbia, Lincoln in his second inaugural address showed that his mind was made up.

Curiously, that speech, with its call to "bind up the nation's wounds," is often cited as evidence of Lincoln's emphasis on reconciliation. But the address also showed Lincoln's theological changes during the war. "Fondly do we hope—fervently do we pray—that this mighty scourge of war might speedily pass away," he said. "Yet if God wills that it continue, until all the wealth piled by the bond-man's two hundred years of unrequited toil shall be sunk, and until every drop of blood drawn with the lash, shall be paid with another drawn with the sword, as was said three thousand years ago so still it must be said, 'the judgments of the Lord, are true and righteous altogether.'"

Was that God's will? How many drops of blood were there? Lincoln's understanding of God had changed his public policy emphases. At first, he had ignored God except when it was politically useful to take His name in vain, and repeatedly sought to control the dogs of war. Then, Lincoln had speculated repeatedly about God's will, as the war dragged on with no resolution in sight. Finally, Lincoln came to believe that a war of attrition and civilian ravishment was militarily necessary and morally defensible, both because such conduct would end the war sooner, and because civilians who had benefited from the bondsman's toil were culpable. Since God spoke through the outcome of battles, each victory gave him greater assurance that the right course of action emphasized iron and blood.

One other aspect of Lincoln's new theology also was crucial. Lincoln for decades had held to the doctrine of necessity, the belief that individual actions were predetermined by some kind of impersonal higher power. The Christian doctrine of Providence differs from such fatalism in that God is not impersonal and His decrees do not rob man of responsibility. Lincoln in his second inaugural address quoted Christ's words, "it must needs be that offenses come; but woe to that man by whom the offense cometh." But Lincoln placed all responsibility on the South, and did not accept that his emphasis on "doing the arithmetic" led directly to those piled-up corpses on the field at Cold Harbor.

That may have been too much for him to bear. His second inaugural address was impersonal, with no reference to himself or his own actions after the opening paragraph. Books like *Abraham Lincoln: The Christian* are probably right to claim that Lincoln was "born again" during the war, but some of the afterbirth stuck to his clothes, and he never entirely shook his earlier fatalism. He wrote to one newspaper editor in 1864 that he was not responsible for devastation: "God alone can claim it." Given Lincoln's tender-hearted tendency to identify with the wounded, he psychologically needed a plaque on his desk that stated, "The buck does not stop here."

The End of the War

Lincoln's theological journey during the war had taken him from initial indecision to a willingness to fight on, for better or for worse. The Bible that he had used for political effect in describing a house divided against itself he now looked to for assurance that he was doing the right thing in blowing up part of it. Sadly, his own familial house was showing wear. Lincoln's oldest son, Robert, at Harvard, was somewhat estranged from his parents; the favorite, Willie, was dead; and Mary Todd Lincoln was exhibiting more intensely the jealousy that sometimes scared those who surrounded her.

The worst explosion came on March 23, 1865, and led to a security letdown that contributed to the president's death. That day Lincoln and Grant on horseback reviewed the troops of General Edward O. C.

Ord. Mrs. Lincoln, arriving late in a carriage alongside Mrs. Grant, received what a messenger thought was comforting news: President Lincoln had given a special permit to the wife of General Charles Griffin, so she would be able to join the two ladies. Mrs. Lincoln, knowing that Mrs. Griffin was a great beauty, was outraged. "Do you mean to say she saw the President alone?" she exploded at Mrs. Grant and the messenger. "Do you know that I never allow the President to see any woman alone?"

When the carriage finally arrived Mrs. Lincoln saw the attractive wife of General Ord riding alongside her husband. Something snapped. Mary Lincoln climbed out of her carriage, stormed over to Mrs. Ord, and, according to Adam Badeau, Grant's military secretary, "called her vile names in the presence of a crowd of officers, and asked her what she meant by following up the President." Mrs. Ord burst into tears. Mrs. Grant defended her and Mary Lincoln turned on her: "I suppose you think you'll get to the White House yourself, don't you?"

Lincoln himself tried to intervene, but "Mrs. Lincoln repeatedly attacked her husband in the presence of officers." Badeau reported that Lincoln "bore it as Christ might have done, with an expression of pain and sadness that cut one to the heart, but with supreme calmness and dignity. . . . He pleaded with eyes and tones, till she turned on him like a tigress and then he walked away hiding that noble ugly face so that we might not catch the full expression of its misery."

By the following month the Lincolns had reconciled, but others had not forgotten. On April 14, when the Lincolns headed to the theater, General and Mrs. Grant did not go with them as originally planned, because Julia Grant refused to spend any more time with Mary Lincoln. (Grant often voiced regret in later years that he had not gone; his presence, and especially that of a military guard, might have thwarted the assassination.) Secretary of War Edwin Stanton and his wife had been invited as well, but Mrs. Stanton also refused to sit with Mrs. Lincoln. Finally, Stanton selected a young major, Henry Rathbone, and his fiancée to go with the Lincolns.

Partway through the play, the member of the Metropolitan Police assigned to guard duty, bored and thirsty, wandered away from his post. John Wilkes Booth fired his fatal shot unimpeded. Major Rathbone did marry his fiancée, but he never lived down or bricked away the events of Ford's Theatre. He became increasingly unbalanced and in 1894 murdered his wife and soon afterwards killed himself. Mrs. Lincoln's mental health deteriorated after the assassination. She was eventually found to be legally insane. She did recall that at Ford's Theatre, just before the assassination, she and the president had talked about a trip they hoped to take to Jerusalem.

The trip that Lincoln did take was into the minds of Americans. His Good Friday death made him an American martyr, but he has resonated so powerfully because he combined appealing qualities from all four of those profiled in the previous chapters: He stood tall like Washington, enunciated American creeds like Jefferson, remained steadfast like Jackson, and joked like Clay. If Jefferson was a Washington in public and an anti-Washington in private, Jackson a Washington both ways, and Clay an anti-Washington both ways, Lincoln was a mixture of all these both in public and private.

What is often ignored when we think of Lincoln as a monument is that he went to Washington as a Clay-lover but found that wheeling and dealing did not answer deeper issues of meaning as the Civil War raged. Profane as a youth, he became devout during the war as he realized its enormity was too big for him to comprehend. His wartime devotion tended to be fatalistic: God ordains whatever happens, and thus whatever happens is right. The Bible, however, teaches that whatever God ordains is right, yet man has the responsibility to choose the right by studying the Bible in order to think God's thought after Him.

The subtle but important difference between biblical and Lincolnesque faiths raises many questions: Because the Union won the war by breaking with constitutional restraints and traditions of humane warfare, were those policies right? Did Lincoln ever put himself under God's authority, or did he come to believe that his high-minded ends justified hellish means? There are many mysteries, but one thing is clear: When Lincoln's assassination left Americans overlooking his disunities and remembering his willingness to give all he had for Union, the bar for presidential successors was raised.

Interlude

CHAPTER 6

Booker T. Washington

We are now about to take a short break from politics, and at the same time probe the further dimensions of leadership and moral vision. In many eras political leaders are expected to provide inspiration, but in late-nineteenth-century America those who most influenced the direction of the nation and the management of its public affairs were most often prominent in fields outside government.

By 1880 it was clear that Congress was out of the business of granting consideration to ex-slaves and in the business of granting favors to business. Would ex-slaves elevate themselves or become a permanent underclass? Would a moral leader emerge from their ranks, one who could help his people move up from slavery without attempting to hide the difficulty of the terrain? Booker T. Washington was that man. But to understand how he became the leading statesman of his time without taking a position with the state, we need to overview his era.

As the Civil War was ending, many Americans in both the South and North hoped that their fellow citizens would accept the verdict and move on. When a constitutional amendment to abolish slavery passed Congress early in 1865, the *Christian Watchman and Reflector* stated that the nation born in July 1776 was now "born again." Such hopes went largely unfulfilled. In the North, would-be dictators argued that the central government should stomp on southern whites and in that way make final anti-slavery victory sure. In the South, some rebels now without a cause resolved to rip out the stitching of anyone who tried to bind up the nation's wounds.

Lincoln's assassination on Good Friday made him a Christ-like martyr among Americans generally, but radicals who feared that Lincoln would revert to moderation once the fighting ended saw the murder as helpful. One radical minister thought Lincoln "too gentle, too lenient to deal justice to traitors" in the way that "the will of God" required. Senator Charles Sumner viewed the assassination as "a judgment of the Lord . . . to lift the country into a more perfect union." Senator Zachariah Chandler of Michigan argued that "the Almighty continued Mr. Lincoln in office as long as he was useful and then substituted a better man to finish the work." (Chandler soon changed his opinion of Andrew Johnson.)

Later in 1865 calls for more punitive actions concerning the South increased. In November, Congressman George Julian of Indiana told his constituents, "It is ordained by Providence that retribution shall follow wrong doing. Thunder in the ears of your President and Congress that you demand the hanging, certainly the exile of the great rebel leaders, the confiscation and distribution of their great landed estates." There turned out to be only one hanging (of the Confederate general who ran the barbarous Andersonville prison) and no confiscation beyond that which the war itself also had effected.

Northern radicals were frustrated, but many of the people they had pledged to help fared worse. Talk was cheap on Capitol Hill as orators listed sins of the South that could be further punished through legislative action. Life was cheap a mile away in "Murder Bay," the area between Thirteenth and Fifteenth Streets a block south of Pennsylvania Avenue, where ex-slaves lived in lean-tos and shacks. The *National Freedman* reported in 1865, "the weather is cold, and they have little or no wood. Snow covers the ground, and they have a scanty supply of rags called clothes. The hospital is crowded with the sick. Government gives them a very, very small allowance of soup. Many will die." Few congressmen showed any personal interest or made individual contributions.

The first big postwar legislative struggle came in February 1866, when Congress passed a bill that gave the federal government total power in the southern states, with federal agents to act as judge and jury. Andrew Johnson, who venerated the Constitution, vetoed the measure. He argued that it represented an "assumption of power by the General Government which [would] break down the barriers which preserve the rights of the States. It is another step, or rather stride, to centralization and the concentration of all legislative power in the National Government."

Johnson pointed out that the vetoed bill would have had arrested southern civilians punished by court-martial. Those found guilty would have had no appeal from those decisions, not even to the U.S. Supreme Court. Johnson also disapproved of the bill's establishment of welfare for ex-slaves. "A system for the support of indigent persons," he wrote, "was never contemplated by the authors of the Constitution." Ex-slaves should emphasize education, Johnson believed. He personally contributed $1,000 to a school for black children in Charleston.

Johnson even had a dream. Knowing that black labor power was essential in the South, he believed that hard work would lead to black economic advancement that would then give ex-slaves the power to demand full political rights. The process would take a generation or two. Johnson told a delegation of black leaders that he wished their goal of full political, social, and economic equality "could be done in the twinkling of an eye, but it is not in the nature of things, and I do not assume or pretend to be wider than Providence."

Radical Republicans had a different view. They used force to place blacks in positions of political leadership for which some were not ready. The corruption of many Reconstruction state governments became legendary. Bribes and payoffs were so common that one South Carolina senator, C. P. Leslie, was able to produce a classic line in their defense: "The State has no right to be a State until she can afford to take care of her statesmen." In South Carolina the Speaker of the House of Representatives lost a $1,000 bet on a horse. Three days later he was voted a gratuity to cover his loss, in tribute to "the dignity and ability with which he has presided."

Johnson's predictions of a southern white backlash proved accurate. The Ku Klux Klan rode, and northern allies of southern blacks moved on to other concerns. The *New York Tribune* a dozen years after the war justified its malign neglect by declaring that "after ample opportunity to develop their own latent capacities" the ex-slaves had proved that "as a race they are idle, ignorant, and vicious." A prediction in *The Nation* proved accurate for many decades: "The Negro will disappear from the field of national politics. Henceforth the nation, as a nation, will have nothing more to do with him."

WASHINGTON'S BOOTSTRAP RELIGION

This was the political environment in which Booker T. Washington grew into leadership. His critics never liked his essential agreement with Andrew Johnson that education and hard work would pave the road to political rights. Some also thought it strange that religion was more important than politics in his life; as Washington's daughter, Portia, said, "We never at home began the day without prayer, and we closed the day with prayer in the evening. He read the Bible to us each day at breakfast and prayed; that was never missed. Really he prayed all the time."

Religion was vital to Washington, but not just any kind, or even any version of Christianity. Washington regularly criticized churches that did not relate the Bible to the problems of this world as well as to the hopes of the next. He fought a two-front war: against atheism and its practical outworking of hopelessness, but also against "sentimental Christianity, which banks everything in the future and nothing in the present."

Washington startled some listeners by stating that "the bulk of our people are as much in need of Christian teaching as any people to be found in Africa or Japan." He joked about an old man who came to a church meeting and said, "I have had a bad time since I was here a week ago . . . I have broken all the Commandments; but, thank the Lord, I haven't yet lost my religion." Washington sometimes despaired at the number of churches that emphasized faith without works and soon became dead.

What Washington wanted was tough-minded Christianity throughout the week: "Our religion must not alone be the concern of the emotions, but must be woven into the warp and woof of our every-day life." He spoke of how Christians should remember not only God's love but also God's holiness, realizing that "If we would live happily, live honored and useful lives, modeled after our perfect leader, Christ, we must conform to law, and learn that there is no possible escape from punishment that follows the breaking of law."

Washington even saw slavery as part of God's sovereign design to bring good out of evil: "We went into slavery in this country pagans; we came out Christians." He told an audience at Carnegie Hall that blacks at least derived from the sadness of slavery "the habit of work." He saw Christianity as the remedy for all social evils, asking and then answering the question, "What is the remedy for lynching? Christian education of the white man and the black man."

Washington taught his students that biblical teaching should be the basis of their work: "I want every Tuskegee student as he finds his place in the surging industrial life about him to give heed to the things which are "honest and just and pure and of good report. . . ." He wanted students to do everything *coram deo,* "in the sight of God": "A student should not be satisfied with himself until he has grown to the point where, when simply sweeping a room, he can go into the corners and crevices and remove the hidden trash which, although it should be left, would not be seen."

LEARNING SELF-DISCIPLINE

Washington's tenaciously held faith grew out of hard experience. He was born on April 5, 1856, in Franklin County, Virginia, the son of a slave mother and a white man from a nearby plantation named Taliaferro, whose last name became the T. in Booker T. Washington. In 1865 nine-year-old Booker, liberated from slavery along with his mother and brother, went to live with a stepfather in West Virginia. There he learned one side effect of freedom: He was put to work in the salt mines, often having to leave for his morning shift at 4 a.m.

How to overcome that? After his shift Booker was able to spend some time at a school run by a literate black ex-soldier hired by poor parents to teach their children how to read. More progress of a sort came after several years, when Booker was able to move from the salt mines to the coal mines. He continued reading whenever he could. He was ready to make rapid progress when in 1872 he heard of the Hampton Institute, a new, higher school for blacks five hundred miles away.

With parental blessings and a few dollars from his older brother, Booker started out, riding when he could, walking often. He slept under wooden plank sidewalks in Richmond and shoveled pig iron to earn money for food. He arrived at the institute in clothes he had worn for weeks. There he received an unusual admissions test: The head teacher told him to sweep and dust an adjoining classroom. He swept it three times and dusted every inch of wood in the room four times. Then, holding his breath, he asked for an inspection.

The teacher examined every corner and rubbed her handkerchief on the table and benches. The handkerchief was spotless. She turned to Washington and said, "I guess you will do to enter this institution." He later remarked that those words made him "one of the happiest souls on earth. The sweeping of that room was my college examination, and never did any youth pass an examination for entrance into Harvard or Yale that gave him more genuine satisfaction."

Washington worked his way through Hampton by doing janitorial work. He became a teacher there, but moved to Tuskegee, Alabama, in 1881 to head an institute newly established by the state legislature. Washington found upon arrival that the supposed school had no building, no land purchased for placement of a building, no equipment, and not even any students.

So he began visiting families in the Tuskegee area, thereby revisiting scenes from his own childhood: the whole family sleeping on the floor in a one-room wooden cabin, the family never eating together but grabbing hunks of bread and fried pork and munching on the way to the hoeing fields. He also saw that formal education by itself did not change lives unless there was the will to work hard in economically productive tasks. (Later, Washington often recalled that in one shack he had encountered a young black who had been to high school and was sitting in greasy clothes amid garbage, studying a French grammar.)

This realization drove him when the Tuskegee Institute held its first class in a church building that July. Washington lined up the students and criticized their dirty shoes and the unmended holes in their clothes. Later, faced with the question of how to feed hungry and penniless students, Washington led them in a "chopping bee," during which students cleared the undergrowth, trees, and shrubs off land that was then to be used for planting food crops.

Some of the students protested, arguing that they had come for an education so they would not have to do manual labor, "slave work." Washington, however, swung his ax vigorously, both showing and telling that "There is as much dignity in tilling a field as in writing a poem . . . It is as important to know how to set a table and keep house as it is to read Latin."

Washington continually stressed the opportunity to make small but significant improvements in any economic situation. In the morning he rode his horse around campus and at evening chapel often reported that he had seen one house run down and another spruced up; one husband and wife were growing peaches on their own soil, but the yard of another house was littered with empty cans of peaches from New Jersey. Washington noted that marriage and family often propelled men to consistent work.

A year after he began the work at Tuskegee, Washington himself was married to Fannie Smith, a childhood sweetheart of his in Malden, West Virginia. They had a daughter, but Mrs. Washington died after two years of marriage. Washington soon married Olivia Davidson, who worked alongside him in building and soliciting funds for the school. During four years of marriage they had two sons, but in 1889, when a fire broke out in their home just after the younger child was born and everyone had to flee to safety, the second Mrs. Washington became seriously ill; Washington took her by train to Boston to receive good medical attention, but she died in a hospital there. Three years later, Washington married Margaret Murray, who was first a teacher and then, at the time of marriage, the principal at Tuskegee. They were married for the next twenty-three years, until Washington died.

Those are the bare details, and Washington's thirteen volumes of papers and several autobiographies, as well as several biographies of him, emphasize his ideas but not his personal life. In *The Story of My Life and Work,* Washington wrote reticently of his "great personal bereavement" when his first two wives died, but gave no specific detail, merely inserting copies of obituaries and tributes by others. He took his children with him on horse rides around campus and trips to other cities, and they later remembered him as a busy but fond father. Later in life Washington developed political enemies who looked for evidence of adultery that could discredit him, but they could not find any. White cultural and political leaders frequently referred to Washington as a "statesman," and he knew that nothing would more quickly reduce his effectiveness than a scandal.

How to Bring About Change

During the Reconstruction era some still believed that the best way for statesmen to push for progress was to move to the District of Columbia. But federal offices were much less active once the tumult of war and early reconstruction ceased. Business hours were such that an official could revive from a late night out by sleeping until nine, and yet be free for a two-hour lunch and a new round of social life beginning at six. Cabinet members often had office hours from ten to twelve in the morning and three to five in the afternoon. When Congress was in session the House and Senate met at noon most weekdays but adjourned quickly, and rarely after five.

In the House chamber, congressmen often read newspapers, trimmed their fingernails, and had spitting contests. Every desk in the chamber had a pink and gold china spittoon next to it to catch tobacco spit, but the floors were still a mess. Visitors who climbed marble stairs to the gallery could shoot at a big rubber spittoon surrounded by a yellow-brown ring. In the Treasury building near the White House, a big wooden box filled with sawdust, at the base of a four-story spiral staircase, served as the main spittoon. The favorite sport of Treasury Department employees was to spit from over a banister several floors up.

Some legislative days included committee meetings and office chores, but constituent service was slight because most voters did not pay much attention to Washington doings or expect much attention. One sport of the period as common as logrolling was walking the mostly uphill mile along Pennsylvania Avenue from the base of Capitol Hill to the Willard Hotel. Congressmen sometimes laid bets on each other's ability to stop in each saloon on the way and have a drink at each establishment. Whoever could reach the Willard without having to take a cab was the winner.

Washington, D.C., was far from Booker T. Washington's Tuskegee. Classes there ignored government and emphasized jobs. Students wrote vigorous essays not on political theory but on concrete subjects like blacksmithing. Students who wanted to give commencement orations on literary subjects were challenged instead to explain why the production of cabbages would be one step on the road to equal rights for blacks.

Washington also tried to shake up the farmers around his institute. Commencement days at Tuskegee were designed to foster transformation among the people of the region. At 3 a.m. farm wagons, oxcarts, and mule buggies started to head to the institute; the line sometimes extended three miles along the road. Close to ten thousand people went through the agricultural exhibits and shops. They saw a young carpenter finishing work on a model house or a mason completing a brick wall. Washington always looked for "a way to make the day of additional value. . . . For many of them it is the one day in the year when they go to school."

Going to school, building businesses, and buying alluvial land that was readily available at $1 per acre around Tuskegee were the ways to fight the sharecropper system, Washington argued. "Buy land," he told farmers. "If you can't buy a hundred acres, still buy land; buy thirty acres; yes, buy one acre and build a house." Take care of that acre, Washington said: "Get land and lie on it. Today you go to town with your wagon empty and come back with the wagon full and your pocket empty. You must go to town with your wagon full of your produce and come back with your wagon empty and your pocket full."

Washington wanted his graduates to be apostles of education, but he also knew from his reading of Paul's epistles that tent-making—having a trade—was essential to independence. He introduced brick-making to the institute in 1883, carpentry in 1884, printing in 1885, mattress- and cabinet-making in 1887, wagon-building in 1888, and tinsmithing and shoemaking in 1889.

In speeches that he gave to publicize the school and raise funds, Washington argued that those who were lazy and made no effort to improve their skills or accumulate property should be scorned. He even told one story in dialect about how a shiftless southern poor white asked a self-respecting old black man for three cents with which to pay his ferry fare across a river. The old black man replied: "I's sorry no to commerdate yer, boss, but der fac' is dat a man what ain't got three cents is jus' as bad off on one side ob der ribber as der udder."

For years Washington told religious listeners not to ignore the present because they had faith in the future. He wanted them to glorify God immediately "by putting business methods into your farming, by growing things in your garden the year around, by building and keeping attractive and comfortable homes for your children so they will stay at home and not go to the cities, by keeping your bodies and your surroundings clean, by staying in one place, by getting a good teacher and a good preacher, by building a good school and church, by letting your wife be partners in all you do, by keeping out of debt, by cultivating friendly relations with your neighbors both white and black."

This message of changing society person by person, heart by heart, was different from that of many previous black leaders who had grown up in the anti-slavery movement. Frederick Douglass, who did not have the Christian base on which Washington would stand, once spoke passionately in Boston's Faneuil Hall as he described bigotry against blacks. He finally cried out, "The Negro has no hope of justice from the whites, no possible hope save in his own right arm. It must come to blood. The Negroes must fight for themselves."

Douglass sat down, his case powerfully made, but then Sojourner Truth raised the eyes of those in the audience with one brief question: "Frederick, is God dead?" Douglass had no answer for her. When Washington became a nationally recognized black leader the tone of the black-white debate changed.

INTRODUCING THE VISION NATIONWIDE

Washington's big national breakthrough came through a speech at the opening of the International Cotton Exposition in Atlanta in September 1895, half a year after Frederick Douglass died. Washington was the first black in decades to speak on a major occasion to a largely white southern audience. After many years of preaching a Christian message, he was prepared to be an overnight sensation. But he had to decide whether to put on a minstrel show for the immediate gratification of some whites, a show of rebellion for the immediate gratification of some blacks, or a display of long-range vision that would challenge both whites and blacks.

Before the speech Washington knelt down with particular fervency "and asked God's blessing upon my effort." Then he got up and argued that blacks were not inferior; that they could or would build strong families, gain solid job-oriented education, and develop economic power; and that they would, after putting those first things first, gain political power. He challenged blacks by saying that the reverse—go for political power now, gain economic power later—would not work. He challenged whites by saying that as blacks followed the steps for advancement, whites would be wrong to get in the way.

Washington was able to say these things in dramatic fashion and with impeccable style. A *New York World* correspondent described how thousands in the audience saw "a remarkable figure, tall, bony, straight as a Sioux chief, high forehead, straight mouth, with big white teeth, piercing eyes, bronzed neck, and his muscular right arm swung high in the air." The reporter noted that Washington's "voice rang out clear and true, and he paused impressively as he made each point. Within ten minutes the multitude was in an uproar of enthusiasm, handkerchiefs waved, canes flourished, hats tossed in the air. The fairest women in Georgia stood up and cheered. It was as if the orator had bewitched them."

What southerners were cheering was a vision of how to end the civil war within their region that had raged throughout the thirty years since General Robert E. Lee's surrender. The greatest applause followed a gesture: Washington thrust his hand above his head, fingers spread out, and said concerning blacks and whites, "in all things that are purely social we can be as separate as the fingers." Then he brought his fingers together into a solid fist, saying that this represented how the races could be united "in all things essential to mutual progress." Whites could have segregation now, if they wished; but instead of supporting suppression, they should turn their attention to mutual economic advancement.

Washington followed his promotion of this long-range vision with an immediate admonition to his own people: Do not emphasize macrosolutions but "cast down your bucket where you are . . . we shall prosper in proportion as we learn to dignify and glorify common labor and put brains and skill into the common occupations of life." This was classic Washington—always long-term satisfaction rather than immediate gratification—and it immediately satisfied the leaders who were listening. As soon as Washington finished speaking the governor of Georgia raced across the stage to shake his hand. Others followed, for *Atlanta Constitution* editor Clark Howell described the speech as "a platform upon which blacks and whites can stand with full justice to each other."

The *Constitution* represented well the goals of the South's white leaders, but black newspapers such as the *Richmond Planet* also made positive remarks. So did newspapers read by northern industrialists such as the *Boston Transcript*, which reported, "The speech of Booker T. Washington . . . seems to have dwarfed all the other proceedings and the Exposition itself. The sensation that it has caused in the press has never been equaled." Washington was providing something for all three of the crucial groups—southern whites, southern blacks, and northern industrialists and investors—that had to cooperate if black economic advance was to come rapidly.

Washington had to give up something to achieve such success, however: the emphasis on political rights that was part of the unfinished agenda from the Civil War era. Others were unwilling to give that up, but Washington was ready: "The wisest among my race understand that the agitation of questions of social equality is the extremist folly, and that progress in the enjoyment of all the privileges that will come to us must be the result of severe and constant struggle rather than of artificial forcing."

Washington's declarations represented one culmination of the 1865–95 era in which economics outweighed politics. The year after his Atlanta speech brought the most hotly contested election in two decades, the McKinley-Bryan battle, and Washington said it did not much matter to blacks. More important than the immediate gratification of political triumphs were the quiet victories: "We find that as every year we put into a southern community colored men who can start a brickyard, a sawmill, a tin shop, or a printing office, men who produce something that makes the white man partly dependent upon the Negro, instead of all the dependence being on the other side, a change takes place in the relation of the races."

While most readers of *The Atlantic Monthly* in September 1896 were debating presidential politics, Washington was crystallizing in its pages his dream of person-by-person economic empowerment: "It is through the dairy farm, the truck garden, the trades, and commercial life, largely, that the Negro is to find his way to the enjoyment of all his rights. Whether he will or not, a white man respects a Negro who owns a two-story brick house."

SPEAKING AGAINST THE GRAIN

Over the following twenty years Washington continued to stroke his audiences, then challenge them. He complimented northern white audiences on the philanthropic aid they had given to blacks, so that their faces glowed. Then he confronted them with their poor record in educational and legal discrimination. Washington complimented a black audience on progress since emancipation so that their faces glowed. Then he commented on the laziness and unreliability of some blacks, and how their lack of industry contributed to prejudice.

Washington also won southern whites to his side by not blaming the South alone for slavery ("The *whole country* was responsible"). He also admitted that Reconstruction was a disaster: "Immediately after freedom we made serious mistakes. We began at the top. We made these mistakes, not because we were black people, but because we were ignorant and inexperienced." Washington then asked white business managers and bankers to allow full opportunity for those who were starting at the bottom and working their way up. "With the exception of preaching the Gospel of Christ," he said, "there is no work that will contribute more largely to the elevation of the race in the South than a first-class business enterprise."

Washington's greatest contributions came when he spoke against the grain, challenging prodigal sons to come home to the biblical morality they had been taught. Once, he told a crowd of five thousand at the Harlem Casino in New York City to "stop staying here and there and everywhere and begin to live somewhere." He talked of the need to save money not in abstract terms but with sympathetic description of the temptations each city store window offered: "The dollars almost jump out of your pockets as you go by on the sidewalk."

Still, Washington always emphasized individual responsibility. He told the Harlem audience, "You men working for rich men here in the city smell the smoke of so many twenty-five-cent cigars that after a while you feel as though you must smoke twenty-five-cent cigars. You don't stop to think that when the grandfathers of those very men first came from the country a hundred years ago they smoked two-for-five cigars."

Washington emphasized individual freedom without neglecting the importance of cultural patterns. The slavery system did give its captives the habit of hard work, he noted, but it also taught them "that labor was a curse. The consequence of the teaching was that, when emancipation came, the Negro thought freedom must, in some way, mean freedom from labor." Since the typical slave saw that plantation owners were educated and did not have to labor in noticeable ways, "education became associated in his mind with leisure."

Finally, Washington emphasized humility over pride. Speaking at the Hampton Institute in 1898, almost a quarter century after he arrived there in rags, Washington said, "The progress along material lines is marked, yet the greatest lesson that we have learned during the last two decades is that the race must begin at the bottom, not at the top, that its foundation must be in truth and not in pretense."

Washington's frequent downgrading of abstract education grated on those who aspired to academic glory. He once wrote of a Yale graduate who went wrong: "Once he gets the idea that—because he has crammed his head full with mere book knowledge—the world owes him a living, it is hard for him to change." Many young men, Washington stated, were "not wholly to blame for their condition. I know that, in nine cases out of ten, they have gained the idea at some point in their career that, because they are Negroes, they are entitled to the special sympathy of the world, and they have thus got into the habit of relying on this sympathy rather than on their own efforts to make their way."

Washington also worried about occupational choices: He was not pleased that "the highest ambition of the average Negro in America was to hold some sort of office, or to have some sort of job that connected him with the Government." He argued that blacks "in the long run can earn more money and be of more service to the community in almost any other position than that of an employee or office-holder under the Government."

Washington acknowledged that the capital city "still has a peculiar attraction and even fascination for the average Negro," but he strove to fight the emphasis on politics: "I never liked the atmosphere of Washington. I early saw that it was impossible to build up a race of which the leaders were spending most of their time, thought, and energy in trying to get into office, or in trying to stay there after they were in."

Making Enemies

Washington's tendency to minimize the immediate importance of national politics alienated those who wanted to work from the top down. Washington wrote that the way for blacks to gain respect from whites was not by legal fiat but by "beginning at the bottom, and working upwards, by recognizing our weaknesses as well as our strength, by tangible evidences of our worthiness to occupy the highest position."

Critics charged him with accepting the removal of civil rights. Similarly, when Washington proclaimed that "my people will be better able to cope with the white man and command his respect when they reach a high state of industrial development," he was accused of excusing those who did not respect blacks as they were.

Washington also alienated those who saw salvation through the arts. William Ferris, author of *The African Abroad,* argued that "the Negro must acquire culture, polish, and refinement, he must acquire an aristocratic, high-bred feeling . . . then we will no longer be a despised but an admired race." This was nonsense to Washington, who countered with his formula: Believe in God, follow God's principles for building strong families and strong businesses, and all the rest will come eventually.

W.E.B. Du Bois became the chief Washington critic. Born in Great Barrington, Massachusetts, in 1868, Du Bois was a product of neither the South nor slavery. He attended school in that small town from age six to sixteen and faced no special discrimination. Specializing in Greek and German at Fisk College in Tennessee, where he went on scholarship, Du Bois wrote a senior essay on Otto von Bismarck. He then received fellowships to study philosophy at Harvard and the University of Berlin, and found himself loving Paris and the art museums of Europe. Du Bois's training was exactly the kind that Washington distrusted.

Du Bois returned to the United States at age twenty-six committed to European notions of broadening the governmental sphere. He became famous upon publication of *The Souls of Black Folk* (1903), a book that criticized Washington's emphasis on economic advancement at a time when political discrimination was deepening. "Manly self-respect is more than land and houses," Du Bois proclaimed. In 1906 he called other opponents of Washington to meetings first in Niagara Falls and then Harpers Ferry, in honor of John Brown.

Instead of throwing down their buckets where they were, Du Bois and his associates issued the Niagara Movement manifesto: "We claim for ourselves every right that belongs to a free-born American, political, civil, and social." Washington, meanwhile, insisted that blacks would find "a safe and permanent place in American life" by avoiding "mere political agitation" and instead "first emphasizing the cardinal virtues of home, industry, education, and peace with our next-door neighbor, whether he is white or black."

The Niagara Movement manifesto provided the ideological foundation for a new organization, the National Association for the Advancement of Colored People. Du Bois in 1909 became the NAACP's director of publications and research, proclaiming that "we shall never cease to protest and assail the ears of America. . . . We want full manhood suffrage and we want it now." Year by year his criticism of Washington became more heated.

The adversaries occasionally met, but Washington refused to play on the NAACP's terrain. Once, when Washington and his critics met at a dinner at Young's Hotel in Boston, each speaker denounced Washington in turn. Finally, called on to respond, he stood and said, "Gentlemen, I want to tell you about what we are doing at Tuskegee." Then, according to onlooker T. Thomas Fortune, "For more than a half-hour he told them of the needs and the work without once alluding to anything that had been said in heat and anger by those to whom he spoke." When Washington concluded his review, he sat down.

The more Washington tried to stay above the fray, the more he was subjected to personal attacks. One of his responses came in a rare aside in his book *The Story of the Negro:* "Any black man . . . willing either in print or in public speech, to curse or abuse the white man, easily gained for himself a reputation for great courage. . . . Another man, who worked patiently and persistently for years in a Negro school, depriving himself of many of the comforts and necessities of life, in order to perform a service which would uplift his race, gained no reputation for courage. On the contrary, he was likely to be denounced as a coward by these 'heroes,' because he chose to do his work without cursing, without abuse, and without complaint."

THE PRICE OF SLEEPLESS NIGHTS

To put feet on his vision beyond the bounds of Tuskegee, Washington founded the National Negro Business League in 1900 and became its president. At Washington's last NNBL convention, in August 1915, seven hundred delegates from thirty different states heard Washington proclaim that development of businesses would lead to educational growth and political freedom. He was pleased to see progress in land owning: The total value of farm property owned by blacks increased by 179 percent—from $177 million to $493 million—during the first decade of the twentieth century.

Success stories emerged in city after city, and Washington highlighted them in his speeches and articles. When he toured Durham, North Carolina, in 1910, Washington was struck by "farms, truck farms, grocery stores, thriving drugstores, insurance houses, and beautiful though modest homes." He also commented on the Gothic Revival building that housed St. Joseph's A.M.E. Church, calling it the finest structure in the South. The North Carolina Mutual Life Insurance Company began in 1898, and by 1911 had five hundred employees, insurance in force of more than $2 million, and an annual premium income of about $250,000. The company followed Washington's principles, even to the point of encouraging its employees to attend church regularly. Many other companies that emphasized family and church also prospered.

Washington pointed to such triumphs of entrepreneurship and contrasted them with government failures in Liberia and Haiti, where blacks had "failed to apply themselves to the development of the soil, mines, and forests. The result is that, from an economic point of view, those two republics have become dependent upon other nations and races. . . . notwithstanding the fact that the two countries have natural resources greater than other countries similar in size." Liberty without virtue led to a new form of slavery.

In his last NNBL speech, in what turned out to be virtually his farewell address, Washington argued that if racial advancement were to come, "We must not be afraid to pay the price of success in business—the price of sleepless nights, the price of toil when others rest, the price of planning today for tomorrow, this year for next year." Those were not mere words for him: Washington's entire life—from his childhood in the mines to his janitorial work at Hampton to his social entrepreneurship at Tuskegee through the frenetic speaking schedule he carried on for his last twenty years—was a testimony to his ability to set aside immediate gratification and concentrate on long-term satisfaction for himself, his family, and his disciples.

Washington's heart gave out on him when he was speaking in New York late in 1915. Doctors there told the almost-sixty-year-old man that he had only hours to live, but he said he did not want to die in a northern hospital. He insisted on heading home to Tuskegee. He was carried to the train at Penn Station and hung on, asking at each station—Greensboro, Charlotte, Atlanta—how far they had come. Washington made it to Tuskegee and died hours after arrival, on November 14.

Tributes poured in from across the country, but writer and editor William Dean Howells, when reviewing Washington's *Up from Slavery*, probably put it best: "What strikes you first and last is his constant common sense. He has lived heroic poetry, and he can, therefore, afford to talk simple prose [and practice] subtle statesmanship." One of the earliest uses of the word "statesman" recorded in the *Oxford English Dictionary*, from 1661, is also appropriate here: "The word Statesman is of great latitude, sometimes signifying such who are able to manage Offices of States, although never actually called thereunto."

Booker T. Washington would have made a great president. Like Andrew Jackson, he was a fully integrated personality who set a course and stuck to it, without distraction or double-mindedness. He expressed faith in God and refused to turn to what some believed was a higher power, government. Like George Washington, he did not write or speak much about the indwelling nature of sin and the need for a Savior, so it is hard to know how deep his Christian faith went, but from all appearances there was bedrock. Whether he saw religion primarily as external good or internal necessity, Booker T. Washington showed no contrast between his public and private duties, and no willingness to concede that the ends of racial equality could justify anything other than the means of statesmanlike uprightness and perseverance.

CHAPTER 7

John D. Rockefeller

Another mode of statesmanship was called for in the late nineteenth century as corporations grew to sufficient size to garner political opposition. Would Americans refrain from the foolish but natural tendency to soak those who had built fortunes by providing improved products? Would business chieftains spend their hard-gotten gains in productive ways? What could business leaders do to grow their corporations without seeding rebellion?

The expansion of enterprise accelerated as the big war was starting. John Brown's raid at Harpers Ferry received big headlines in 1859, but another event that year had a long-run significance equally as great.

The successful drilling for oil at Titusville, Pennsylvania, set off a rush for "black gold" throughout western Pennsylvania. Just as in the California gold rush ten years before, entrepreneurs and fools both rushed in, and fortunes came and disappeared easily. One journalist wrote, "Almost everybody you meet has been suddenly enriched or suddenly ruined (perhaps both within a short space of time), or knows plenty of people who have."

Newspapers printed stories of money and sex. Edwin Drake, the discoverer of Titusville oil, lost all he had and plodded the streets of New York in an old coat, while others with sudden oil riches shopped in brothels until they dropped. One farm owner, "Coal-Oil Johnnie," used the proceeds from oil wells on his property to load his shirtfront with diamonds and his hands with hundred-dollar bills for tips to chorus girls. In three years he tossed away half a million dollars (the equivalent of tens of millions today) and was virtually bankrupt.

The record for the most rapid rise and fall probably went to Henry R. Rouse, who so enjoyed viewing his gusher that he lit a cigar to celebrate. When a spark suddenly set the pooled oil on fire, he ran through the flames and, severely burned, fell near the edge of the inferno, but with the presence of mind to fling his wallet outside the fire. Rouse's friends dragged him out. He retained consciousness long enough to dictate his will.

Accidents like these did not keep away speculators. They built hurriedly and haphazardly, not worrying about inefficiencies and losses because the potential gains were so great. Those who thought about God at all while the good times rolled typically saw him as a great sugar daddy who gave and gave without asking for responsible behavior. Once the fury diminished, however, there would be room for someone who did not take God's abundance for granted, and who paid close attention to details.

John D. Rockefeller was such a person. Born in upstate New York in 1839, he grew up in a torn household where he regularly saw acute evidences of sin. His father, "Big Bill" Rockefeller, styled himself a businessman but was really a gambler and con man who flashed a roll of bills when he made a financial killing and ran away each time he lost his latest haul. Big Bill was indicted for rape in 1849 but avoided arrest and moved his family to another New York town and then on to Cleveland.

The abrupt moves left his wife and children not only morally but also financially embarrassed. Frugality and saving became not only a moral imperative but a physical necessity as well. John's churchgoing mother held the family together and taught all her children to be steady rather than spectacular. She "never tolerated any wasteful thing," Rockefeller recalled many years later. She also required attendance at Sunday school and services. Big Bill did not go, for, as his son put it, he "was not a Christian man."

Rockefeller was baptized at the Erie Street Baptist Church in Cleveland in 1854, quickly started teaching Sunday school, and "was contented and happy . . . with the work in the church. That was my environment, and I thank God for it!" In no other place besides home, Rockefeller said, did he feel so at ease. He also had to earn a living, so at age sixteen he spent a sweltering summer fruitlessly knocking on doors of firms throughout Cleveland. He finally gained a clerk's position on September 26, 1855, and for the rest of his life celebrated that day as his turning point.

Rockefeller loved life as a clerk because he prized order, system, and measuring. A childhood schoolmate later noted that young Rockefeller had played in ball games if needed, but "what he really liked to do was to keep the tally sticks, cutting a notch in the stick for every run that came in. . . . He never made a mistake." At work he demonstrated that same thoroughness, scrutinizing every bill: "The bill had to be accurate in every detail before I O.K.'d it to be paid."

Rockefeller's work habits were in one sense a continuation of his tally-stick record-keeping, but his precision represented a Lincolnesque honesty that went two ways. Rockefeller's first partner, Maurice Clark, recalled that Rockefeller "was methodical to an extreme, careful as to details and exacting to a fraction. If there was a cent due us he wanted it. If there was a cent due a customer he wanted the customer to have it." Lincoln stories emphasized the rail-splitter's precision at always leaving the customer whole; customers were not so pleased when a businessman took extra steps to ensure that his firm was left whole.

Rockefeller's early job habits stayed with him for a lifetime. When he was almost eighty he exclaimed, "How many times I have dreamed . . . that I was still trying to collect those old bills! I would wake up exclaiming: 'I can't collect So-and-So's account.'" Rockefeller kept precise records of his contributions as well. From December 1855 to April 1856 he received close to $95 for four months work and dispensed $5.88 in charity, some to church members ("to a poor man in church, .25 . . . to a poor woman in church, .50") and some to missions, including twelve cents to the Five Points Mission in New York City.

Rockefeller also gave his money directly to the Euclid Avenue Baptist Church in Cleveland. He considered contributions to church a good investment, because, as he wrote to a friend, he needed "good preaching to wind me up, like an old clock, once or twice a week." Rockefeller most enjoyed hearing sermons that gave him precise lists of obligations and restrictions. He was less interested in talk of God's grace.

Love and discipline are both needed in the raising of a child who feels comfortable with himself but not so comfortable that aspirations disappear. It is not clear how much love Rockefeller received, but he did receive discipline and later disciplined himself by, among other things, abstaining from tobacco, alcohol, caffeinated products, and—from all available evidence—prostitutes. Rockefeller avoided debt and bought inexpensive "clothing such as I could pay for, and it was a good deal better than buying clothes that I could not pay for." Some of his cost shavings became legendary. He did not miss a train even when he had to bolt from a railroad station's dining room because "the boss with the lantern on his arm shouted 'All aboard!' But before going I'd stuff my cheeks with food (I always had a good big mouth), then spend a long time after I got aboard the train eating what I had carried away."

Rockefeller prided himself on obeying the letter of the law, whether that law was biblical or congressional. He loved skating and constructed a yard beside and behind his home that could be flooded during the winter and turned into an ice rink. One Sunday the weather turned cold and Rockefeller wanted to flood a pond to create a smooth surface for the next day's skating, but he did not want to have such work done on the Sabbath. Rockefeller's employees did the flooding, under his direction, in bitter cold shortly after midnight.

Putting Aside Immediate
Gratification in Business

Rockefeller's devotion to following the law was not casual. Neither was his attention to detail. Since Cleveland was close to the oil fields, those seeking quick fortunes in the 1860s patched together refineries there and in a dozen other cities. Rockefeller in 1863, having paid for a substitute to take his place in the Civil War, organized a partnership for fighting the oil wars. Even during the oil boom's most rapturous moments, when money flowed and others thought it foolish to pay attention to economy, he wasted not and later wanted not.

Economy: When a refinery needed new installations and repairs, Rockefeller bought pipes and joints himself rather than contracting out to a plumber, and saved half the cost. Economy: When more barrels were needed, he had employees make top-notch, well-glued white oak barrels for one dollar each rather than buying them for $2.50. When dozens of new barrels were needed quickly, Rockefeller himself came to the shop at 6:30 a.m. to help out.

Rockefeller's company not only built its own barrels but also manufactured its own sulfuric acid, recovering it after use. At a time in Cleveland when small refiners let their gasoline—the major oil product was kerosene used for lamps, and in the pre-auto age gasoline was a by-product—run into the Cuyahoga River, Rockefeller's company found ways to use all their by-products in fuel or lubrication. Rockefeller wasted no food in traveling. He wasted nothing at home.

Rockefeller scorned producers who kept no books and tossed aside expensive equipment that could have been fixed. "The Oil Region was a mining camp" that needed to become a business, he concluded: "It has always been my rule in business to make everything count." His goal was to make small but steady gains, avoiding large gains in one transaction followed by large losses.

From 1868 to 1873 oversupplies of oil relative to market demand sent prices plummeting. Only those refiners who had learned to be provident rather than prodigal could survive. Rockefeller began to buy up small Cleveland refineries in a way that was economically rational, and beneficial to owners ready to relinquish ownership, but not pleasing to those who wished to remain independent. Those who accepted stock in Rockefeller's new company, Standard Oil, often became rich. Those who would not cooperate lost out.

Once Rockefeller gained dominance in Cleveland he offered merger deals to leading companies in other cities. Stating that he had nothing to hide, Rockefeller allowed owners of those companies to inspect Standard's books, analyze the economies he had effected, and then realize that Standard could undersell them and drive them from business. Many owners sold out to Rockefeller in return for a block of Standard stock, at fair prices but loss of pride. It was inevitable, Rockefeller argued: The market system had to reward ruthlessly those who attained the greatest efficiency, and cast on the scrap heap of production those who fell short.

Rockefeller's wage record was satisfactory, given the economics and poverty of the era. The salaries he paid were at or better than the going rate. After his initial years in business Rockefeller faced no strikes. He paid his bills exactly on time and gained a good reputation with suppliers. As his agent T. H. Wheeler put it, Rockefeller "wanted every one who dealt with him to make a profit and be satisfied."

Rockefeller's economy and efficiency made a huge difference in the lives of American consumers. Before the 1870s, nighttime meant bedtime for all but the rich. Abraham Lincoln, the stories went, educated himself by the flickering light of the fireplace, but many people did not even have that opportunity much of the time. Whale oil and candles were too expensive to use for ordinary activities such as reading. In the 1870s, however, with the lowered price of kerosene meaning that one cent per hour could dispel darkness, middle- and working-class people could let there be light.

Why, then, did some people consider Rockefeller to be a prince of darkness? Envy played a factor, but concerning his business competitors, it was true that Rockefeller's "rising tide lifts all boats policy" was only for boats that made him captain. He took secret rebates from railroads and thought that reasonable because large shippers rightfully should receive "more consideration than the smaller and less regular shippers."

Rockefeller was flabbergasted by those who argued that the rates should be the same for all. He asked, "Who can buy beef the cheapest—the housewife for her family, the steward for a club or hotel, or the commissary for an army?" Then, the logical parallel: "Who is entitled to better rebates from a railroad, those who give it for transportation 5000 barrels a day, or those who give 500 barrels or 50 barrels?" If the family went meatless or the small company could not compete, so be it.

CONQUERING THE WORLD

Once Rockefeller succeeded in largely unifying and increasing the efficiency of American production, he set out to beat the world. In the 1870s, Arabian oil still lay untouched under the desert and the United States had virtually a monopoly on the production of oil for western Europe and Asia. During that decade U.S. exports of kerosene almost quadrupled to 367 million gallons, with Standard Oil the standard carrier. The export surge owed much to that company's ability to stand by its name and set the standard in quality for world markets.

Here's where another aspect of Rockefeller's consistency became crucial. Petroleum had long been known for its usefulness in lamps because it "gives a clear, brisk light," as S. P. Hildreth wrote in the *American Journal of Science* in 1826. The problem, however, was that petroleum needed to be purified, and purification was erratic. Kerosene ("coal oil") on the eve of the Civil War was three times less expensive than whale oil, but poorly refined kinds were known to blow up. "Beware of cheap oils," one newspaper article noted. Consumers worldwide yearned for reliability.

This Rockefeller provided: Laboratories established in each Standard refinery tested the oil repeatedly. A central laboratory in New York checked samples of all exports. If tests showed any problems, the refinery that had made the oil was called on the carpet, while the marketing department rolled out the red carpet for any customers who complained. Standard quickly replaced any sub-Standard oil. The 1880s brought competition from Russia, but quality assurances, plus repeated lowering of prices, helped to beat back that threat. European consumers found that oil from Baku did not burn as brightly or as long as that shipped by Standard.

Do away with more lamps, more refills! Buy Standard! The 1890s brought competition from Burma and the Dutch East Indies, but from 1880 to 1900 American kerosene exports doubled again, to 740 million gallons. Some people had scorned Rockefeller's tally-stick mentality. But without close accounting, without sorting through even the sweepings from his factories for tin shavings and solder drops, without using the waste (culm) from coal heaps to fuel his factories, he would not have been able to sell oil at close to a nickel per gallon, and by doing so create and then preserve hundreds of thousands of jobs for Americans. Even with Standard's quality lead, a rise of one cent per gallon would have lost it much of the world market.

What Price Economic Victory?

As Standard was bestriding the earth like a colossus, however, a new question was arising: Did America want a colossus? How disciplined should the economy be? Efficiencies created lower prices, but they also could lead to decreased work forces. That seemed to many Americans a good trade because those whose work was rendered superfluous could find other jobs where they would be more productive. But those left out always complained.

Rockefeller, winning worldwide, began having serious trouble at home in 1878, when a Clarion County, Pennsylvania, grand jury indicted him and eight other Standard officials for conspiring to achieve a monopoly. Specifically, Standard was accused of working out secret rebates with railroads so that it could ship its product more cheaply than competitors could. The case was settled out of court in 1880 when Standard agreed to full publicity for all rates and an end to rebates.

The great journalistic attack commenced in 1881 when Chicago writer and lawyer Henry Demarest Lloyd blistered Rockefeller in an *Atlantic Monthly* lead article. The article had many factual errors, but its major indictment was chilling to those who believed that government should promote the survival of endangered species of companies. "How seldom I had an unbroken night's sleep, worrying about how it all was coming out," Rockefeller said in 1906. "Work by day and worry by night, week in and week out, month after month. If I had foreseen the future I doubt whether I would have had the courage to go on."

Lloyd began his attack by showing how major railroads secretly granted lower rates to Standard and other large corporations. He went on to detail how the competitive advantage allowed by those rates enabled Standard to knock out smaller competitors and establish a virtual monopoly. Lloyd then charged that Standard and similar companies held onto their power by bribing journalists and legislators. He also attempted to show that state governments were so corrupt that only Washington's intervention could set things right.

Rockefeller agreed with only one part of Lloyd's analysis: Yes, Standard had battered its competitors. To use today's language, Rockefeller acknowledged that a heavyweight boxer had roughed up a bantamweight, and that was not a pretty sight. But, Rockefeller insisted, Standard did not hit below the belt. It broke no laws. It did throw around its economic weight, but the only reason it could do so was because Standard stressed efficiency and frugality.

Rockefeller also noted that he was the victor and others could have been. He emphasized that Standard itself had faced a squeeze from the Pennsylvania Railroad and associated freight lines in the 1870s but had moved quickly to develop new pipeline technology and lay down lines. Others that were agile could have done the same, acquiring a fortune considered outrageous but nevertheless earned through hardworking days and sleepless nights. Why should they now suffer slings and arrows?

That was the question Rockefeller asked—Bill Gates might ask similar questions now—but cold logic did not make winners popular among those who were envious or fearful. The charge that most rankled Rockefeller was that he had used the power of government to suppress potential competitors. He differentiated Standard from corporations that were always asking government for special favors such as tariff increases, subsidies, land grants, and tax underassessments. Standard, he pointed out, merely wanted to be left alone to throw its weight around—and why not, since each pound of muscle was hard-earned? To maintain independence Standard used lobbying tricks, sure, but its goal in relation to government was defense, not offense.

Rockefeller also noted Standard's need to protect itself from legislators who had found that blackmail could pay, and pay well. Other testimony from the time supports this concern. When Theodore Roosevelt was in the New York legislature during the early 1880s, he estimated that a third of his colleagues were corrupt. He cited bills that corporate backers had paid them to sponsor, with ambiguous wording that could confuse honest legislators. But Roosevelt also noted that for every rotten bill invented by corporate interests there were at least ten designed ostensibly to restrict those interests. Their sponsors even received favorable publicity for introducing them, but there was a catch—they "had not the slightest intention of passing them, but wished to be paid not to pass them."

That was Rockefeller's argument, and a public relations expert might have found a way to have him phrase it in politically potent, Jeffersonian language: Government, hands off our yeoman handiwork! But Rockefeller could not honestly play that game because, in his experience, small business was not the hero. Given international competition, he believed that concentration in the oil industry was inevitable. He saw Standard, with its quality control and frequent lowering of prices, as a public servant.

Rockefeller, above all, was a man of vision, a vision of efficiency. From childhood through old age, in business and in church activities, he wanted to show in his records that nothing was wasted, much was constructed, and the bigger the better. "Mere money-making has never been my goal," he said: "an ambition to build" was his motivating force. In building, Rockefeller's goal was never to beggar his neighbor, but to buy him out on the road to maximum production discipline.

Standard efficiency did create a potential political problem, however. Americans sympathized with small business but not big. They wanted business leaders to have the liberty to build, but they wanted them to lead honorable lives. Railroad public relations officials throughout the last half of the century tried hard to allay public concerns and humanize their industries.* Standard's executives saw such

*See Olasky, *Corporate Public Relations: A New Historical Perspective* (Hillsdale, NJ: Lawrence Erlbaum Associates, 1987).

needs also, and they had one easy recourse: John D. Rockefeller himself was not, personally, a frightening individual.

DISCIPLINED AND UNOSTENTATIOUS

The life-styles of Rockefeller and some of the tycoons of our era could not be more different. Rockefeller was in church every Sunday, unless traveling, and frequently went to church suppers and picnics, but not to theaters. His journalistic reading was the *Cleveland Leader* and the *Baptist Standard*. He did read a novel once—*Ben Hur*—and said he enjoyed it.

When Rockefeller moved to New York City in 1884 he maintained patterns of domesticity, leading family prayers at seven-thirty sharp each morning. His children grew up wealthy but generally unspoiled. Once, when spending requests were too high, Rockefeller said, "Who do you think we are, Vanderbilts?" He taught a Sunday school class, "Don't let good fellowship get the least hold on you. . . . [E]very downfall is traceable directly or indirectly to the victim's good fellowship, his good cheer among his friends, who come as quickly as they go." Family remained.

Rockefeller's plainness puzzled reporters who expected a giant or an ogre. They seemed surprised to find just a man who was, to quote a reporter from Joseph Pulitzer's *World* of March 29, 1890, "well but plainly dressed, a little above the average height, well proportioned, weighing probably 180 pounds, with an intelligent and pleasant countenance, fair complexion, sandy hair and mustache intermixed with gray, a somewhat prominent nose, mild gray eyes, and an agreeably expressive mouth."

Many reporters were prepared to comment archly about the anticipated fanciness of Rockefeller's clothes, yet they ended up noting that he dressed neatly but abstained from rings or necktie pins. Those who investigated further found that Rockefeller bought new suits when the old ones were getting shiny, and that he preferred cloth coats (with plain sweaters, if needed) to fur coats. Reporters often described Standard as a terror, but Rockefeller as a terrier: He might bite and hold on, but he was not Rock the Ripper.

Reporters who were hoping that Rockefeller would throw lavish parties with dogs dressed in tuxedos were disappointed to find that he was early to bed, early to rise, and eager to avoid society functions. They chronicled that he enjoyed rowing, driving a buggy with his family, and walking in the woods, and that he preferred bread, milk, and apples to the creations of French chefs. Reporters on Pulitzer's *World* were told to skewer the wealthy, but even they had to acknowledge that Rockefeller was "modest, retiring, gentle-mannered, and without the human vanities that we associate with great millionaires."

If all of the new business elite had been like Rockefeller, some class animosities of the 1890s could have been avoided. But as it was, New York boasted a legendarily expensive dinner for dogs, and even socially backward Washington had balls where guests drained hundreds of cases of champagne and hundreds of gallons of terrapin soup. Jewelry fiends like Mrs. Leland Stanford, wife of a multi-millionaire senator, wore $250,000 in gems when she went out, kept sixty different diamond rings, and served tea from a pot of solid gold.

But Mrs. Rockefeller dressed plainly, like her husband, in contrast with the trends reported on by journalist Frank Carpenter: "We are lavishing fortunes on clothes. There is enough silk worn here every winter to carpet a whole state; there are pearls by the bushel, and diamonds by the peck. . . . The older the woman, the more giddy she seems to be. She cuts her dresses an inch lower at the bust for every extra ten years, and I blush for the fair sex when I look at the décolleté corsages and fat bare backs of the powdered old dames." (Carpenter concluded, "Fortunes are spent in paint and powder every season, and had I the income from the rouge alone, I would not have to work to support myself.")

Rockefeller and his family were not like that. But Rockefeller also was not forthcoming with reporters, some of whom noted that he answered questions literally and dodged implications. The *New York Sun* in 1898 characterized his responses as slow, sparing, and "seldom in response to the meaning of the question put." But what many reporters ended up noticing, instead of cautious responses or displays of wealth, were Rockefeller's eyes: "deep-set, rather small, of a steel-gray color, and quizzical, except when he is aroused from the seeming apathy that his face usually expresses. Then the eyes become very bright and look straight at his questioner."

FORESIGHT IN BUSINESS, NOT ELSEWHERE

Within his sphere of using American resources and making this nation's industry the world's standard for excellence, Rockefeller showed great foresight. Look, for example, at his record during the 1880s, when, over the objections of many Standard managers, he pushed the company to expand beyond its Pennsylvania and West Virginia holdings to the new Lima field in Ohio. Objections to that move came largely because the base of the Lima oil was sulfur rather than paraffin, which meant that kerosene made from Lima oil coated lamp openings with a film of soot.

Rockefeller, however, had confidence that Standard chemists would find ways to use the Lima crude, and he was right. Lima oil, turned into lubricants, axle grease, Vaseline, paints, and varnishes, became profitable. The Lima field bridged the era between the decline of the eastern fields and the opening of those in Texas. If Rockefeller had not gone ahead, Standard would have had trouble obtaining enough raw materials when the advent of automobiles turned gasoline into a major product. Without Rockefeller's leadership this century's huge economic boom, which with rare exceptions has ended poverty among Americans who work hard and build strong families, would have been delayed.

It was natural that from 1880 on Rockefeller would receive pleas to show leadership on public policy questions, including issues of poverty-fighting and education. His instincts on anything economic were good. In 1887, when he sent a young man $50 he made it a recorded loan, so that Rockefeller would have an IOU: "It will be injurious for him to receive from others what he can in any way secure for himself by his own efforts." He criticized one urban mission for its "policy of feeding all" who came; it would be far better to "give them work and make them earn their food."

Rockefeller's grasp of those fundamentals, however, did not help him to be as successful in his philanthropic work as he had been within the oil industry. With ample tithing money, and wanting to do something major for the Baptist churches that had comforted him for decades, he decided to branch out from his quiet church-giving and make a big splash by funding the creation of a major new Baptist university.

Rockefeller looked for advice about university-building from fellow Baptists who had advanced degrees and distinguished academic reputations, such as William Rainey Harper of the Morgan Park Theological Seminary in Chicago and Augustus H. Strong, president of Rochester Theological Seminary. The first problem he ran into, however, was that there was no single standard for purity within university circles, as there was within Standard Oil's business.

Conservative ministers considered Harper to be a loose constructionist concerning Scripture. Harper did not surprise the conservatives when he proposed that Rockefeller's millions should fund an institution under Baptist auspices but secular in tone. After all, if the Bible could not be trusted, the next best option was to trust the best and brightest brains that money could buy.

Strong, on the other hand, was orthodox in his faith and tough-minded in his analysis of what a Christian university should be. He argued that the university's tone should be explicitly and aggressively Christian, with only Christian professors allowed. The Harper versus Strong debate was theologically nuanced and beyond Rockefeller's grasp, so he turned to a third man, Frederick T. Gates.

LETTING SOMEONE ELSE MAKE THE DECISION

The choice was curious. Gates for years had been attracted by the social and moral teachings of the Gospels, while quietly doubting their central point, the divinity of Christ. After serving as a pastor in Minneapolis he had found his real gift in fundraising for Baptist institutions. He wore costly clothes to give the appearance of success, always expressed radiant geniality, and spoke of the high-minded merits of contributing, never mentioning that a particular gift could serve the public relations interests of the donor. (As Gates wrote, the donor's "own mind will suggest to him the lower and selfish ones. But he will not wish you to suppose that he has thought of them.")

Gates later published his Machiavellian rules for successful solicitation, the tenth of which was, "Let the victim talk freely, especially in the earlier part of the interview, while you use the opportunity to study his peculiarities. Never argue with him. Never contradict him. . . . If he is talkative, let him talk, talk, talk. Give your fish the reel, and listen with deep interest."

Gates, who first met Rockefeller to request funds for one of his projects, had discerned that Rockefeller, despite his expressions of nonchalance, was worried about his public image and his private giving. Gates listened, and realized that tithing decisions had been easier for Rockefeller when they involved dimes and quarters rather than millions of dollars. Gates understood that Rockefeller was being called to be a statesman, but all he really knew was the oil business and the Baptist Church.

Once Gates sensed that Rockefeller was sure of himself in business but unsure concerning philanthropy, he reeled him in, and Rockefeller soon hired Gates to be his primary grant-maker. This meant that Gates could play the decisive role in determining the nature of the university to be created. He proceeded carefully because Rockefeller definitely did not want to finance what was clearly heresy.

Rockefeller even expressed initial interest in Strong's charges that Harper was weak theologically, but showed little patience for what seemed to be theological nuances. Rockefeller liked to hear a rousing sermon that gave him precise marching orders. Furthermore, Strong's suggestions that Rockefeller might be funding a university to improve his public relations infuriated him. Rockefeller did not want to admit his desire for a kinder and gentler press.

Rockefeller's Christianity, as it turned out, did not go very deep. He liked a precise listing of dos and don'ts in church. He believed in and practiced family values. But there is no indication that he ever developed a clear sense that God—and not man's work, however meticulous—saves sinners. Nor is there evidence of Rockefeller developing a Christian worldview, a sense of how the Bible can be applied thoughtfully not only in church and family devotions, but in all aspects of life and within every department of a university.

Without that understanding, and with a need for praise, Rockefeller was easy game for Gates, who put into play one thing he had learned about his prize catch by listening, listening, listening. The secret was this: Rockefeller had moved to New York City but was still suspicious of the East and did not want to be seen as abandoning his midwest roots. Gates, playing off Rockefeller's unease, convinced him that the new university should be in the wholesome Midwest.

That decision, of course, favored Harper, the theologically liberal Chicagoan, over Strong, the theologically conservative New Yorker. Personal issues also played a part—Rockefeller enjoyed meeting with Harper, who chatted about surface issues, and grew tired of Strong, who pushed Rockefeller to think about the deeper questions of theology—but once the decision about location, location, location was made, Gates's route to control was greased.

Gates's prominence meant that theological liberalism would be in the saddle. The executive board of the Education Society, which Gates made the central instrument of Rockefeller's giving, proposed that the new institution be under Baptist auspices but "conducted in the spirit of the widest liberality." Religion would be centered in the Divinity School, and the rest of the university would be thoroughly modern. Rockefeller approved, and did not even visit the campus until it was six years old in 1896. Then he heard the students sing,

> *John D. Rockefeller, wonderful man is he*
> *Gives all his spare change to the U. of C.*

Not everyone thought Rockefeller's educational philanthropy was wonderful. As Gates acknowledged in 1896, Rockefeller "received many letters from every part of the country complaining of the attitude which the University has seemed to take regarding the Bible." But the University of Chicago was not intended to uphold biblical truth, Gates responded, because Rockefeller had "founded in Chicago a secular institution of learning. He had no thought of the University entering the theological arena."

Of course, by not entering that arena, the University of Chicago went with the flow. University professors from 1890 to 1910 endorsed evolution and other anti-biblical themes. Rockefeller complained only when actor Joseph Jefferson was invited to give a speech to the students. Harper sent Rockefeller an apology, noting that he did not think that by the invitation "we would be understood to be endorsing the theatre in general." Harper concluded abjectly, "the whole event must be regarded as a mistake."

Thus soothed, Rockefeller kept giving. From 1890 to 1910 he gave about $35 million to the university; all others combined gave about $7 million. Rockefeller had built a university that would teach anti-biblical ideas, but he could take comfort in not endorsing the theater in general. Rockefeller's final grant of $10 million to the university, in 1910, carried with it only one stipulation: 15 percent of that gift had to be used to build and furnish a university chapel, because "that building which represents religion ought to be the central and dominant feature of the University group."

WHY STATESMEN NEED VISION

For Rockefeller, the chapel—not the workplace or the classroom—was Christianity. Church attendance, tithing, accuracy in accounts, and the avoidance of theater (along with dancing, drinking, smoking, and cardplaying) constituted holy living, with the life of the mind and most other human activities relegated to individual taste. Such thought led to the development of a culture that showed sound morality in many respects, but lacked deep roots and was easily toppled when new social and intellectual forces arose.

What Rockefeller could have used, after his tremendous economic success, was a vision for a Bible-based, free market society. He understood microeconomics and microethics—pricing and marketing decisions within the firm; fair dealing with employees, suppliers, and customers; tithing and not lying. But he did not have a vision for the way an economy could be efficient without thwarting small businessmen, and the way a college could challenge socialist ideologies by emphasizing biblical help for the poor through compassion rather than forced redistribution.

Instead, he listened to Gates and other advisors who proposed that Rockefeller respond to critics not by enunciating a different vision but by making placating contributions. Ironically, such attempts did not bring Rockefeller glowing reviews, and sometimes even prompted the opposite. Rockefeller in 1905, stung by more books attacking him, sent $100,000 for missions to the liberal Congregationalist denomination. He may have expected to hear earth's version of a heavenly chorus. Instead, all hell broke out. Led by Washington Gladden, moderator of the National Council of Congregationalists, thirty ministers proposed that the denomination should turn down Rockefeller's "tainted money" and remain "pure."

As debate spread nationwide Russell Conwell, the minister/public speaker and founder of Temple University in Philadelphia, called Rockefeller "a generous Christian man." Senator Robert La Follette of Wisconsin, however, spit scorn: "I read yesterday that Rockefeller has been to prayer-meeting again. Tomorrow he will be giving to some college or university. He gives with two hands, but he robs with many. If he should live a thousand years he could not expiate the crime he has committed. There is only one way—eternity the time; and as to the place, you can guess that. He is the greatest criminal of the age."

He was not. Rockefeller was a man who gained great wealth by paying attention to small things; a world now sliding on oil owes debts of economic gratitude to him. By making it possible for poor as well as rich people to have light at night in the nineteenth century and mobility in the twentieth, he was one of the great philanthropists of his age. In his philanthropy through contributions, however, Rockefeller did not pay attention to critical matters. Foundations he set up with much of his money, like his university, eventually turned their attention to undermining the market system that he had mastered.

Overall, Rockefeller kept close accounts, wanted to be judged by those accounts, and expected others to do the same and be evaluated the same way. He appeared to like the idea of God also keeping close accounts because he believed he would come out fine on the balance sheet. He was a fair man to deal with, a man of his word, but it was important to check his words very carefully to see what loopholes he left himself. He perceived the Bible as a handbook for moral instruction, but perhaps not as a book that displays man's sinfulness and desperate need for God's grace.

Rockefeller set a high standard of hardheadedness for his business successors to follow, but his vision of pure, coal-hard efficiency also created a risk that they would appear to be hard-hearted. Booker T. Washington successfully moved during the 1890s from his specific calling as a headmaster and social entrepreneur to a wider post as a statesman. Rockefeller also had a nineteenth-century gyroscope that kept him faithful in his marriage and in his work, but he was out of his league when dealing with issues of society and culture that would become central during the twentieth century.

Act Two

(1885–1963)

CHAPTER 8

Grover Cleveland

While national attention lay elsewhere during the 1870s and 1880s, those who sought national office were often seen as cynics out to defeather the American eagle in order to cushion their own nests. Mark Twain fricasseed Washington in his novel *The Gilded Age*, and British observer James Bryce generalized that American politicians simply thought of high office "as a means of gain." Reporters joked about Congressman "Pig-Iron" Kelley of Pennsylvania, who took Henry Clay to the extreme by combining high tariff agitation with sexual prowling: "When he goes into society he backs women into corners and asks them their opinion of the duty on steel rails." Senator Joe

Brown of Georgia was a favorite because of his bald head and flowing beard, which he clutched with both hands when he became excited during debate.

Hypocrisy seemed dominant. The Grant administration was the most corrupt in American history to that point, and no one seemed to care all that much. A wheeler-dealer who emerged during that period, Senator James G. Blaine ("Blaine, Blaine, monumental [or continental] liar from the State of Maine," his enemies chanted), became the Republican candidate for president in 1884. There were small lies as well: Although the Senate restaurant went officially "dry," not selling liquor, a senator who winked at a waiter and asked for "cold tea" would be brought a teacup half filled with whiskey. By the 1880s bathrooms in the Capitol actually had bathtubs, and an average of fifty congressmen each day bathed in nine tubs, some made of marble. Yet many journalists concluded, they could not wash off the dirt that was a feature of political hog-trading run rampant.

What Bryce and other political scientists began to note, even amid the slow pace of Washington life, was that the stakes of national politics were quietly growing. The first ten amendments to the Constitution had been checks on federal power, but six of the next seven (beginning with the slavery-abolishing Thirteenth Amendment, adopted in 1865) contracted the ability of state governments to legislate within their own domains and gave more authority to Washington. The growth of big business was beginning to tilt some liberals to call for a bigger government to counterbalance private strength. Both liberals and conservatives called for honesty in government, but few thought they would obtain it.

And Washington itself was growing: The district's population, which had risen from 3,000 in 1800 to 8,000 in 1810, 40,000 in 1850, and 61,000 in 1860, rose to 109,000 in 1870 and 200,000 at Grover Cleveland's inauguration in 1885. Gothic-style stores and offices replaced Henry Clay's former home off Thirteenth Street. A boardinghouse keeper received $64,000 for a house she had bought twenty years before for $4,000. Sanitation also improved, as open sewers and swamps were covered over and drained. Workmen even put the finishing touches on the long-languishing Washington Monument. Capped off at 555 feet in 1884 and opened to the public in 1888, it was the tallest structure in the world, beating out the spire of the Cologne Cathedral by forty-three feet.

Washington and the entire country, it seemed, could follow the Washington Monument and point heavenwards—or America could wallow in political and social muck. When journalist Frank Carpenter described the Capitol at night, he pointed in both directions. On the one hand, he wrote, "The Capitol at night is a magnificent sight. From its perch on Capitol Hill it is visible for miles, looking like some great illuminated temple or banqueting hall. Its hundreds of windows blaze with light, and a spiral flame of burning gas jets runs about its dome." The view of Washington from the Capitol held romance: "Long lines of light mark its broad avenues. Crescents and rings of gas flames show its numerous circles, and constellations like those overhead tell the location of its squares and parks."

But on the other hand, Carpenter wrote about thinly veiled ads in the *Washington Star* that suggested immorality in the houses just off those broad avenues: "Wanted—By two sisters, two large unfurnished rooms, where no questions will be asked." "Personal—A widow lady desires a gentleman to assist her financially." "Wanted—Room for gentleman in home of a discreet young widow, where he can enjoy all the comforts of a home." Carpenter and others yearned for a throwback president, a second George Washington, who could fight for both private and public virtue.

Ironically, the man who brought a sense of honor back into the national government, Grover Cleveland, knew from his own past about sexual arrangements such as those advertised in the *Star*, and the importance of avoiding them. Cleveland in many ways was not what he appeared to be. When citizens met him—280 pounds with brown hair, blue eyes, and a drooping brown mustache—they saw a slow-moving, bulky body and did not expect aggressiveness on the job. But Cleveland as mayor, governor, and then president typically worked every day except Sunday from 9 a.m. to 1 or 2 a.m. (with time out only for ample meals) and was willing to make tough decisions every hour of the day. As president, he skipped Washington socializing and moth-balled the *Dispatch*, the presidential yacht.

Cleveland had practiced being out of the swing of things while serving his apprenticeships as mayor of Buffalo and governor of New York. In Buffalo, because he stood against raids on the public treasury, he gained the nickname "Veto Mayor." In Washington, opponents called him the "Veto President." Cleveland's political enemies taught their children to sing,

> *A fat man once sat in a President's chair, singing Ve-to, Ve-to, Ve-to.*
> *With never a thought of trouble or care, singing Ve-to, Ve-to....*

But if what Cleveland did during his six busy workdays did not trouble him, it was because on the seventh he worshipped at the First Presbyterian Church.

Such worship was crucial for Cleveland, son of a biblically orthodox minister. Cleveland did not worship the doting grandfather god that was beginning to dominate some aspects of American Christendom. He also did not bow to the subjective self-selected god peeking out from the pages of theological tomes devoted to "higher criticism." He worshipped the God of Scripture, saying, "the Bible is good enough for me, just the old book under which I was brought up. I do not want notes, or criticism, or explanations about authorship or origin."

Cleveland believed in a Lord who proclaimed objective truth and challenged men to do their duty. He emphasized duty frequently in both his public pronouncements and private letters during the 1880s and 1890s: "We have not permitted duty to country to wait upon expediency . . . I am sure I never was more completely in the right path of duty than I am now." After leaving office in 1897, he wrote of his "consciousness of duty well and faithfully performed. Popular applause is, of course, gratifying; but there are times when a man's own satisfaction with his conduct is a better criterion of real merit."

That sensibility dominated Cleveland's public policy work. His friend Richard Gilder explained that "the 'preacher blood' of the President has told in him more and more as his public and private responsibilities have increased." Personal setbacks pushed Cleveland forward to an even greater sense of obligation. In 1893, when he fought off cancer by having his left upper jaw removed, Cleveland wrote to Thomas Bayard, ambassador to England, "I see in a new light the necessity of doing my allotted work in the full apprehension of the coming night."

CHOOSING BETWEEN THE TWO WAYS

That work began when Cleveland was born on March 18, 1837, to a devout mother and a minister father. Cleveland later summarized his childhood years in central New York State, near Syracuse, by writing, "I was reared and taught in the strictest school of Presbyterianism." Family devotions, Sunday school, and three church meetings on Sunday made up part of that strict school.

Young Cleveland studied the Westminster Shorter Catechism and found some of the memorization difficult, but as president he told reporters that he could recite it from beginning to end. He wryly commented, "those are not apt to be the worst citizens who were early taught, 'what is the chief end of man?'" (The catechism answer is, "To glorify God and to enjoy him forever.")

Cleveland credited the "precious precepts and examples of my early days" for "every faculty of usefulness I possess, and every just apprehension of the duties and obligations of life." As a teen he began taking a lively interest in political and ethical questions. With other students at his preparatory school he organized in 1853 a debating society that examined topics such as whether "Roman Catholic institutions are a menace to the interests of the Union." Cleveland, as judge in the debate, decided the question in the negative. Another day Cleveland argued that an attorney should not defend a man whom he knows to be guilty.

Cleveland planned to go to college, but when he was sixteen his father died and he needed to work to obtain money for himself and his family. In 1853 and 1854, Cleveland was an assistant teacher at the Institution for the Blind in New York City. Fanny Crosby, the blind writer of hymns such as "To God Be the Glory," was another assistant. The job was hard but the location good for a young man exploring low-rent taverns (no proof of age necessary in those days) and torn between street life and higher callings.

The tension was such that a sermon he heard from famed preacher Henry Ward Beecher at Beecher's Plymouth Church in Brooklyn stayed with him for over half a century. Beecher, Cleveland remembered much later, compared two men, "one laden like a beast of burden with avaricious plans and sordid expectations, and the other with a light step and cheerful determination, seeking the way of duty and usefulness and striving for the reward of those who love and serve God, and labor for humanity."

It was the old story of immediate gratification versus long-term satisfaction, but Beecher observed the burdens carried by those on the path of the avaricious and sordid, compared to the "light step" of those striving for God's reward. Cleveland, trained for godly usefulness but titillated by the sordid, said, "I have never for a moment lost the impression made upon me by the vivid contrast thrillingly painted in words that burned between the two careers, nor have I ever failed to realize the meaning of the solace in death of the one and the racking disappointments in life and despair in death of the other."

Tired of big-city poverty, Cleveland planned to head west. He stopped off in Buffalo to see an uncle, who persuaded Cleveland to stay and helped him get a job as a law office clerk. Cleveland began studying and in 1858 was admitted to the bar. He gained a reputation for working late over lawbooks and performing reliably in court, but he also became known for going out later to drink and sometimes fornicate. Cleveland did not marry until 1886, when he was forty-nine. During his twenties and thirties it seemed that, in a sense, he was trying to combine the two lives of which Beecher had spoken. That was an experiment that would both propel and come back to haunt his political career.

Friends made in both parts of his life helped Cleveland gain election as sheriff of Erie County in 1870. The good salary the job brought evidently attracted Cleveland to it, but there was a downside: The sheriff also had to serve as hangman. After one drunkard, Patrick Morrissey, was convicted of driving a bread knife into his mother's breast, Cleveland in 1872 had no trouble pressing the lever that sprang the trap and left Morrissey dangling.

A case in 1873, with saloonkeeper Jack Gaffney sentenced to die for killing a friend in a dispute over cards, bothered Cleveland more, since the hanging would leave behind a widow and young children. Some said that Gaffney was insane and should not be hanged, so Cleveland obtained a stay of execution from the governor and impaneled a jury to examine Gaffney's claim. But when the jury decided that Gaffney indeed was sane, Cleveland again did his duty.

Cleveland quietly practiced law during the late 1870s, but his reputation for honest diligence at work pushed him to the fore in 1881 when Buffalo's Democratic Party leaders were looking for a clean successor to a scandal-ridden mayor. Elected to office, Cleveland vetoed a board of aldermen's agreement with a street-cleaning company that included ample payoffs to the aldermen themselves; Cleveland called it "the culmination of a most bare-faced, impudent, and shameless scheme to betray the interests of the people, and to worse than squander the public money."

Cleveland also vetoed city donations to the Firemen's Benevolent Fund and to a veterans organization, then personally made a donation to the latter. Government was to govern and not do charity, he explained. Cleveland's willingness to resist demands for government handouts made his name known throughout New York State. When Democratic leaders in 1882 looked for a gubernatorial candidate to run against Republican corruption, they tapped Cleveland.

Once elected, he vetoed attempts by localities to get the legislature to use state money for local projects. American government, he believed, should remain decentralized. His most famous veto was of a popular five-cent-fare bill that reduced the cost of riding on New York City's new elevated railroads, in part because railroad investors had risked their money in an unproved endeavor and deserved their profits. He also argued that since the state had entered into a contract that allowed the railroad to charge ten cents per ride, it was bound to abide by it: "The State should not only be strictly just, but scrupulously fair." Cleveland sent out his veto message and went to bed thinking his political career was over, but the next day press and public saw him as a profile in courage.

"MA, MA, WHERE'S MY PA?"

Then came 1884, and the decision by Republican Party leaders to nom-
inate Blaine, who was corrupt enough for the *New York Times,* Repub-
lican-leaning in those days, to call him "a prostitutor of public trust, a
scheming jobber, and a reckless falsifier." The evidence for Blaine's
most blatant offense—when Speaker of the House fifteen years before,
he had received payoffs for aiding the Little Rock and Fort Smith
Railroad—included letters he had written to a railroad executive, one
of which had the postscript "Burn this letter." Democrats countered
with a governor admired for honesty, Grover Cleveland.

Cleveland's nomination came on July 11, with crowds chanting that
rhythmic line about a monumental, continental liar. Some pro-Cleve-
land marchers pulled out pieces of paper and set them on fire, yelling,
"Burn this letter." But Democratic leaders felt burned on July 21, when
tales from Cleveland's nightlife of the previous decade displayed the
fallibility of "Grover the Good."

The story was this: Cleveland in 1874 had sexual relations with a
widow, Maria Malpin, who became pregnant. Since she had slept with
others Cleveland's paternity was not certain, but he gave the child his
last name and monetary support. Maria, financially whole but emotionally troubled, became an alcoholic and suffered a mental breakdown. Cleveland arranged for her institutional care and his son's
adoption by a western New York couple.

Today, such efforts would mitigate the scandal and even negate it
for many reporters. Then, Buffalo Baptist minister George Ball, who
had uncovered the story, argued that voters would have to choose
"between the brothel and the family, between indecency and decency,
between lust and law." C. W. Winchester, a Buffalo Methodist minister, preached a sermon about "Absalom the Fast Young Man," with
Absalom just happening to weigh about 280 pounds and possessing a
drooping brown mustache.

Cleveland's defenders acknowledged the fornication but said it was
long past. They noted that Cleveland had never invited a woman "in
any way bad" to the governor's mansion. Republican crowds countered
by chanting, "Ma, Ma, where's my Pa? Gone to the White House, ha,

ha, ha." Minister Henry Ward Beecher bemoaned the frequency of fornication but told one reporter that if every New York voter who had committed adultery would vote Democratic, Cleveland would win the state in a landslide.

The election in many ways came down to lesser-of-evil discussions: Which was worse, fornication or financial corruption? The 1884 campaign was the first since 1828 (when John Quincy Adams was charged with pimping and Andrew Jackson with wife-stealing) in which talk of sex played a large role. Republicans tried to equate Cleveland's earlier history of tavern tippling and fornication with moral looseness among Democrats generally. Republicans in Protestant areas also stressed the tendency of urban Catholics to join with southerners in voting Democratic. Discussions of denominational voting patterns and alcohol-prompted illicit sex came together in a famous Republican banquet attack on "Rum, Romanism, and Rebellion."

Democrats successfully made their own connections. They said that Blaine's bribe-taking was consistent with the Republican emphasis on Henry Clay–like economic intervention through differential tariffs and internal improvements. Blaine wanted more power for Washington. More power inevitably attracts the interest of those who want to use that power for their own advantage. Such forces offer bribes. Cleveland himself called the Republicans merely "a vast army of office-holders" who displayed "impatience of constitutional limitations of Federal power." He said that Republicans wanted "to extend the scope of Federal legislation into the domain of State and local jurisdiction."

The election was a cliff-hanger, but voters narrowly chose Cleveland over Blaine, sexual sin confessed over theft disputed. When Cleveland, known as a Presbyterian, arrived in Washington, residents expected him to attend the famed and fashionable New York Avenue Presbyterian Church that Lincoln had attended. Cleveland chose the First Presbyterian Church and its fiery old Pastor Sunderland, who had been his mother's minister in Batavia, New York, many years before. Sunderland, startled, told a reporter that he had opposed Cleveland's election, "and now this man, whom I said was not fit for the White House, heaps coals of fire on my head by coming through the church door. . . . The President knew well what I had done."

Cleveland was as unpretentious in decorating as in churchgoing. On his way to interviewing Cleveland, journalist Frank Carpenter observed, "The hall and the stairs that brought us to the President's offices are covered with an old piece of carpet which was good once, but which has been patched, sewed, and resewed. It would not bring fifty cents at an auction." At the president's stables south of the White House, Carpenter noted, "Many a man in Ohio has vehicles just as fine as those of President Cleveland, which show no glint of gold or silver trimming. His horses are just good plain roadsters."

STEWARDING RESOURCES

As president, Cleveland tried to steward the nation's resources as he stewarded his own. He sharply criticized the "vicious paternalism" that would arise if citizens developed "the hope and expectations of direct and especial favors." Cleveland saw government's calling as "the enforcement of exact justice and equality" before the law. He fought against undiscerning pension expansion, high tariffs, and other budget items that promoted specific rather than general welfare.

Pensions represented one major threat to the maintenance of small government. Originally, Civil War pensions were granted only to soldiers and sailors (and their widows and children) whose war service left them so disabled that they were unable to work. By 1885, however, fraud was rampant and the pension rolls numbered 325,000. Thousands of able-bodied men received pensions. Thousands more gained support because of problems incurred in civilian life. Thousands received funds by lying or faking. Even deserters had pensions.

Beyond pension board laxity stood the problem of special pension bills: Veterans with claims so lacking in standing that even lax pension authorities refused them appealed to friendly congressmen or senators. They often received special pension approval in logrolling sessions attended by only a few members. In one six-month period the House alone passed over four thousand pension bills. No president from 1865 to 1885 had ever vetoed one.

Cleveland vetoed special pension bills 108 times between March 10 and August 17, 1886. He noted that a whole lot of lying was going on, and the Bible said such fabrications should be fought. He also gave specific reasons for vetoes. One claimant never actually enlisted, but was riding to enlist (he said) when injured. Another claimant had been injured at home by a Fourth of July explosion. A third actually served and contracted diarrhea, which he said led to an eye disease twenty years later. When Cleveland issued vetoes in all such cases Republican newspapers accused him of mean-spiritedness. The *New York Times* said he was "sending the destitute, aged mothers of soldiers to the poorhouse, in order that the Democratic party may gain a reputation for economy."

To show Cleveland's mean-spiritedness, some newspapers gave examples of pension bills he had vetoed. One of the press favorites was the pension of Sallie Ann Bradley, an Ohio woman who said her husband had died as a result of wounds suffered during the war. Furthermore, she claimed, two of her four sons had been slain in battle, and of the two who survived, an exploding shell had ripped off the arm of one, and the other had lost an eye in battle. They could not earn enough to sustain their aged mother. And President Cleveland, the brute, would not allow Mrs. Bradley to have a pension.

As the post-veto furor raged, a Wilmington, Ohio, newspaper investigated the claim. It found that Mr. Bradley had not died from Civil War wounds. He had "choked to death on a piece of beef when gorging himself while on a drunken spree." Two of the sons indeed were dead, but one had died during an epidemic after the war and the other had committed suicide while drunk. None of the arms of the two surviving sons had been torn off by a shell. One son, a shoemaker, had lost an eye, but he had lost it "while working at his trade from a piece of heel nail striking it when repairing a pair of boots." The two surviving sons were able to support their mother, if they wished to do so.

The Clinton County *Democrat* concluded that perhaps Mrs. Bradley should receive financial help, as perhaps tens of thousands of others should, but if so the issue should be debated, not handled in a lying fashion. If one widow is to be pensioned just because of her widowhood, the newspaper concluded, "there should be a bill passed to put them all on the list. But it is not from any love of Sallie Ann Bradley that all this bluster is being made, nor because she is any more worthy of a pension, but because it is hoped that by misstating the facts a little political capital may be made."

Congress was not ready until the next century to pass a widows' pension bill, but in 1887 it did pass a bill ostensibly to end hypocritical claims, not by tightening rules but by opening the doors wider. Veterans who claimed an inability to work for any reason whatsoever, including old age, could receive pensions under the new legislation. Parents and widows of dead veterans could also receive pensions. Given the breadth of involvement in the Civil War, the dawn of what would amount to almost a national welfare system was at hand.

Not quite. Cleveland vetoed the dependent pension bill, arguing that only those with disabilities incurred because of service should receive pensions. Otherwise, he maintained, the pension program would become a welfare system, and the greatly increased army of claimants would be officered by those who "put a premium on dishonesty and mendacity." Cleveland believed that churches and community groups, not government, should take the lead in fighting poverty, and he did not want federal efforts to loom over the local.

Congress sustained Cleveland's veto, and the *Washington Post* applauded his fight against what it considered a reckless piece of legislation. Cleveland also battled to prevent government hiring of inferior candidates for jobs because of their backgrounds. Republican lobbyists were demanding that Union army veterans receive absolute preference, but Cleveland was willing to give preference only when candidates were equally fit, with fitness strictly determined. This was biblical fairness, and Cleveland won that battle too.

Tariff wars animated debate throughout Cleveland's terms as they had during Jackson's. In 1885 the average rate was over 46 percent, virtually unchanged since the Civil War. Tariffs had been raised then to bring more money to the government and to pay off particular political interests. During the 1860s southern opponents of such measures were not around to get in the way of northern industrialist interests. But in 1886, Cleveland argued publicly that tariffs were not a protection for but a tax on American consumers: A tariff was "paid by them as absolutely . . . as if it was paid at fixed periods into the hands of the tax-gatherer." Reduction of tariffs was a poverty-fighting device that would "cheapen the price of the necessaries of life."

Cleveland also was a successor to Jackson in vetoing bills for internal improvements, particularly notorious pork barrel bills involving rivers or harbors. He argued that those who would gain from such improvements should pay for them. Overall, Cleveland vetoed twice as many as did all twenty-one of his predecessors combined. He took some political heat for supposedly obstructing government processes and standing in the way of progress, but he constantly explained that he was fighting attempts by some people to use government power to confiscate the work of others.

MARRIAGE, AND A DIVORCE FROM POLITICS AS USUAL

In 1886 also, Cleveland's life changed as he married Frances Folsom, the graceful and pretty twenty-two-year-old daughter of a law partner who had died eleven years before. Press publicity that year was intense, and not only because Cleveland was the first incumbent president to be married in the White House. Cleveland had become administrator of his late partner's estate, serving essentially as a guardian for Frances, so there were whispers about whether the middle-aged man had acted improperly. Gossips even speculated about the physical safety of slight Frances because of Cleveland's bulk.

Cleveland, however, had known his new bride since she was a baby, seen her when she attended Central High School in Buffalo, and visited her (with chaperones) when she attended Wells College in Buffalo. Press reports certified that all was aboveboard. Marriage itself seemed to tame what was left of Cleveland's savage beast. After a year of domesticity Carpenter wrote, "He has become gentler and more polite. . . . Instead of appearing to be bored with his state dinners, he apparently finds them agreeable. At the last big evening reception, he did not look straight ahead and plunge unseeing through the crowd as before, but stopped now and again to say a gracious word to one or another of his guests."

Marriage also humanized Cleveland in the public's eye. In 1887, when he stood for principle over "expedience and sentiment," he was not tagged as often as cruel and mean-spirited. That year Congress voted to send $10,000 of free seed to drought-stricken farmers in west Texas. Cleveland vetoed the bill, arguing that "the lesson should be constantly enforced that though the people support the Government, Government should not support the people." Cleveland noted that "Federal aid, in such cases, encourages the expectations of paternal care on the part of the Government and weakens the sturdiness of our national character."

Cleveland argued that Washington help to the needy, however benevolently intended, would "destroy the partitions between proper subjects of Federal and local care and regulation." Such aid also reduced among Americans "that kindly sentiment and conduct which strengthens the bond of a common brotherhood." Cleveland challenged volunteers to come forward, and they did. The *Dallas News* and the *Louisville Courier-Journal* were among the newspapers that promoted relief funds. The *Courier-Journal* editorialized that "Kentucky alone will send $10,000 in seed or in money . . . to justify the President's contention that the people will do what is right."

Clara Barton, president of the American Red Cross, also called on private sources to do the job: "The counties which have suffered from drought need help, without doubt, but not help from Congress." Volunteer contributors from across the country responded. West Texas eventually received not $10,000 of federal funding, but over $100,000 in private aid.

Cleveland's emphasis on restraining government spending boosted his popularity during his last two years in office. Marriage covered over the "Ma, Ma, where's my Pa?" cries. Cleveland's advisors argued that he should run a "good feelings" reelection campaign, making prime use of his young wife and not stressing controversial issues such as tariff reduction. Cleveland, however, insisted that his marriage remain largely private and his vigorous positions on the tariff abundantly public. "I do not wish to be reelected without having the people understand just where I stood," he said, "and then spring the question on them after my reelection."

Republicans in 1888 put forward for president a much stronger candidate than they had in 1884, a former Union general unmarred by corruption, Benjamin Harrison. The campaign was intense. Harrison gained support from corporations looking for governmental support and tariff increases. Cleveland demanded that tariffs be cut, and called the law in place a "vicious, inequitable, and illogical source of unnecessary taxation." He showed how tariffs, like other taxes, gave politicians power to issue favors and exact bribes. Republicans responded with scare tactics: Cleveland's proposed reforms would lead to wage reductions, job loss, and even starvation, they proclaimed.

Harrison won a narrow victory. After the election, Cleveland expressed his continued concern: "The fortunes realized by our manufacturers are no longer solely the reward of sturdy industry and enlightened foresight . . . they result from the discriminating favor of the Government." Over the next four years Cleveland maintained his opposition to government moving from promotion of the general welfare to support of specific payoffs, whether to politically preferred companies or poor individuals. He complained whenever he saw the government entering "gratuitously into partnership with these favorites, to their advantage and to the injury of a vast majority of our people."

Cleveland also emphasized personal philanthropy, and contributed to a wide variety of charities, including projects recommended by Booker T. Washington. He proposed that business leaders "do something for humanity and the public good" by being honest on the job and charitable off it.

SECOND EFFORT

In 1892, Cleveland ran against Harrison again. During the campaign, instead of backing off, Cleveland again called for lower tariffs. He pointed out that high tariffs were not yielding dividends for workers. Cleveland's case in point was the just-concluded Homestead strike, in which ten persons died on July 6 as steel workers pushing a strike at a Carnegie plant in Pennsylvania traded shots with 270 well-armed Pinkerton guards.

The guards had been brought in to facilitate the plant's reopening with new workers, but Homestead employees argued that such strikebreaking was a betrayal of Carnegie's pledge to Congress that higher tariffs would lead to higher wages. The McKinley tariff of 1890 had indeed reworked tariff schedules so that as lower manufacturing costs in other parts of the world pushed steel prices downward, the U.S. tariff would constantly increase. The result of government's preferential treatment, Cleveland said, was death at Homestead, the "abiding place of high protection." He argued that increased government involvement in the economy since the Civil War was creating a "widening rift between rich and poor."

Cleveland was reflecting here the biblical emphasis on fairness to the poor as well as rich. Departing from conservatism's frequent defense of corporate prerogatives, he called Carnegie's hard line on wages, after soft treatment by Congress, "the tender mercy the workingman receives from those made selfish and sordid by unjust governmental favoritism." He suggested that Washington governmental halls were not and never would be a friendly place for the poor. Once the door was opened to raids on the U.S. Treasury, Cleveland figured, those with better know-how and lobbying skills would get in first.

Cleveland defeated Harrison in another very close contest, becoming the first president to return to office after a four-year furlough. (His two terms, separated by Harrison's, have bedeviled schoolchildren memorizing presidents' names and orders: Was Cleveland both the twenty-second and the twenty-fourth president?) During his second term, while critiquing corporate attempts to manipulate government and use force to maintain power, Cleveland also refused to let unions rule by economic strangulation. He ordered government troops to maintain law and order during the Pullman strike of 1894, thus angering radicals who refused to let the trains run on time and the mail go through.

Overall, a biblical sense of duty ruled Cleveland, and he expected others to perform their contractual duties as well. During Cleveland's second go-around, however, the Democratic Party began to turn around, in a way subtle at first but speeding up so that in 1896 and thereafter it became a whirlwind.

The change was almost 180 degrees. From Jackson to Cleveland the Democratic Party's paramount principles had been fixed. Democrats insisted on strict construction of the Constitution so that Washington's power was strictly limited. The goal was to protect ordinary citizens—yeomen farmers, urban laborers, small merchants—from discrimination. This discrimination could most readily arise if governmental power grew, and if those best positioned to manipulate it were able to build public-private partnerships.

From Jackson to Cleveland the political agenda for strict constructionists was clear. First, Democrats favored low taxes and tariffs so that government would not have a big pot of money that would inevitably attract flies. Second, Democrats demanded that internal improvements be financed privately or on the local or state level. Third, Democrats wanted business to be largely unimpeded by governmental regulation and also unpropelled by government favoritism. Behind these ideas was a theology: that man is sinful, that power corrupts, that leaders should not be led into temptation, that giving them control over a big pot of money at their right hand was likely to deliver many to evil.

In Cleveland's time, however, the left wing of the Democratic Party pointed to the growth of corporations such as Standard Oil and argued that those big organizations, through fair or foul means, would put smaller organizations out of business unless government stepped in. Such concentration of power in government would not be as dangerous as people of an earlier age had thought because there was enough natural virtue in leaders as well as followers to make concentrations of governmental wealth safe for democracy.

Cleveland's popularity and strength of character helped to hold the line against tendencies toward governmental growth during his first term. While Cleveland and his vetoes were sidelined from 1889 through 1892, however, Congress increased pension payments and other expenditures, passed tariffs so high that imports decreased sharply and government revenues decreased, and reduced the government's gold stock by requiring government purchases of silver. Those economic errors, along with turmoil in international financial markets, scared businessmen. Shortly after Cleveland took office the panic of 1893 ended years of economic growth and led to a political panic that led some to see weird panaceas as common sense.

Cleveland's second term was wrecked by continuing economic depression. Perhaps 20 percent of the industrial labor force was unemployed during the winter of 1893–94. Problems did not melt away with the coming of spring. Farmers also suffered greatly, as commodity prices decreased and foreclosures soared. Politicians made appeals to inflate the currency by having the federal government abandon the gold standard, adopt an inflationary "bimetal" silver and gold standard, and then decree that silver was worth almost twice as much as it had been. This would make farm debts, payable in gold, decrease in real value.

Cleveland, as always, was for long-term satisfaction, not immediate economic gratification. Furthermore, he did not want government fiat to create either winners or losers. He argued that abandonment of the gold standard would impair confidence in the currency and further disrupt business. Above all, for Cleveland a contract was a contract: Those who borrowed money were morally bound to pay it back in real value, and those who saved it should reap benefits. In 1894 he vetoed a bill that would have expanded silver coinage and led to "the cheapening of the dollar."

The battle intensified in 1895 as Cleveland attacked critics of the gold standard, insisting that inflation would injure "the poor, as they reckon the loss in their scanty support, and the laborer or workingman, as he sees the money he has received for his toil shrink and shrivel in his hand when he tenders it for the necessities to supply the humble home." Pro-inflation leaders shot back with personal attacks. In January 1896, Senator Ben "Pitchfork" Tillman of South Carolina called Cleveland a "besotted tyrant" who was "self-idolatrous . . . an arrogant and obstinate ruler." Tillman promised to stick his pitchfork into Cleveland's "fat ribs."

The hits kept coming. Governor John Altgeld of Illinois, a radical Democrat, attacked Cleveland at a Jefferson Day banquet, explaining that "To laud Clevelandism on Jefferson's birthday is to sing a Te Deum in honor of Judas Iscariot on a Christmas morning." Support for Cleveland within the Democratic Party plummeted, as proponents of quick fixes gained popularity amid depression. The Democrats endorsed a silver standard and looked to inflate the size of the federal government. They nominated as Cleveland's successor the silver-tongued silver advocate William Jennings Bryan, a man who also applied Scripture to politics, but in a very different manner than did Cleveland: Bryan spoke of God's love but never emphasized man's sinfulness and the need, therefore, to limit the power of sinners in government.

The two Democrats also differed stylistically. Cleveland spoke plainly and calmly; Bryan was an orating tornado. After service in Congress, Bryan spent the mid-1890s lecturing throughout the South and West on a simple cure for rural debt: Abandon the gold standard, promote inflation. As he moved away from the biblical equation of justice as fulfillment of contracts by both rich and poor, Bryan adopted the rhetoric of class conflict: "the idle holders of idle capital" versus "the struggling masses."

By the time 20,000 people gathered in Chicago for the 1896 Democratic convention—they would have to be reached without a microphone—Bryan was ready. His penetrating voice reached throughout the hall. The excitement was greatest when Bryan, calling "the moneyed interests" latter-day Pontius Pilates, concluded with strong Christian symbolism: "You shall not press down upon the brow of labor this crown of thorns. You shall not crucify mankind upon a cross of gold."

Awed journalists searched their minds for glowing descriptive expressions. Mark Sullivan described how Bryan's speech "brought tears to the eyes of men and caused women in the gallery to become hysterical." Charles Warren described what happened after the speech: "There was a pause. Then occurred a wild and hysterical uprising; waves of deafening cheers and yells swept from end to end of the building and back again, unceasing in their tumult." Harry Peck also wrote of "tumult like that of a great sea thundering against the dikes. Twenty thousand men and women went mad with the irresistible enthusiasm." One senator simply said, "Glorious."

Bryan, whom Cleveland termed a "demagogue and insolent crusader," received the nomination. Cleveland in his speeches had criticized those from all walks of life who used government to gain special advantages, but for Bryan the chief distinction was not one of character but one of class. He asserted that "the producing masses of this nation and the world" were in his corner, opposed by those who for their selfish interests demanded a gold standard. Bryan lost the election but won the hearts of Democrats, while Cleveland retired to Princeton, New Jersey.

Cleveland opposed Bryan's campaigns both in 1896 and 1900, contending that "the safety of the country is in the rehabilitation of the old Democratic party. It would be a difficult task to do this, at the end of four years of a Bryan administration and its absurdities, for which the Democratic party would be held responsible. . . . I am afraid that the Republicans cannot be dislodged until Bryanism and all in its train is abandoned if not expressly repudiated." Cleveland thought he saw Bryanism repudiated in 1904 when the Democrats turned to a conservative candidate, but that turned out to be a short-lived trend. First Theodore Roosevelt, then Woodrow Wilson spent the next twenty years fighting or embracing aspects of a Democratic Party that was no longer Jackson's or Cleveland's.

Grover Cleveland died in 1908. His last words were, "I have tried so hard to do right." He had. A prodigal son who fathered a child out of wedlock, he tried to do right in making sure that his son grew up in a strong adoptive family. A rocklike constitutionalist, he fought those who planned to stretch the Constitution's meaning by transferring tax money to influential individuals and groups. Cleveland provided integrity at a time it was desperately needed, but had trouble holding the allegiance of those who wanted not good government but a government that would feel their pain. He had many of the qualities of a George Washington but not the stature gained by successful military leadership. Cleveland thus could start the second age of the presidency down the right road, but his route could readily be abandoned by those who would follow.

CHAPTER 9

Theodore Roosevelt

The campaigning of William Jennings Bryan sent Cleveland into political exile and propelled Theodore Roosevelt into national prominence. Republican candidate William McKinley exuded dignity as he sat on his front porch and received delegations of visiting citizens, but Bryan during a four-month campaign in 1896 visited some 250 cities and gave speeches whenever his train stopped. Republicans needed energetic orators to hit the hustings, and Theodore Roosevelt was McKinley's most energetic surrogate both in 1896 and as vice presidential candidate in 1900.

Roosevelt, born in 1858 to a mother who had been a Georgia plantation belle, was particularly close to his father, who came from a New

York Dutch Reformed (Calvinistic) background and was a partner in an importing firm. Theodore Roosevelt, Sr. was also a teacher and mentor of poor children at mission Sunday schools, a distributor of evangelical tracts, and a founder of the New York Children's Aid Society, which under the leadership of Charles Brace sent orphaned and abandoned children to adoptive homes on upstate and midwestern farms.

Theodore Roosevelt, Jr. began to memorize psalms and hymns at the age of three, and later in his childhood spent an hour every Sunday evening with his father, discussing the sermon they had heard earlier that day. "Teedie," as he was called, was required to listen diligently to the sermon and study its biblical citations so that he could outline the major points of the minister's argument later on and evaluate its validity. (Those who knew Roosevelt as an adult said he had an extraordinary biblical knowledge and could "repeat at will long portions of Scripture.")

Roosevelt as an adult was always proud of his father, "the best man I ever knew." He spoke of how Theodore, Sr. regularly volunteered for person-to-person charitable work, devoting himself to "getting the children off the streets and out on farms." Like his father, Roosevelt for seven years taught a Sunday school class for poor children. The paternal relationship was particularly strong because of doctor's orders: Teedie, with asthma so severe that it seemed he would become a lifelong invalid, was homeschooled all the way to college. Some elite schools during the 1870s were already starting to relativize ethics, but physical necessity gave Theodore, Sr. the opportunity to instill in his son a strong sense of objective right and wrong.

Teedie Roosevelt built himself up physically through calisthenics and boxing. He entered Harvard in 1876 and did well in his studies, but during his sophomore year came "sharp, bitter agony," as Theodore, Sr. developed a malignant tumor and died, at age forty-six. Theodore, Jr. wrote immediately after the burial, "if it were not for the certainty, that as he himself has so often said, 'he is not dead but gone before,' I should almost perish." In his diary shortly afterwards Theodore Roosevelt asked God's help in fulfilling a pledge to his father to abstain from sexual intercourse until marriage.

The vow was very important to Roosevelt on three levels: obeying God, honoring his father, and developing self-control. The next diary page after the pledge features a large blot of ink, but Roosevelt later wrote that he remained "perfectly pure" during his college years. He did get drunk when he was initiated into the Porcellian, a prestigious club. He found the action so embarrassing and the hangover so bad that he resolved never to overindulge again.

Roosevelt's one constant yearning, from soon after he first saw her in 1878, was to marry Alice Hathaway Lee, then a perky seventeen-year-old with honey-colored hair, pink cheeks, and a golden smile. Roosevelt wrote of their first meeting, "As long as I live, I shall never forget how sweetly she looked, and how prettily she greeted me." At twenty TR was a thorough romantic.

The next two years for Roosevelt were a rush of wooing, winning, and producing an honorable record that would make him worthy of such a bride. Roosevelt woke up early, studied hard before breakfast, and worked hard in the morning so that in the afternoon he could head to Alice's house a few miles away. He took long walks with her, played whist with her, and told her ghost stories. Sometimes he despaired and wrote in his diary, "I did not think I could win her, and I went nearly crazy at the mere thought of losing her." She turned down his marriage proposal and he, unable to sleep, wandered night after night through the wintry woods near Harvard.

In January 1880, however, Roosevelt was able to write in his diary, "after much pleading my own sweet, pretty darling consented to be my wife. . . . Oh, how I shall cherish my sweet queen! How she, so pure and sweet and beautiful can think of marrying me I can not understand, but I praise and thank God it is so." They were married on Theodore's twenty-second birthday. She was nineteen. He was on top of his world following graduation, and even the boredom of a short stint in law school could not subdue the pleasure of marriage to Alice.

But there was more. Roosevelt decided to do what gentlemen in Jefferson's day had felt obliged to do, but a century later rarely contemplated: At age twenty-three he ran for election to the New York State Assembly and won. In Albany, Roosevelt's constant motion and high-pitched reformist rhetoric made such an impression that at age twenty-four he became minority leader. To the amusement of some and the satisfaction of others, he brought to bear the Bible on all kinds of issues that had previously been seen as readily compromisable. "Mr. Roosevelt keeps a pulpit concealed on his person," critics proclaimed—and he had great fun.

Satisfied in marriage, able to concentrate his energies on work, Roosevelt seemed to do everything—walk, talk, think—at a pace much faster than others. Reporters called him "the Cyclone Assemblyman." They enjoyed writing about his huge energy that was apparent even on off days, which could be used for climbing a mountain or playing ninety-one games of tennis.

Speed and newfound stamina set Roosevelt apart, but so did a willingness to talk about right and wrong even when he realized he was in the wrong. His faith was most evident after Grover Cleveland's veto of legislation Roosevelt had supported, the "five-cent bill," which lowered the price of railroad rides at the cost of violating pledges made to railroad investors. Roosevelt announced, "I have to say with shame that when I voted for this bill I did not act as I think I ought to have acted.... We have heard a great deal about the people demanding the passage of this bill ... but we should never yield to what they demand if it is wrong." For Roosevelt, as for Cleveland, a deal was a deal; to negotiate for a square deal was fine, but to demand a new one was wrong.

HEALING WOUNDS BEYOND HEALING

Early in 1884, Roosevelt at age twenty-five was on fire, working a dozen hours a day on legislative business, enjoying "my own sweetest little wife," and looking forward to the birth of their first child. Suddenly, on Valentine's Day, everything changed. Alice died immediately after giving birth; Bright's disease was the official cause. On the same day Roosevelt's mother died of acute typhoid fever. His faith that he was getting a square deal out of life faltered. When Alice "had just become a mother," Roosevelt wrote, "when her life seemed to be but just begun, and when the years seemed so bright before her—then, by a strange and terrible fate, death came to her. And when my heart's dearest died, the light went from my life forever."

Roosevelt told a friend that his pain was "beyond all healing," and that "time will never change me in that respect." Yet, there was healing. Roosevelt was left with an infant daughter, but he felt incapable of taking care of her—his sister Anna took the baby in temporarily—and of carrying on any normal life in New York. His money would have allowed him to ride on a disordered, urban playboy carousel, but instead he rode into the wilderness, often spending fourteen hours a day in the saddle on a Dakota Territory cattle ranch in which he had invested. Roosevelt learned to drown his sorrow in forthright action, observing after a buffalo hunt that "Black care rarely sits behind a rider whose pace is fast enough." He stopped second-guessing himself or God.

When Roosevelt, turned twenty-seven in years and older than that in self-awareness, came back late in 1885 from one of his Badlands trips, he encountered twenty-four-year-old Edith Carow. Edith was a childhood playmate and a teenage friend who had long felt that she and Theodore were made for each other. He had always liked her character and her wisdom, but had dropped her as soon as Alice took his breath away. Edith was not unattractive, but her steely blue eyes and firm jaw (mitigated by a sweet smile) promised a different type of relationship than he had had with the charming and sometimes childlike Alice.

Roosevelt, pondering his future, realized that his faith in God and God's precepts remained, but that he himself had changed in many regards from romantic to realist. He and Edith were married in 1886, and Alice came with them to a new home, Sagamore Hill, at Oyster Bay on the Long Island Sound. Five more children came: Theodore, Jr., Kermit, Ethel, Archibald, and Quentin. Roosevelt called them his "blessed bunnies" and romped with them inside and out. He taught his children what he tried to teach the country: "Nothing is worth having or doing unless it means effort, pain, difficulty." But he was joyful in the chase, and had a way of turning seriousness into sport.

Seeing Poverty and War Close-up

His new family convinced Roosevelt to settle down in the familial East rather than the Wild West. With home life once again in order, he moved to the task of ordering city, state, and nation. Roosevelt's first return to politics was a near miss: He ran unsuccessfully for mayor of New York, but impressed editors such as Joseph Bishop of the *New York Evening Post* with his "inflexible honesty, absolute fearlessness, and devotion to good government which amounts to religion."

From 1889 to 1897, Roosevelt practiced his newly hardened religion first as a member of the Civil Service Commission in Washington, then as police commissioner in New York. He pleased his children by taking them to police headquarters, although they were disappointed to learn that their father did not wear a high helmet and a blue uniform with silver buttons. Much of Roosevelt's education came by night, though: He often walked the streets with journalist friends Jacob Riis and Lincoln Steffens to learn about poverty and crime close-up. He came away from that observation more convinced than ever that success for both rich and poor involved putting off unethical immediate pleasures to follow God's rules, which would lead to long-term enjoyment.

Like Andrew Jackson early in the century, Roosevelt ran into a battle about Sunday closings. German brewers organized a parade to protest Roosevelt's orders that the police enforce the law, and sarcastically invited the commissioner to sit on the reviewing stand. Roosevelt surprised the marchers by showing up and then giving his broad smile as the first banner came into view, with its large letters proclaiming DOWN WITH TEDDY! "*Wo ist* Teddy?" shouted the banner carriers, and he responded in German, "*Hier bin ich*," "Here I am." Roosevelt leaned over the railing, beaming, and the marchers cheered his courage.

Roosevelt's combination of biblical understanding, experiential grounding, and guts helped him to be an extraordinarily effective pro-McKinley speaker in the 1896 campaign. He criticized "socialists who are always howling about the selfishness of the rich." He emphasized that a poor person's enemy is the "leader, whether philanthropist or politician, who tries to teach him that he is a victim of conspiracy and injustice, when in reality he is merely working out his fate with blood and sweat as the immense majority of men who are worthy of the name always have done and always will have to do."

Called to Washington in 1897 to become assistant secretary of the navy, Roosevelt learned how to move fast and minimize bureaucracy. While purchasing merchant ships on the eve of the Spanish-American War that could rapidly be converted into cruisers, Roosevelt paid $500,000 for a Brazilian ship but made it a condition that the vessel arrive under its own steam at a specific point by a specific date. As ship dealer Charles Flint admiringly wrote, "In one sentence he thus covered all that might have been set forth in pages and pages of specifications, for the vessel had to be in first-class condition to make the time scheduled in the contract! Mr. Roosevelt always had that faculty of looking through details to the result to be obtained."

Roosevelt talked over his work with his wife, Edith, and valued her advice: "Whenever I go against her judgment, I regret it." When the Spanish-American War began in 1898, however, he turned down her request that he stay in Washington. Since Roosevelt had agitated for war he said he could not stand being called an "armchair and parlor" warrior who would send others to fight in his stead. He enlisted, saying, "my power for good, whatever it may be, would be gone if I didn't try to live up to the doctrines I have tried to preach."

Few Washington officials a century ago approved of his logic, and few would now. "I really think he is going mad," one bureaucrat said, and another merely asked, "Is he quite mad?" Secretary of the Navy John D. Long noted in his diary, "He thinks he is following his highest ideal, whereas, in fact, as without exception every one of his friends advises him, he is acting like a fool." Long concluded, "He has lost his head," but noted concerning his criticism, "how absurd all this will sound if, by some turn of fortune, he should accomplish some great thing and strike a very high mark."

ONE SHINING MOMENT, AND THEN MORE

Roosevelt aimed high and struck high. He led soldiers (many of whom he had convinced to enlist) up Kettle Hill east of Santiago, Cuba, on July 1. Mauser bullets killed men all around him, but he shamed the terrified into following by rasping at them, "Are you afraid to stand up when I am on horseback?" Kings in the Old Testament were to lead their armies themselves, and Roosevelt sent no surrogates. A bullet grazed his elbow, but he killed a Spaniard and listened to Mauser shots that sounded "like the ripping of a silk dress."

Then it was on to San Juan Hill about seven hundred yards away. Roosevelt started briskly but forgot to order his soldiers to follow him, so only five did. Two were shot while Roosevelt rushed back to his regiments and yelled, "Are you cowards?" Then he gave the order, riding his horse ahead of the troops under heavy fire up the hill, until the Spaniards at the top gave up or ran. "I would rather have led that charge than serve three terms in the United States Senate," Roosevelt wrote.

The nation's newspapers gave the exploits of Roosevelt and his "Rough Riders" front-page placement. The *New York Sun* reported, "Bullets were raining down on them, and shot and shell from the batteries. . . . Up they went in the face of death, men dropping from the ranks at every step. Roosevelt was a hundred feet in the lead . . . shouting for the men to follow him. . . . Finally his horse was shot from under him. He charged up the hill afoot. At last the top of the hill was reached . . . the position won."

Roosevelt's political elevation was instant. He returned home to New York just in time to be nominated for the governorship in 1898 by a corrupt Republican Party that needed him to avoid being swept out of office by the backlash from a canal contract scandal. Roosevelt was dynamic on the stump, but he also benefited from the introduction one of his sergeants, Buck Taylor, provided: "Ah want to talk to you about muh colonel. He kept ev'y promise he made to us and he will to you. When he took us to Cuba he told us . . . we might meet wounds and death and we done it, but he was thar in the midst of us. When it came to the great day he led us up San Juan Hill like sheep to the slaughter and so he will lead you."

After Roosevelt was elected and Republican control was saved, however, he had to fight state party leader Thomas Platt concerning legislation. Platt was known as "the Easy Boss," but he was a hard-nosed critic of William Jennings Bryan. So was Governor Roosevelt; only their methods of opposition differed. Roosevelt favored steps that would slow down the "rush toward industrial monopoly" by keeping big corporations from using their size, Rockefeller-style, to beat out their less efficient, smaller competitors. Not having seen how regulation can so easily harass businessmen, he had a much more optimistic view of its possibilities than most people of a philosophy similar to his have today. Roosevelt argued that government should not stop competition, but should "make the chances of competition more even."

Bunk, Platt said: Get the government involved, and bureaucracy will make the countryside unsafe for enterprise. Platt succeeded in getting Roosevelt out of the way by having him selected as President William McKinley's running mate in 1900. Roosevelt had no yearning for the understudy office, believing that four years in a do-nothing position would hurt his chances for the presidential nomination in 1904. McKinley advisor Mark Hanna opposed the choice for the opposite reason: "Don't any of you realize that there's only one life between this madman and the Presidency?"

Others were also worried by someone who tried to apply the Bible. In 1899, Governor Roosevelt stunned humanitarians and some politicians by allowing a woman to be sent to the electric chair for the first time in New York history. He said the woman had been justly convicted of murder, and the Bible did not say that only men should not kill. But popular pressures overrode all hesitations, and the forty-two-year-old Roosevelt as the new century began saw himself potentially elevated to high national office, and sidelined.

Roosevelt spoke on both domestic and foreign policy during the campaign of 1900. As Bryan emphasized class differences and called for federal action to redress economic grievances, he also began moving the Democratic Party from its traditional states' rights emphasis to a power-centralizing approach. Roosevelt argued that government could play an anti-trust role but should avoid the type of extensive government regulation that Bryan demanded. He said, "If Bryan wins, we have before us some years of social misery not markedly different from that of any South American republic." Since competition made for economic progress, a wise government might act to increase competition but should never do the opposite.

Roosevelt also opposed Bryan's criticism of military spending and said that his foreign policy closely resembled Thomas Jefferson's, "whose accession to the Presidency was a terrible blow to this nation." During the campaign Roosevelt did not hide the criticism of the renowned Jefferson that he had bravely presented at the Naval War

College in 1897: Jefferson's attempt to avoid war by not building big fighting ships had actually precipitated the War of 1812 by making America virtually defenseless in the shipping lanes.

Uniting Christian and Republican Influence

Mostly, however, Roosevelt in 1900 campaigned on the Bible. He gave speeches and published articles with explicit titles such as "The Eighth and Ninth Commandments in Politics." He described how any kind of economic preferment because of political ties "comes dangerously near the border-line of the commandment which, in forbidding theft, certainly by implication forbids the connivance at theft, or the failure to punish it."

Roosevelt's mind worked concretely. He gave neither the politician nor the journalist leave to dance around honesty: "Under the higher law, under the great law of morality and righteousness, he is precisely as guilty if, instead of lying in a court, he lies in a newspaper or on the stump." Cynical observers like British writer John Morley found distasteful Roosevelt's combination of whirligig speaking style and scriptural quotations; he called Roosevelt a combination of "St. Paul and St. Vitus." But Roosevelt's biblicism not only neutralized much of Bryan's economic rhetoric, but also displayed a social vision that undercut Bryan's moral appeal.

Boss Platt had figured out how to get Roosevelt out of the way in New York, but he had not figured on an assassination. Six months after Roosevelt became vice president, President McKinley was shot while working a reception line in Buffalo. Roosevelt and his family were vacationing in the Adirondack Mountains when news that McKinley was dying arrived. Roosevelt rode a swaying wagon down a narrow mountain trail, boarded a train waiting at the county station, and took the oath of office on September 14, 1901, in one room of a house, with McKinley's body in another room. Roosevelt at age forty-two was the youngest man ever to become president.

Roosevelt became known as a trust-buster during his first term because he favored action against very large corporations that worked to reduce competition. What he became most passionate about, however, were not big economic issues but social issues involving questions of family and sexual morality.

The primary job of government, he said, was not to bring "economic justice" but to provide for the common defense against attacks on decency such as "rape, or the circulation of indecent literature . . . or gross cruelty to women and children, or seduction and abandonment, or the action of some man in getting a girl whom he had seduced to commit abortion." None of these crimes was beyond that into which ordinary people could fall, if they did not fight against "the wild-beast qualities of the human heart." But there was a way out: "Fear the Lord and walk in his ways."

Midway through his presidency Roosevelt specified two cases where he had been asked about pardons and had lost his temper: "One where some young roughs had committed rape on a helpless immigrant girl, and another in which a physician of wealth and high standing had seduced a girl and then induced her to commit abortion." In those situations he not only turned down the requests for pardon, but also "wrote to the individuals who had asked for the pardon, saying that I extremely regretted that it was not in my power to increase the sentence. I then let the facts be made public, for I thought that my petitioners deserved public censure."

Throughout his presidency Roosevelt strongly emphasized male responsibility. He saw as symbols of irresponsibility the burlesque theaters and gambling rooms that stood a few blocks from the White House. He was not amused that congressmen and others patronized the nearby Lyceum Theatre, where "nightly can be seen peroxide blonde burlesque troops in astonishing displays of female nether extremities." Nor was it good news that the adjacent red-light district featured streets that at night were, according to one guidebook, "conveniently dark—possibly to enable 'statesmen' to prowl about without too much publicity."

Roosevelt himself did no prowling, even though it was the custom for many affluent men to have a mistress. He was authentically a family man in his forties with a loving wife and fun-loving children. (John Kennedy, the youngest president next to Roosevelt, would try to bring off that appearance.) During Roosevelt's second term, his youngest son, nine-year-old Quentin, formed with other children a "White House Gang." Roosevelt led them on a "pirate expedition" down the Potomac, encouraged their play in the White House attic, and otherwise gave them the run of the White House.

Roosevelt drew the line, however, when Quentin thought his privileges gave him free rein everywhere. Once, when the children left muddy footprints in the corridors of what is now the Old Executive Office Building next to the White House, and were brusquely told to leave, they retaliated by standing on the White House lawn and using hand mirrors to flash blasts of reflected sunlight into the office windows of their insulters. Soon, a military aide strode across the lawn to them and told them to pay attention to some semaphore signals that would soon begin from the roof of the office building. He translated for them as the soldier on the roof signaled with flags: "YOU UNDER THE TREES. ATTACK ON THIS BUILDING MUST CEASE IMMEDIATELY. CLERKS CANNOT WORK. GOVERNMENT BUSINESS INTERRUPTED. REPORT WITHOUT DELAY FOR YOU KNOW WHAT. THEODORE ROOSEVELT." Quentin received a severe talking-to and never acted up in that way again.

Many adults, however, shirked their responsibilities and acted up in adulterous ways. Roosevelt always tried to keep those realities in mind. When asked about government aid to widowed or deserted mothers with children, he emphasized that "care must not be given in such way as to encourage the man to shirk his duty. His prime duty is to provide for his wife and his children; if he fails to do so, the law should instantly seize him and force him to do so." Roosevelt thought that those who impregnated and ran should be treated severely, because American society would fall if such activity ever became general: "The man has not merely grievously sinned against another human being, but has grievously sinned against society. . . ."

Troubled by a rising divorce rate, Roosevelt argued that "Not only easy divorce, but the shameful shirking of duty by men and women which leads to such divorce and to all kinds of domestic unhappiness . . . should be unsparingly condemned." Speaking against the proto-feminism of the Progressive Era, he said that "any attempt to bring about the kind of 'economic independence' which means a false identity of [male and female] economic function spells mere ruin."

Helping the Poor

One guidebook from the beginning of this century described Washington as "this gay, high-colored, aristocratic city, possessing many of the attributes of her monarchical sisters of the Old World, rivaling the Rome of the Caesars in her magnificent entertainments." President Roosevelt, however, saw himself as a defender of an old Jerusalem threatened by chaos, rather than the creator of a new Rome.

He especially did not want the government to become the furnisher of bread and circuses. Roosevelt's prime political concern became the defeat of not only William Jennings Bryan but a growing socialist movement as well. The U.S. Socialist Party would stumble during World War I and shoot itself in its left foot as internal struggles grew with the emergence of Soviet communism. Before the war, though, it was making deep inroads in many cities, and Roosevelt went after it. "Socialists and others really do not correct the evils at all, or else only do so at the expense of producing others in aggravated form," he said. Roosevelt saw socialism as the political manifestation of covetousness. Like all sins in this life it could not be stopped, merely contained.

What containment meant in practice was that Roosevelt was willing to accept very limited governmental action in specific circumstances—where it would increase rather than decrease competition. When those who dreamed of a welfare state asked him for support, however, Roosevelt chastised them for "mere sentimentality." He noted, "None of us should be hard-hearted, but it is no less desirable that we should not be soft-headed." His progressivism was based on the understanding, gained by Jacob in the Book of Genesis, that it would be necessary to wrestle all night to receive a blessing.

Roosevelt noted in 1907, in a speech against "deadening socialism," that "the only permanently beneficial way in which to help any one is to help him help himself; if either private charity, or governmental action, or any form of social expression destroys the individual's power of self-help, the gravest possible wrong is really done to the individual." Sin could overturn good intentions. The practice of philanthropy, Roosevelt insisted, required "incessant supervision lest it lose all vitality and become empty and stereotyped so as finally to amount to little except a method of giving salaries to those administering the charity."

Roosevelt argued that socialism could be fought most successfully by applying biblical ideas about helping the poor. The greatest hope lay through "voluntary action by individuals in the form of associations," particularly when the goal was "that most important of all forms of betterment, moral betterment—the moral betterment which usually brings material betterment in its train." Church- and community-based charity of the right kind was essential. Those who truly wanted to help had to stand "against mere sentimentality, against the philanthropy and charity which are not merely insufficient but harmful."

In response to those who thought that would-be helpers, even when naive, should be cheered, Roosevelt argued, "I really do not know which quality is most productive of evil to mankind in the long run, hardness of heart or softness of head." He took such a message directly to the helpers, telling an audience at the New York City YMCA that the Bible tells each of us "to stretch out his hand to a brother who stumbles. But while every man needs at times to be lifted up when he stumbles, no man can afford to let himself be carried, and it is worth no man's while to try thus to carry someone else." Governmental aid, he stated, should be limited and "extended very cautiously, and so far as possible only where it will not crush out healthy individual initiative."

Mere economic redistribution would not help. It might be politically popular, but the leader who appealed to covetousness "is not, and never can be, aught but an enemy of the very people he professes to befriend.... To break the Tenth Commandment is no more moral now than it has been for the past thirty centuries." Some were sarcastic. Speaker of the House Thomas B. Reed congratulated Roosevelt on his "original discovery of the Ten Commandments." But Roosevelt pointed out that politicians who preached covetousness might lead a poor person "to hope for redress elsewhere than in his own industry, honesty, and intelligence." Ideas had consequences.

Roosevelt's way of analyzing poverty issues carried over into other areas as well. He always insisted on clear and concrete applications of biblical commandments. He typically noted, "The Eighth Commandment reads: 'Thou shall not steal.' It does not read: 'Thou shall not steal from the rich man.' It does not read: 'Thou shall not steal from the poor man.' It reads simply and plainly: 'Thou shall not steal.'"

POST-PRESIDENCY DRIFT

When Roosevelt retired in 1909, he thought it was for good. He wrote about the importance of personal morality among statesmen: "A nation must be judged in part by the character of its public men...." He became president of the American Historical Association and emphasized the responsibility of men of letters not to cut themselves off from life around them and biblical morality. (Roosevelt as president had shown how to stage an historical commemoration. He knew that in 1807, Jefferson, having deliberately kept his navy weak, had put forward the disastrous Embargo Act. In 1907, Roosevelt had a large navy to show off, so he sent sixteen battleships on a fourteen-month round-the-world trip described as a goodwill tour, which it was: Countries saw that if they did not bear goodwill toward the United States, they might suffer.)

Roosevelt kept speaking out and coming back to some basic biblical themes concerning the relation of private and public ethics. In five lectures that he gave at Pacific Theological Seminary in 1911, he emphasized "the harm done by the practice among so many men of keeping their consciences in separate compartments; sometimes a Sunday conscience and a week-day conscience...." In "The Public Servant and the Eighth Commandment," he continued to emphasize that there was no preferential option for the poor, and that it was wrong for the politician to "do something that is just a little bit crooked" to benefit either corporate or labor union interests.

Roosevelt also wrote essays on subjects such as "deliberate sterility in marriage," in which he criticized those who were deliberately childless. Such a decision, he wrote, was due to "coldness, to selfishness, to love of ease, to shrinking from risk, to an utter and pitiful failure in sense of perspective and in power of weighing what really makes the highest joy and to a rooting out of a sense of duty, in a twisting of that sense into improper channels."

When individuals did their duty, a nation could be saved. Duty involved taking biblical risks, which included having children. Did it also include returning to politics? In 1912, Roosevelt's handpicked successor, William Howard Taft, disappointed him. Roosevelt also disliked Woodrow Wilson, calling him a "Byzantine logothete" (by which he meant that Wilson's speeches had little substance). If Roosevelt could wait until 1916, the Republican nomination and probably more time in the White House were well within reach. But a fight with Taft seemed likely to split the Republicans and elect Wilson.

Roosevelt's reasons for not waiting seem to have been personal rather than political. Early on he had been a man in a hurry, from the time he had become minority leader in the New York legislature while barely out of college. Alice's death, and his subsequent remarriage and family growth, had given Roosevelt a longer-run perspective. But as he felt old age approaching he lay aside his telescope and lost the ability—which given his fast-pulsed nature was always hard for him—to "wait on the Lord." His closing campaign was the statesman's equivalent of what Dylan Thomas would write:

> *Do not go gentle into that good night.*
> *Rage, rage against the dying of the light.*

Once Roosevelt put himself into a rage, he could then readily convince himself that holding off in this situation was immoral. He ran a third-party campaign so frantic that he sometimes fell into the promise-making that he had avoided in previous contests. With William Howard Taft not a lame duck officially but a dead duck politically, Roosevelt worried more about his competition to the left—a Democratic Party with a Wilson face but a William Jennings Bryan heart, and the surging Socialist Party candidacy of Eugene Debs. Under such pressure Roosevelt sometimes pandered, rhetorically accepted a far greater degree of government economic intervention than he had allowed during his administration.

The campaign itself was spectacular. In other presidential elections of the twentieth century—1948, 1968, 1980, and 1992 being particularly memorable—a third candidate in the race has received at least 5 percent of the popular vote. In the 1912 election, both third- and fourth-party candidates (Roosevelt and Debs) did so, with Roosevelt finishing far ahead of Taft. Neither Taft nor Debs talked about the Bible that much during the campaign, but each of the top two finishers, Wilson and Roosevelt, repeatedly did. Wilson won with 42 percent of the popular vote.

Roosevelt's greatest triumph of the campaign came when he was shot in the chest on his way to an auditorium to give a speech. Coughing and putting a hand to his mouth to see if there was any blood, he saw no red and decided the bullet had not hit a lung. He then walked onto the stage, raised his hand to silence the crowd, and announced he had just been shot. He even held up the metal eyeglasses case and the folded manuscript that had slowed down the bullet on its way to his chest and probably kept it from killing him. He then delivered a stemwinder: If Taft Republicans slanted laws to favor the rich, and Wilson Democrats slanted laws supposedly to favor the poor, Americans would become divided, haves against have-nots, one nationality against another. Roosevelt said, "When that day comes then such incidents as this tonight will be commonplace in our history." He then headed to the hospital, and electoral defeat.

Politically frustrated, Roosevelt left the country to go on an expedition up the Amazon River that nearly killed him. Broken in health, and having broken the Republican Party, he was in no position to run for president in 1916; Roosevelt had to watch helplessly as a man he despised was reelected. He called Wilson "the worst President by all odds since Buchanan, at heart neither a gentleman nor a real man . . . always utterly and coldly selfish . . . a silly doctrinaire at all times and an utterly selfish and cold-blooded politician always."

When the United States entered the world war in 1917, Roosevelt, worn-down as he was, volunteered to recruit and lead a regiment as he had in the Spanish-American War. Although President Wilson did not keep faith with those who voted for him because "He Kept Us Out of War," he did keep Theodore Roosevelt out of war. Roosevelt pleaded and pressed but Wilson, whether for political or military reasons, refused. Roosevelt's sons all served, and his youngest, Quentin the former prankster, was killed.

Unable to contribute to winning the war on the battlefield, Roosevelt tried to help win the peace by aiming his oratorical guns once again at the left. He spoke frequently in 1917 about how America's great enemy was socialism, not because that movement legitimately could help the poor but because it represented "an effort to enthrone privilege in its crudest form." Roosevelt noted the existence of political payoffs and corporate swindles, but argued that there is "no greater example of a corrupt and destructive privilege, than that advocated by those who say that each man should put into a common store what he can and take out what he needs." He wanted Americans to fight socialism not because it was inefficient but because it was immoral, a theft of "the earnings of the intelligent, the foresighted, and the industrious," and a blow to self-reliance.

Roosevelt also emphasized in his last two years the role of churches in teaching right and wrong. One memorable article in *Ladies' Home Journal* in 1917 tried to explain why promoting church attendance was good public policy: "In this actual world a churchless community, a community where men have abandoned and scoffed at or ignored their religious needs, is a community on the rapid downgrade." Even though some individuals or families could remain apart from worship and yet be excellent citizens, "this does not affect the case in the world as it now is, any more than that exceptional men and women under exceptional conditions have disregarded the marriage tie without moral harm to themselves." American movement away from biblical religion "if at all common," Roosevelt insisted, "means the complete moral disintegration of the body politic."

But Roosevelt's own bodily health was disintegrating all the while. In late November 1918 he told a visitor, "No matter what comes, I have kept the promise I made to myself, when I was 21, that I would work up to the hilt until I was 60, and I have done it. And now, even if I should be an invalid—or if I should die, what difference would it make?" Roosevelt had run the race. Having braved the Badlands, the African and Amazon jungles, and American politics, he died in January 1919, at age sixty, in his own bed, in his family home.

Theodore Roosevelt was mourned not only for his vibrant personality, but also because he followed in the Jackson and Cleveland tradition of taking stands in defense of ordinary people against what appeared to be special interests. Roosevelt never seemed a humble man in his statesmanship, but he energetically followed the biblical precepts of fair play and honesty. Broken by his first wife's death, Roosevelt renewed his life in the Badlands and for the next quarter century set a pace in devotion to his new family and his new public roles that few others have equaled. Both publicly and privately he put into practice his professions of faith, and when he put the lives of others on the line he did the same with his own. He became a president who addressed not only questions of economics but difficult social issues as well, upgrading the presidential podium into a bully pulpit.

CHAPTER 10

Woodrow Wilson

Grover Cleveland and Theodore Roosevelt each moved toward maturity in the 1870s and 1880s, propelled in one case by a child born out of wedlock and in the other by a wife dying during childbirth. Thomas Woodrow Wilson, on the other hand, gained self-discipline early on, in the eyes of observers. He seemed so much like an upright if slightly dull Presbyterian professor that he was a favorite speaker at commencement exercises and was eventually named the president of Princeton University. But, in a clear example of personal changes affecting public policy, he went through what might popularly be called a midlife crisis and came out of it at least partly liberated in his own eyes from the constraints of marriage, biblical teaching, and conservative politics.

Wilson was born in Virginia in 1856, two years before Roosevelt, and also into a deeply religious family. "Teedie" Roosevelt paid close attention to Sunday sermons so he could answer his father's questions. "Tommy" Wilson probably paid even closer attention, because the minister, Joseph Wilson, was his father.

Those sermons were different in at least one important respect from those Teedie heard. Roosevelt came to believe in staying close to God's commands as a way of fighting sin that would always be indwelling. Tommy, however, absorbed his father's concentration on not only sin but the opportunity for believers to achieve virtually total harmony with God in this life, if their faith is strong enough. At age seventeen he wrote about how he would "attain nearer and nearer to perfection."

Tommy's mother, Jessie, was also crucial in his development. When Joseph Wilson moved to an Augusta, Georgia, pulpit in 1858, the church ladies gave Mrs. Wilson small welcoming presents of fruits and preserves, until they realized that such gifts hurt her pride. On a boat trip everyone except the Wilsons was eating cake on the deck, but when Jessie was offered a piece she replied, "No, thank you. I couldn't eat it for anything—not here on the deck." From the time Woodrow Wilson was a teenager, she was chronically ill and depressed, but no organic cause was ever found for her symptoms.

Tommy, like Teedie Roosevelt, was tutored mainly at home, but young Wilson did not learn to read until he was twelve. He later said that he was not taught to read because his father wanted to teach him whatever was important to know about the outside world, and did not want him to learn about it from others. It also appears that Wilson was dyslexic; throughout his adult life he remained a slow reader, making up in academic doggedness what he lacked in speed. In any event, as a child he developed an active fantasy life, and it stayed with him longer than usual. At age seventeen, Wilson entered Davidson College in North Carolina, he was still spending much time in an imaginary world he created, where he was Commodore Lord (sometimes Vice Admiral) Thomas W. Wilson, Duke of Carlton (sometimes Eagleton), responsible for writing rules and regulations for the Royal United

Kingdom Yacht Club, and reports to the Navy Department about his war against pirates.

Wilson wanted to fight against pirates of various kinds. In 1876, when he was nineteen, he declared in an essay entitled "Christ's Army" that the real war was between Christ and "the Prince of Darkness": "Will any one dare to enlist under the banners of the Prince of Lies, under whose dark folds he only marches to the darkness of hell? For there is no middle course, no neutrality." That attitude, along with Wilson's confidence that he understood what the right course was, has led many historians to call Wilson a Calvinist, a term often used to label a person who is adamant concerning biblical application. It's always vital, however, to ask whether such a person is unwilling to bend concerning God's words, or his own words.

Wilson transferred from Davidson to Princeton, at that time still a country college to which many southern scions came. Its stone buildings stood bare, its campus almost treeless. Near the buildings sat whitewashed brick latrines, built when every wooden outhouse became material for bonfires, and sometimes every little breeze seemed to whisper some unpleasant odor. Although chapel services included preaching about honesty, "shanannigagging" (copying another student's paper) was widespread. Sophomores and others often put more imagination into attacking the classes above or beneath them than into their schoolwork, with letters six inches high displayed on posters knocking freshmen who were "Puerile Pukes of Low Degree" or "Lineal Descendants of Balaam's Ass." Hazing was common, although it received criticism when a freshman shot a sophomore in the legs with a revolver.

Amid hijinks and lowjinks, Wilson's seriousness stood out. He had few friends but was admired for his outstanding oratorical ability. He won awards in public speaking contests, organized the Liberal Debating Club, and became known as a student willing to challenge authority. He became managing editor of *The Princetonian*, then in its third year as a fortnightly newspaper, and changed its pattern of coverage. Volume two had paid attention to the religious life of the campus, but *The Princetonian* under Wilson virtually ignored religious practice, except to suggest that college prayer meetings be reduced from four to two per week, and to wonder whether too many Princeton scholarships were given to candidates for the ministry.

Sexual and Theological Temptation

Wilson experienced the tensions of biblical application as he tried to deal with sexual impulses. While a teenager he had some "love adventures" in Columbia, South Carolina, where his father had become a theological seminary professor. When he was twenty-two Wilson wrote about God and sex at religious camp meetings, where passions awakened sometimes led to kissing: He argued that it was not right "to blame the young men and women for yielding to a temptation which everything conspires to make almost irresistible. I know well enough that I could pretty safely predict my own course under such circumstances."

At age twenty-three Wilson fell in love with his nineteen-year-old cousin, Harriet Woodrow, a talented singer. He pursued her so ardently, on at least one occasion loudly cheering her singing as others politely applauded, that he embarrassed her. For that and other reasons, including her reluctance to marry a cousin, she rejected him. He retaliated—as he did against all who disappointed him—by calling her "heartless." When he recalled that period four years later in a letter to his wife-to-be, Wilson wrote, using italics, "I was absolutely *hungry for a sweetheart.* ... Seriously, I *was* in need of a sweetheart." In 1883, after study at the University of Virginia Law School, and while suffering through boredom as a lawyer in Atlanta, Wilson found a sweetheart in Ellen Axson, a Georgian lady who expressed total devotion for him.

The two were married in 1885, despite his "poor prospects" as a graduate student at Johns Hopkins. They soon had three daughters, and Ellen Wilson devoted herself to being a wife, mother, and career helper. She made her own clothes and dresses for her daughters during years of family financial stringency, and kept doing so long after her husband earned a good salary. She took care of household chores and business transactions, and reviewed her husband's outlines before he went out lecturing.

Wilson's theological views were affected during these years by a case involving his favorite uncle, James Woodrow, a seminary professor who had come to believe that Darwin was right on the origin of species and the Bible was wrong. The issue came to a head in 1888 when Uncle Woodrow, outed as a Darwinist and ousted from his professorship, appealed to the General Assembly of the Southern Presbyterian denomination. During that Baltimore convention Wilson was "sitting on the edge of his chair and all but cheering" at Uncle Woodrow's attacks on orthodoxy, but the General Assembly by a vote of 65–27 supported the dismissal. Wilson wrote in his journal that he was still "orthodox in my faith," yet had become "unorthodox in my reading of the standards of the faith," particularly those parts of the Westminster Confession that dealt with the creation of the world.

After short teaching stops at Bryn Mawr and Wesleyan, Wilson from 1890 to 1902 was professor of jurisprudence and political economy at Princeton. He became an elder in his Presbyterian church and offered in his classes a generally conservative perspective on the American constitutional framework. His oratorical ability brought him many offers to give guest lectures at other universities, but he began to write to his wife about the sexual temptations he felt while on his lecture swings, and his need to control "the riotous elements in my own blood." When Wilson lectured at the New York Law School, he took the train back to Princeton in the evening rather than staying overnight in the city. When he lectured in Baltimore in 1894, Wilson wrote to his wife that he had walked up and down the streets looking into each pretty face that passed.

Wilson's letters about "all the roving, Bohemian impulses" he was having weighed down Ellen Wilson, especially since her husband paid no attention to her own concerns. When a friend died Ellen Wilson wrote to another friend, "I cannot shake off for a moment the weight it had laid upon my spirits, all the more so perhaps because for Woodrow's sake I must not show it. He is almost terribly dependent on me to keep up his spirits and to 'rest' him as he says. So I dare not have the 'blues.' If I am just a little sky-blue he immediately becomes blue-black!"

GOD AND MAN AT PRINCETON

When the Presbyterian-based Princeton in 1902 needed a president who could give good speeches, Wilson was a logical choice. His inauguration came on a brilliant October day, with the Pennsylvania Railroad running a special train to the village of Princeton, and dignitaries on hand including Grover Cleveland, Booker T. Washington, Mark Twain, and J. Pierpont Morgan. Wilson gained as enthusiastic a reception as Booker T. Washington had won seven years before in Atlanta. One spectator, George Watt, wrote that Wilson "was faultlessly dressed and gave the impression of immaculate cleanliness. His figure was erect but supple; and he seemed very tall because of his slenderness. . . . He spoke without the slightest effort in a voice as clear as any bell. Both his enunciation and pronunciation were perfection."

Wilson quickly moved to minimize the college's theological heritage, announcing that Princeton "is a Presbyterian college only because the Presbyterians of New Jersey were wise and progressive enough to found it." Even though he was ordained a Presbyterian ruling elder in 1897, Wilson eliminated Bible classes at Princeton soon after becoming president. Some churchmen opposed being marginalized, but others had become convinced (as had Rockefeller) that God was the god of the chapel, and other gods should dominate the laboratories and lecture halls. Wilson eventually gave in to some objections by reinstating Bible teaching, but only outside the normal curricular structure. Through such organizational changes he began to convey his belief that fact and faith were two different ships, probably passing in the night.

Wilson began to sneer at orthodox Christians who proclaimed a unity of fact and faith, and told one of his daughters that hell was only "a state of mind." Soon he began twisting Scripture during his Princeton chapel talks. For example, one Wilson sermonette turned a statement by Jesus about the centrality of objective truth—John 6:63, "the words that I speak unto you, they are spirit, and they are life"—into a celebration of personal subjectivity. Wilson said, "The 'spirit' spoken of in the text [is . . .] the spirit which translates all law into privilege . . .

by satisfaction of inborn instincts." It was God's will for us that such instincts be satisfied, and even if biblical law had to be broken in the process, people made God happy by satisfying their instincts.

Wilson's instinct, like that of many other men, was toward adultery, and as his fidelity to Scripture became looser, so did his fidelity in marriage. The fifty-year-old Wilson had a stroke in 1906 that left him blind in his left eye and with periods of numbness in his right arm. Ellen Wilson wanted her husband to have any pleasure that might relax him. She even encouraged him to meet women who were more frivolous and "gamesome" than she was. She told a cousin, "Since he has married a wife who is not gay [that is, playful], I must provide him with friends that are." She and his doctor urged him to get some rest and relaxation in a warm place, where he would be off by himself and would have no social duties, not even a wife and daughters to concern him.

Wilson chose Bermuda. There he met Mary Allen Hulbert Peck, born in 1862, married in 1883, widowed in 1889, and remarried in 1890. Mrs. Peck had spent every winter from 1892 in Bermuda, while her husband remained in Pittsfield, Massachusetts, where he was president of a woolen manufacturing company. She told all her Bermuda friends that her husband was stingy and refused to give her money, but every winter she rented a luxurious house in Bermuda and arrived with her own maids. In 1907 she was known to leading lights and visitors to Bermuda as a vivacious forty-five-year-old who smoked, danced well, and stirred the souls and bodies of middle-aged men.

Wilson enjoyed talking with Mrs. Peck so much in early 1907 that he arranged to once again leave his family in Princeton and come back to Bermuda in January and February 1908. After a month of long walks and poetry reading with Mrs. Peck on the island, Wilson was writing her a note addressed to "my precious one, my beloved Mary." Meanwhile, he wrote to Ellen and his daughters that he was resting comfortably. Church fidelity also suffered: During Wilson's visit in 1907 he preached a sermon at one church, but during his 1908 trip he stayed away from church altogether. He wrote to Mrs. Peck that she was a "veritable child of nature. . . . There is an air about you like the air of the open, a directness, a simplicity, a free movement that links you with wild things that are yet meant to be taken into one's confidence and loved."

Later in 1908, Wilson confessed wrongdoing to his wife and asked her to forgive him for his emotional estrangement. "God give you the strength to be patient with me," Wilson wrote. "I have never been worthy of you." She did forgive him, and he did not return to Bermuda in January 1909. Later that year, however, Wilson wrote to Mrs. Peck that he had thought of her "a thousand times." At the end of 1909 and in January 1910, when Mrs. Peck had an apartment in New York City at 39 East Twenty-seventh Street, it seems that their relationship intensified once again, with Wilson apparently visiting her alone at least half a dozen times.

Wilson's earlier resolution to avoid placing himself in the path of sexual temptation in New York City vanished, and his biographer August Heckscher is among those who have concluded that during this period, "Wilson saw his relations with Mary Peck enter a new phase, in all probability changing from a romantic friendship into a love affair."

JUSTIFYING INFIDELITY

Wilson had become loose in his general theology, but until 1908 he always stressed that personal morality should be based on God's commands, which were good for all times and all places. As his desires began to direct his behavior, however, he modulated that emphasis on personal virtue. In 1908, after his Bermuda interlude, Wilson lectured Princeton seniors graduating that spring about the way ethical standards were changing. He suggested that students grow up and out of a straightforward Ten Commandments understanding, and realize that ethical situations are "complicated by a thousand circumstances." Later that year Wilson began to emphasize a new, relativistic standard.

In October 1908, in a speech at Pittsfield, he went all the way, suddenly claiming that public fidelity was crucial but private fidelity was not: "If there is a place where we must adjourn our morals, that place should be in what we call the private life. It is better to be unfaithful to a few people than to a considerable number of people." No longer should voters examine personal morality as a clue to fitness for office: "There are so many men who are good in their private lives who are unwise in public affairs and purposes. Men who are saints in private lives may be poor leaders."

Just as Wilson in one sense had established a cover with his wife ("I'm trying so hard") that would then justify a lapse, so at age fifty he began putting together a portfolio of statements that would position himself well to gain support from progressives. Until 1908, Wilson was known as a conservative Democrat, an opponent of William Jennings Bryan, unions, and big government. But from 1908 onwards Wilson de-emphasized the idea of progress coming from the competition of private interests and spoke largely about the need for all to conform to a public morality defined in liberal terms.

The change at first came primarily in speeches. Wilson told the American Bankers Association that business morality should be evaluated not in terms of the biblical fulfillment of contracts ("thou shalt not steal") but through an analysis of the way that corporations might contribute to "social reintegration." In 1909 and 1910 he proclaimed a communitarian gospel: "Christianity came into the world to save the world as well as to save individual men," so souls should be seen "not as if they were units, but as if they were subordinate parts of great complicated wholes." This was popular talk in the Progressive Era, but it was opposed to the biblical morality that Grover Cleveland and others in the nineteenth century had practiced.

How Wilson's subordination worked out in practice became apparent when Dean Andrew West, his opponent in a Princeton dispute about the future of the graduate school, asked Wilson to keep promises he had made concerning location and financing. Wilson responded that in the larger interests of the college he would break his promises, for "there are after all two moralities, public and private." West retorted, "Which one are you going to use on me?" Wilson was liberated: His theology had loosened over time, his marital vows were becoming elastic, and, hoping to have his way politically at Princeton, he felt free to maneuver regardless of previous commitments.

Eventually Wilson's Princeton associates caught on, and after eight years his presidency ended in a shambles. Wilson wanted to set up residential colleges as a way of reducing the influence of social clubs akin to modern fraternities, and he wanted a new graduate school on a plot of land of his choosing. Both of his initiatives failed, but it was his action after defeat that astonished supporters and prefigured the way he would act toward the end of his eight years as president of the United States. Wilson went into a rage, attacking Princeton publicly in a speech at Pittsburgh in April 1910, and privately complaining about the college he once loved: "How full the place is of spiteful hostility to me. It is a dreadful thing to be hated by those whom you have loved and whom you have sought to serve unselfishly. . . ."

MINISTER TO THE STATE

The defeat and subsequent outburst, like his League of Nations loss nine years later, ennobled Wilson in the eyes of his backers, for he had portrayed his Princeton fight as a battle for democracy against the snobbery of social clubs. Wilson's eloquent public speaking also attracted the attention of politicians looking for not only a fresh face but also a melodious voice. As democrats and demagogues yearned for Wilson he yearned for the opportunity to be a "minister to the state. . . an instrument of judgment, with motives not secular but religious." Wilson said he could be one "who conceives in his mind those reforms which are based upon the statutes of morality; who tries to draw society together by a new motive which is not the motive of the economist or of the politician, but the motive of the profoundly religious man."

Politicians had mixed feelings concerning their new find. Wilson was not a glad-hander—editor William Allen White said that Wilson's handshake felt "like a ten-cent pickled mackerel in brown paper"—but, oh, could he give a speech! New Jersey Democrats, reeling under charges of unethical conduct, made Wilson their gubernatorial candidate. Wilson won big in 1910 and saved many local Democratic politicians, but one stalwart said he gave them "the creeps. The first time I met him, he said something to me, and I didn't know whether God or him was talking."

If Wilson was a god, he was like those of Greek mythology: Flattery could win a pass into the inner circle, candor a dismissal. Over the next decade his theology and politics continued to move far from their Calvinistic roots. Wilson maintained faith in a divine will, but he no longer took God's word in the Bible as the concrete expression of His will. This meant that Wilson could redefine morality to his own liking; in time, he could even substitute his own thought for God's and then believe himself to be infallible.

Wilson's talk in 1910 on "The Clergyman and the State" showed how he had redefined morality to allow for his own practice. "Sin is, in almost all its forms, selfishness. It is not always enlightened selfishness, but it is always selfishness," he said. Were those who thought themselves above selfishness—say, men comforting unhappy women who said they were trapped in bad marriages—therefore not sinners? Wilson went on to emphasize collective rather than personal ethics, with a person like himself at the fulcrum of change: "The whole morality of the world depends upon those who exert upon men that influence which will turn their eyes from themselves."

Wilson was justifying his conduct with Mrs. Peck and his political movement to the left, but he knew that many would find neither justifiable. Once Wilson became New Jersey's governor he ceased his adultery with Mrs. Peck, although they continued to correspond. She wrote to him that she was moving toward a divorce, and supporters of Wilson's prime opponent for the Democratic nomination in 1912, Champ Clark of Missouri, circulated rumors of the Wilson-Peck trysts. That April someone stole Wilson's briefcase from a Chicago hotel room in an apparent attempt to gather letters or other incriminating information. When Mrs. Peck obtained her divorce in July, Wilson indicated that he did not want to resume their affair but he sent her money, perhaps out of sympathy, perhaps out of fear that she would sell his love letters.

After Wilson gained the nomination he heard that Elihu Root, the Republican senator from New York, knew of a letter concerning the Peck divorce that might name the presidential candidate as a contributor to the breakdown of the Pecks' marriage. Root, a former secretary of war and secretary of state who won the Nobel Peace Prize in 1912, knew how to wage political war, and Wilson hurriedly wrote to the former Mrs. Peck, now Mary Hulbert again. He warned her to be very careful: "Malevolent foes" were out to get him, and questions "of life and death" were at stake.

Wilson won the nomination because he appealed to both wings of the Democratic Party: Cleveland remnants saw him as a trustworthy religious man who had long praised private enterprise, and Bryanites discerned the progressive trend of his speeches. He was a compromise choice on the forty-sixth ballot at a weary convention, but Wilson saw it all through the eyes of faith in himself and faith in a God who had anointed him. He told an aide who had worked almost sleeplessly for two weeks before and during the Democratic convention, "I wish it clearly understood that I owe you nothing. Remember that God ordained that I should be the next president of the United States. Neither you nor any other mortal could have prevented that."

Wilson was so rhetorically brilliant and in tune with the politically progressive trends of his era that usually skeptical reporters cheered his orations and wrote cheerleading accounts. Once it became evident that Wilson's extramarital interests would not be reported, election to the presidency in 1912 turned out to be easy, with Taft and Roosevelt at each other's throats. Wilson's rhetoric was sometimes breathtaking: He predicted that "the community will turn to him almost as they would turn for salvation, go to him for those deep counsels which transcend all circumstances." Yet he was such a splendid speaker that his audience, as at a good movie, was willing to suspend disbelief.

PROPHET, PRIEST, AND PRESIDENT

Wilson's declarations that the good news was at hand continued in his first inaugural address. "The feelings with which we face this new age of right and opportunity sweep across our heartstrings like some air out of God's own presence," he said. Wilson prophesied a new freedom for administrators within "the great Government"—capital G, like God. He gave Government a task that required omnipresence: "To purify and humanize every aspect of our common life. . . . To lift everything that concerns our life as a Nation to the light that shines from the hearthfire of every man's conscience and vision of the right."

Wilson, wanting the air from his own presence to sweep across Congress, called it into special session on April 8. He became the first president since John Adams to restore the old monarchical practice of speaking before the assembled legislators to make them begin their work with his agenda. The next day he went to the Capitol to consult directly with members of Congress; since Lincoln's time presidents had often finagled but had officially stood by, positioning themselves as executives waiting for Congress to legislate. But Wilson, energetic like Roosevelt, went right at his goal of obtaining something old within the Democratic Party agenda, tariff reduction, and a few things new, legislation to increase Washington's economic power.

His moral slippage did not hinder Wilson during the tariff debates, where he stood like Andrew Jackson, the original stone wall, in opposition to the Henry Clay–like program of heavy, politicized tariffs. Any other position would have torn apart the Democratic Party, but Wilson did more than go through the motions. His task in one regard seemed easy: A Congress with a Democratic majority in 1911 and 1912 had passed three bills lowering tariffs but President Taft, loyal to the Whig-Republican legacy, had vetoed them all; with Taft out of the way a 300-pound obstacle was removed. Yet, now that tariff reduction was politically likely, lobbyists for the sugar, wool, and even Bible-publishing industries, worried about foreign competition, doubled their pressure. Wilson, to his credit, took on these special interests, stating that Washington had rarely seen "so numerous, so industrious, or so insidious a lobby."

With Wilson refusing to compromise on his determination to eliminate tariffs on wool and (in three years) sugar, his Democratic majority held firm, placing many products on the free list and reducing overall tariffs from an average of 40 percent to 25 percent. This was a great achievement in the Democratic, small government/lower taxes tradition, but when Wilson signed the bill in October 1913, he said that he felt "like a man who is lodging happily in an inn which is half way along the journey." The rest of the way became, counter to the Jackson-Cleveland tradition and Wilson's own past, an establishment of staging areas for government expansion.

First among the beachheads was establishment of a graduated income tax: The poor and the middle class paid zero; those with incomes of $20,000 to $50,000 (wealth in those days) paid one percent; income over $500,000 was taxed at 6 percent. Earlier in his career Wilson had called such differentiation unjust, but the new Wilson put pragmatism first. He discerningly forecast higher rates to come but noted that opposition would be minimal if the graduated rate "began upon somewhat moderate lines."

The old Wilson also had opposed bills providing government credit for farmers, declaring (like Cleveland), "I have a very deep conviction that it is unwise and unjustifiable to extend the credit of the Government to a single class of the community." That conviction disappeared as Wilson signed the Federal Farm Loan Act. His signing of the Adamson Act, by which the federal government for the first time told private businesses (in this case, railroads) how long their employees could work and what they had to be paid, also represented a change from earlier professions. Neither of these laws had large immediate effects, but they set precedents that became central to New Deal and Great Society approaches.

Other parts of the Wilson domestic legacy, such as the establishment of the Federal Reserve System and the Federal Trade Commission, are more difficult to assess, but they were all part of a trend of slow government expansion. Wilson's soul mate in that process was Edward House, an unofficial political advisor who often went by the honorary title of Colonel. House, the youngest and most loved of seven sons, summarized his vision in a novel he had published in 1913, *Philip Dru, Administrator: A Novel of Tomorrow.* The hero, Dru, the youngest and most loved of seven sons, leads a revolution and becomes temporary dictator of the United States, implementing radical changes and then benignly turning over his power to a newly elected government. Wilson administration goals were not as spectacular, but both Wilson and House saw government as not just a protector of individual freedom but a provider of social progress. That very positive light is hard to recapture at the end of the political century they wrought.

Life in the White House, with Colonel House's omnipresent flattery, only increased Wilson's arrogance. Increasingly, he styled himself a new messiah and argued that under his leadership a new age could commence on demand. Sometimes he was childish. When Walter Hines Page, the American ambassador to Great Britain, brought to a Washington meeting perspectives the president did not want to hear, Wilson "sprang up, stuck his fingers in his ears, and, still holding them there, ran out of the room," according to Page's account.

Wilson also refused to pay attention to what was happening to his wife. Ellen Wilson in 1913 began to have serious kidney problems, but Wilson kept insisting that nothing was wrong. He wrote to Mary Hulbert in June 1914 that "there is nothing at all the matter with her organically." On July 28, Wilson wrote to a political ally that the weather, not physical ailments, was troubling his wife. Wilson was deeply involved with news of the beginning of war in Europe when Ellen Wilson died of kidney failure on August 6. Before losing consciousness, she told the attending physician, "Doctor, if I go away, promise me that you will take good care of Woodrow."

NEW MARRIAGE, NEW TERM

Wilson had often said that he could not live without a sweetheart, and in March 1915, little more than half a year after the death of his wife of three decades, he met and fell hard for forty-two-year-old widow Edith Galt. Wilson was soon writing her about how he, half awake in the early morning, imagined their next time together: "I could feel your breath on my cheek, our lips touched, and there was all about me the sweet atmosphere that my Darling always carries with her." She responded in kind; once, after he sent her some silk stockings, she wrote that she was in her wrapper with the stockings on, and ready to give him in her imagination "a fond and very tender kiss my precious Woodrow, before we put out the light—and I feel your dear arms "fold round me."

Meanwhile, the remnants of adultery had to be cleaned up. On May 31, Mary Hulbert came to the White House for frank discussions, and several weeks later Wilson came up with $15,000 to buy several mortgages she held on a New York property. Throughout the summer gossip flowed. William McAdoo, the secretary of the treasury who had cemented a political alliance with Wilson by marrying one of his daughters, received an anonymous letter saying that Mary Hulbert had displayed letters Wilson had sent her and intimated that the $15,000 was a payoff. McAdoo told Wilson about the letter at lunch on September 18. Later that day Wilson rushed to Mrs. Galt's home.

Their discussion was lengthy. Judging by a letter he wrote her the next morning, he told Mrs. Galt of his affair with the then Mrs. Peck, and that the letters in his former lover's possession "disclose a passage of folly and gross impertinence in my life. I am deeply ashamed and repentant." Wilson also explained to Mrs. Galt his way of dealing with such error: "I have tried to expiate folly by disinterested service." His public professions were an attempt to prove to himself and others that he was still righteous despite what he knew was sin.

When Mrs. Galt said she would still marry him, Wilson sent her a letter of enormous relief. Wilson stated that her love "brought me to the startling, humiliating discovery that I was allowing myself to be dominated by fear and the desire to conceal something which no doubt everybody who has trusted and believed in me probably has a right to know, unless I am to play the hypocrite." Wilson wrote that he had been "acting the part of coward" out of fear that public admission "might make the contemptible error and madness of a few months seem a stain upon a whole life." He resolved that he would no longer "live under the domination of such a fear and allow it to govern the whole course of my life. . . ."

Mary Hulbert was the odd woman out. In October she wrote forlornly to Wilson of his new love, "She is very beautiful. . . . The cold peace of utter renunciation is about me. . . . It is rather lonely, not even an acquaintance to make the air vibrate . . ." Regardless of her loneliness, Mary Hulbert maintained tight lips and tight control of the letters. Stories about Wilson's personal life during the 1916 election never reached critical mass.

Wilson's new propensity to do whatever it took to retain power, however, grew to huge and historic size during the election campaign. No president before Wilson ever ran on an anti-war platform and soon after reelection led the United States into war. But in 1916, Theodore Roosevelt and Senate leader Henry Cabot Lodge were calling for tougher policies toward Germany, and Charles Evans Hughes, who won the Republican presidential nomination early in June, also talked tough. Later that month Democratic convention keynote speaker Martin H. Glynn, arguing that neutrality within the American tradition went along with motherhood and apple pie, cited examples of presidents who maintained peace even when provoked. After each mention he said—and the delegates, with uproarious enthusiasm, began chanting along—"But we didn't go to war."

That became the theme of the Wilson campaign and its most effective slogan: "He kept us out of war." Privately, Wilson told Secretary of the Navy Josephus Daniels, "I can't keep the country out of war." Publicly, while not making an ironclad guarantee, he proclaimed himself to be the alternative to Republicans who would draw America "into the embroilments of the European War," and he had his followers incessantly talk up that "kept us out of war" slogan and plaster it on billboards throughout the country. The Wilson of a decade earlier would have considered this deception wrong, but Wilson in 1916 knew that it would be a close election, that most Americans did not want to enter a European war, and that God wanted him in his position even if he had to break God's law in the process.

Few Americans knew about Wilson's theological or personal infidelity, and they thought they could trust his pledge. Wilson, however, was, in the words of his secretary of war, Lindley Garrison, a man of high ideals and no principles.

He Led Us into War

Wilson's second inaugural address on March 4, 1917, ended in a furious burst: "Men's hearts wait upon us. . . . I summon all honest men, all patriotic, all forward-looking men to my side." One month later Wilson formally went back on his implied pledge and led the way into war. There is still a debate as to whether changes in German strategic thinking—primarily the move to more aggressive submarine warfare—during the months after the election forced Wilson's hand, but what is clear is that during the campaign he knew his peace campaign was a fraud.

Characteristically, Wilson offered no apology, but a new, far-from-Calvinistic theology within which Americans headed to Europe were "Christ's soldiers" engaged in a holy mission. Wilson preached utopian progressivism, most notably in his claim that the war among European powers was the "war to end wars," one that would "make the world safe for democracy." Because Wilson no longer believed that all people were naturally sinful, he saw the German people as good and their leaders as the source of corruption. When Wilson asked Congress for a declaration of war, he argued that militarism was the enemy, suggesting that the military balance of power did not matter as long as Germany was a democracy. The French and British thought differently: For them, the problem was power, and as long as Germany thought it could overpower its foes, ordinary citizens—not just leaders—would want it to do so.

War was hell for soldiers in the trenches of Europe, as neither side could break through. For those who had long demanded government control of the economy, however, economic mobilization for war was heavenly. Washington officials took charge of the economy and railroad transport. Financier Bernard Baruch gained effective control over war industries, and Wilson's son-in-law McAdoo loomed over the railroads and financial matters. As an aptly named contemporary book, *How America Went to War: The Giant Hand,* put it, "As to the control of American business, it became absolute. There was no freedom of individual enterprise. The control was autocratic, as powerful as any which ever reigned in the Russia of the Romanoffs." Baruch and others often said "you should" rather than "you must," but what Wilson's appointees called "the big stick behind the closet door" and "the pistol in the hip pocket" were always within reach.

War expenditures (in 1917 dollars) totaled $22 billion—the figure does not include veterans' benefits and other costs that came in after the war—which equaled all federal expenses from 1789 up to April 6, 1917, when war was declared. Government powers increased in noneconomic ways as well. Under provisions of the Sedition Act (the first one since John Adams), Wilson officials jailed dissenters and closed down their publications. Meanwhile, the inventor of modern public relations, Edward Bernays, toiled in Wilson's Office of War

Information, learning how "the conscious and intelligent manipulation of the organized habits and opinions of the masses is an important element of democratic society." Bernays, believing that there is "no being in the air to watch over us," argued that public relations counselors earn their pay "by making the public believe that human gods are watching over us for our own benefit."

PRESIDENT OF THE WORLD

The war ended with German exhaustion on November 11, 1918. Fresh American troops had made a difference at the end, and Wilson headed to France to win the peace with a fresh approach. He played designated savior as a million Parisians chanted "Wilson, Wilson," and Prime Minister Georges Clemenceau of France said, "I do not think there has been anything like [Wilson's reception] in the history of the world." With his hubris at its height, Wilson even claimed direct divine inspiration for the League of Nations agreement: It came about "by no plan of our conceiving but by the hand of God who had led us into this way. We can only go forward, with lifted eyes and freshened spirit, to follow the vision." (Wilson was far from omniscient, though. He did not even know the geography and demographics of one "country" he abstractly stitched together, Czechoslovakia.)

Wilson told Felix Frankfurter he was "the personal instrument of God" in Paris, but after the 1918 congressional elections, when many of his supporters were voted out of office, he was barely the personal instrument of the United States. Domestic suspicion hindered his international efforts; French leaders were not going to put their trust in a plan that had no force behind it and would probably not have U.S. Senate support. Wilson's flights of rhetoric at meetings did not help his reputation with European politicians. Prime Minister David Lloyd George of Great Britain believed that Wilson "regarded himself as a missionary whose function was to rescue the poor European heathen from their age-long worship of false and fiery gods."

As Lloyd George put it, Clemenceau "would open his great eyes in twinkling wonder" when Wilson began orating, as much as to say:

"Here he is off again." Wilson's "most extraordinary outburst," according to Lloyd George, came when he explained the failure of Christianity to achieve its highest ideals. "Jesus Christ so far [has] not succeeded in inducing the world to follow His teaching," Wilson stated, "because He taught the ideal without devising any practical scheme to carry out His aims." In Lloyd George's account, "Clemenceau slowly opened his dark eyes to their widest dimension and swept them round the Assembly to see how the Christians gathered around the table enjoyed this exposure of the futility of their Master."

Curiously, in some history books Wilson is called a Calvinist president, but his emphasis on lions lying down with lambs through his own efforts rather than God's was the exact opposite of biblical approaches. Nor could Wilson fulfill his promises: When he eventually made concessions to political realities, politicians who had acknowledged their limitations in the first place scorned him. Clemenceau sarcastically summed up his experience: Wilson "talked like Jesus Christ but acted like Lloyd George." Lloyd George himself prophetically stated that the peace conference merely set the stage for the next generation's world war: "All a great pity. We shall have to do the same thing all over again in twenty-five years at three times the cost."

Wilson did not have omniscience and the League of Nations covenant was not inspired, but Wilson seemed to consider it inerrant. His refusal to compromise in the slightest doomed the effort to make the United States a league member. "The stage is set, the destiny disclosed," he said upon submitting the treaty to the Senate early in 1919, but the campaign for the league ripped wide his prophetic mantle. Wilson traveled the country by train during that summer, hoping to rally the country to his side, but the postwar credibility of a man who had last stumped the country on a no-war pledge was not too high. Wilson's statements that "The light streams upon the path ahead, and nowhere else" seemed arrogant to all but his true believers. He was making little headway, and in September came the crushing blow: Wilson suffered a stroke—an occlusion of the right middle cerebral artery—that paralyzed his left side.

Trying to Hold On

It was time again for secrecy; Edith Wilson told reporters that improvement in her husband's condition was just around the corner. Secretary of State Robert Lansing suggested that the incapacitated president step down temporarily, but Wilson's doctor would not sign a certificate of disability and cabinet members were afraid to force the issue.

Even then Wilson refused a compromise that would have allowed for adoption of the League of Nations treaty, with reservations that would preserve American sovereignty to the satisfaction of a crucial swing vote of Republican senators. In January 1920 he reiterated his refusal even to discuss any changes. By March, White House publicists were announcing that Wilson was working at his desk every day from nine-thirty on, but Wilson actually stayed in bed most of the time, able to get angry but no longer physically or politically able to get even.

Wilson's departure from reality became most evident when he tried to have his operatives gain him the Democratic nomination for a third term. Even his doctor saw no choice but to inform party leaders that Wilson was "permanently ill physically" and failing mentally. Wilson had long been fascinated with Ouija boards and superstitions. He considered thirteen his lucky number, remarking that he had thirteen letters in his name, was the thirteenth president of Princeton, and was chosen as president during his thirteenth year on the faculty. Wilson retained such superstitions despite his stated belief in God's providence, and they did go along with his new theology: Since the Bible was not clear, he looked for clarity elsewhere. In 1920, when he did not find it, and when voters in the fall election firmly repudiated the Democratic Party and its pro–League of Nations platform, Wilson increasingly cursed his "bad luck" and became morose.

Wilson survived until February 1924, and apparently remained unrepentant to the end of his life. He at times regained enough of his old fire to declare that others were proceeding outside God's will. "I have seen fools resist Providence before, and I have seen their destruction," he told well-wishers shortly before he died, and he was apparently not speaking about himself. "You can't fight God," he told his followers at the end, and perhaps he did have his own rise and fall in mind.

What led to his fall? Woodrow Wilson, like Thomas Jefferson, came to believe that the rules constraining ordinary mortals need not affect him. Proud and arrogant as he grew older, Wilson saw himself as beyond a literal reading of Scripture: His was a high and lonely destiny. While he could not be totally explicit in his public pronouncements, he drifted with liberal seminaries and churches into a thoroughly modern millennialism. Wilson displayed certainty, but it was certainty in his own rectitude rather than God's. His adamancy became arrogance because it was founded not on God's words but his own. Feeling predestined to lead the lesser folk, Wilson could run as the anti-war candidate and, post-election, demand a war to end wars. Feeling predestined to lead the world, he insisted on getting his way with the League of Nations, and ended up with both a personal and institutional collapse.

Wilson left a legacy that went far beyond the problems that arose from his League debacle. After the war ended in November 1918, the wartime industrial and propaganda czars went home. And yet, as journalist Mark Sullivan noted a few years later, "they remembered. Never again was life quite the same. Never again in any ordinary business or walk of life could they feel themselves geared into the immensity of things, the pace, the high momentum they had experienced in Washington. They learned that the legend about Cincinnatus, to be true, should be modified. Cincinnatus, in his farm on the Tiber, kept his hands on the plow, his eyes on the furrow—but he mused on Rome, as about an old love never to be recaptured."

For some, after a time, the old love was recaptured. The greatest long-term consequence of Wilson's modest start-ups of new domestic programs, and his intensive buildup of wartime order, may have been that the projects and the vision were there to recapture during the New Deal. In 1933, Franklin Roosevelt's administration, with generally good intentions amid a national crisis, declared war on the Depression and tried to implement Wilson's World War I regime during peacetime. The graduated income tax became significant, wages and hours became heavily regulated, and two of Wilson's key wartime subordinates, Hugh Johnson and George Peek, were put in charge of American industry and agriculture.

And there was a deeper, but hard-to-measure outcome as well. Up to Wilson's time citizens believed that a president was bound by his word. Wilson lowered expectations. At a time when schoolchildren still learned about young George Washington's supposed words, "I cannot tell a lie," their parents began wondering whether presidential practice had changed.

CHAPTER 11

Franklin Roosevelt

When Woodrow Wilson entered the White House in 1913 he had to manufacture a sense that government action was necessary. When Franklin Roosevelt took office twenty years later, a consensus for rapid change of some kind already was present. Unemployment had risen from 1.6 million in 1929 to 12.8 million (25 percent of the labor force) early in 1933; many more were semi-employed. As fruitless job-hunting went on month after month, observers noted desperation among family heads now dragging their tails: "Fear driving them into a state of semi-collapse, cracking nerves; an overpowering fear of the future [as they watched] their children growing thinner and thinner."

Roosevelt was the president who gave many of those individuals new hope amid depression, and a decade later confidence during war. He was not a likely choice as a tribune of the poor. From soon after his birth on January 30, 1882, Franklin Roosevelt traveled frequently by train with his affluent parents. Young Roosevelt rolled through cities and countryside in his father's private railroad car, well supplied with servants and a chef so there was no need even to eat in public establishments. He sat with the high and mighty, not the lowly. (On a trip to Washington, Franklin's father took him to shake hands with a weary Grover Cleveland, who said, "I'm making a strange wish for you, little man, a wish I suppose no one else would make. I wish for you that you may never be President of the United States.")

Years later Roosevelt loved campaigning for vice president in 1920 from a private railroad car. He was free to walk through small towns, but he rarely did so. Instead, he averaged seven speeches a day from the back of his railroad car, and fit in local references sent by his advance man, reporter Steve Early. Roosevelt often spoke about what a great opportunity he had to get out of an office, travel through the country, and hear directly in voters' homes their hopes and fears.

Roosevelt lost that election, and a year later came down with polio. From then on it was harder to carry on the ruse about easy, firsthand observation of how the other half lived. From then on Roosevelt was even more dependent on what he could view out the windows of his railroad cars. Nevertheless, he still saw himself as having tight personal communication with his fellow Americans. In 1938, while traveling from Georgia to Washington by train and discussing the criticism he faced on Capitol Hill, Roosevelt peered out the window at some poor folks who were waiting for his train to go by. He then commented, "*They* understand what we're trying to do."

Washington reporters affectionately joked about FDR's train window understanding. The correspondents treated him favorably even when their publishers were hostile, but even they snickered quietly when Roosevelt told an anecdote detailing his conversations with mechanics and other workingmen who dropped in on him. Associated Press veteran Merriman Smith later wrote that Roosevelt "claimed a lot of friends in comparatively low stations of life. I regarded them as his imaginary playmates."

Roosevelt merged lack of contact with a great show of friendliness that pulled in votes. He could love one and all among the "ordinary people," some journalists observed, because they were all imaginary playmates. He had the brilliant politician's ability to appear to be bonding with people while remaining thoroughly aloof. Playwright and presidential speechwriter Robert Sherwood spoke of FDR's "thickly forested interior." Eleanor Roosevelt said of her husband of four decades, "He had no real confidantes. I don't think I was ever his confidante, either."

Growing Up with Confidence

Roosevelt had no confidants but a lot of confidence. His playmates were imaginary but, from a young age, he believed in himself. He grew up that way not only because of class privilege and the expectation of being served, but also because of his theology and his expectation, similar to Woodrow Wilson's, that he was chosen to perform great services to mankind.

Franklin Roosevelt particularly learned to think that way during his college preparatory experience at the Groton School in Massachusetts. Nine of every ten students at Groton were members of *Social Register* families. Many of them left as partakers of the social gospel. Endicott Peabody, founder and headmaster of Groton, was a disciple of Charles Kingsley, founder of the Christian Socialist Movement in England. Peabody, in turn, became a lifelong influence on Roosevelt and many others. (When Roosevelt held private services in Washington before his inauguration and on other major occasions, he asked the Reverend Peabody to conduct them.)

Peabody proclaimed not only the social gospel but also social universalism—the belief that it was unfair for anyone to be poor, and that government's task was to eliminate this unfairness by siding with poorer over richer, worker over capitalist. The influence of Peabody's faith is evident in notebooks Franklin kept at Groton on a variety of political issues. For example, Franklin proposed the development of unions backed up by governmental arbitration boards as the way to "resist unjust exactions by the employers." Unjust exactions by unions did not receive emphasis.

Roosevelt went, per custom, from Groton to Harvard, there becoming editor in chief of the student newspaper, the *Crimson.* He was not overly concerned with his studies and graduated with a C average, but led an active social life. Acquaintances and distant relatives like Corinne Alsop, one of Theodore Roosevelt's nieces, privately called him "the feather duster" because he was handsome, chatty, and apparently superficial. But one of his society girlfriends, Alice Sohier, later said, "In a day and age when well-brought-up young men were expected to keep their hands off the persons of young ladies from respectable families, Franklin had to be slapped—hard."

At Harvard, Roosevelt's most vivid moment involved a brief encounter with the poor. Hurrying to South Station in Boston for a train to New York and a social weekend there, he carried his heavy suitcase aboard a streetcar. A wheel of the streetcar broke a few blocks from the station, so Roosevelt jumped out and started running, only to crash his suitcase into a small Italian boy. The child's mother leaned out of a tenement window and started yelling, so Roosevelt took from his pocket a new dollar bill and waved it in front of the boy; money, in Roosevelt's experience, always garnered a respectful response.

In this case, however, the boy proudly knocked the bill from Roosevelt's hand and called him a rich bully. When a crowd began to gather, Roosevelt picked up his suitcase, leaving the dollar in the gutter, and tried to walk away quietly. But some men from the crowd followed. He started running. They chased him. Roosevelt thought of throwing away his suitcase, "but I had my dress clothes in it." He leaped onto his train as it was pulling away, with pursuers shaking their fists from the platform and yelling. Roosevelt later told this story to show that his life had not been as sheltered as some supposed, and that he was able to escape from tight fixes.

Roosevelt graduated from Harvard in 1904 and married his even-more-sheltered cousin Eleanor Roosevelt in 1905. By 1914 they had four children, but Eleanor had also come to believe, as she later told her daughter Anna, that sex was "an ordeal to be borne." Franklin went through what he saw as his own ordeals: classes at the Columbia University School of Law, passing the New York bar exam, some indifferent lawyering which contributed to his growing reputation as a dilettante. Roosevelt came alive occupationally only when he entered politics, using his name to run successfully for state senator in 1910.

A Communitarian Ethos

The Groton influence of Endicott Peabody showed in a speech Roosevelt gave at the People's Forum in Troy, New York, in 1912. There he declared that western Europeans and Americans had achieved victory in the struggle for "the liberty of the individual," and that the new agenda should be a "struggle for the liberty of the community." The wrong ethos for a new age was, "every man does as he sees fit, even with a due regard to law and order." The new order should be, "march on with civilization in a way satisfactory to the well-being of the great majority of us."

In that speech Roosevelt outlined the philosophical base of what would eventually become the New Deal. He also forecast the rhetorical mode by which "community" could loom over individual liberty. "If we call the method regulation, people hold up their hands in horror and say 'un-American,' or 'dangerous,'" Roosevelt pointed out. "But if we call the same identical process co-operation, these same old fogeys will cry out 'well done'. . . . Cooperation is as good a word for the new theory as any other."

The difficulty, Roosevelt felt, lay in gaining enough political power to force others to cooperate, and in this regard Roosevelt decided to go far beyond what Endicott Peabody had taught. Leaders of New York City's Democratic machine, Tammany Hall, had seen how Theodore Roosevelt boosted the electoral base of the state's Republicans. To add state power to their local power, they were eager for a Roosevelt of their own. Franklin, with his pretty face, distinguished name, and patrician persona, was perfect for Tammany, which could give him votes and muscles in return—if he would make a deal.

At first Franklin would not. As a new state senator in 1911 he led a rebellion against the bosses. Journalists at the Legislative Correspondents' Association annual dinner described Roosevelt's ambition in song:

> *Said Franklin D.: "There's got to be*
> *Some new insurgency,*
> *We've got some boys to make a noise*
> *And leader I will be."*

The revolt, however, ended in defeat for the insurgents, as Tammany withdrew its original nominee for the Senate and substituted one who was worse. The reporters' song told of how Franklin D.

> *Can't compete with Tammany . . .*
> *Skies are clearin', keep on cheerin', Tammany.*

The newsmen saw Roosevelt insisting on good public relations for himself but ready to give up substance.

As journalists predicted, Roosevelt soon made his peace with corrupt bosses: "To have success, I believe in unity," he said. Over the years Roosevelt displayed his increasing ability to go along to get along. On July 4, 1917, he was the principal speaker at the Society of St. Tammany celebration in New York City, even though Tammany was working against a reform candidate for mayor that year. A newspaper photograph from the event shows Roosevelt and Tammany Hall head Charles Murphy standing together, with Murphy still wearing his embroidered Tammany sash and Roosevelt holding his rolled tightly in his fists. On the floor of the 1920 Democratic convention the two men spent much time together, signaling to their followers that an arrangement had been reached.

By then Roosevelt had gained a reputation in Washington through service as assistant secretary of the navy, the same post that the Republican Roosevelt had held on his way to the White House. There was a major difference, however: Theodore Roosevelt used every opportunity (such as the absence of his boss) to push the navy toward the aggressive posture it would adopt once the Spanish-American War began. Franklin Roosevelt charmed people into friendship but did not take the risks that would lead some to dislike him but all to respect him.

ADULTERY AND ITS OUTCOME

As Roosevelt's prospect for political happy days increased, his opportunities for domestic cheer diminished. Franklin and Eleanor Roosevelt were opposites in temperament: He was a balloon threatening to float away, she had psychological burdens so large that she wanted someone lighthearted to make her more buoyant. The union of opposites made sense, in theory: She would steady him, he would help her fly. In practice, the union did not work. Franklin was continually flirtatious, and Eleanor felt increasingly inadequate and lumpish.

The marriage as marriage essentially ended when Lucy Mercer entered it. From a distinguished Maryland Catholic family that had become poor, she came into the Roosevelts' life in 1914, when she was twenty-three. Eleanor, who described Lucy as "fair, slender, full-breasted and smiling," employed her as a social secretary. One friend remembers her sitting on the Roosevelts' rug, spreading invitations, bills, and letters on the floor and piling them neatly. Another called her smile "the most beautiful and winning I have ever seen."

She won Franklin Roosevelt. He ran to Lucy's arms often, especially during the summers when Eleanor and the children went off to their summer home on Campobello, a small island just off the coast of Maine, but in Canadian waters. Eleanor's cousin Alice Roosevelt Longworth supported his adultery, inviting both Franklin and Lucy to her home for dinner. Alice said of Franklin, "He deserved a good time. He was married to Eleanor."

The crisis came on September 20, 1918, after Roosevelt returned ill from an inspection trip to Europe and Eleanor unpacked her husband's travel bags as he lay ill with pneumonia. She discovered letters Lucy had sent him and confronted her husband. Eleanor said he could have a divorce if he wanted one. But Roosevelt's key advisor Louis Howe told him to count the political costs. Roosevelt's mother, Sara, who gave her son a substantial allowance that allowed him to live as a lord and not a minor bureaucrat, told him to count the economic costs. If he said yes to divorce, she insisted, he would be saying no to her dollars.

Roosevelt also apparently assessed the effects upon his five children, whom he enjoyed immensely. Threatened with a cutoff of much that was dear to him—fame, fortune, children—he cut off Lucy. A marriage of convenience and shared ambition replaced what initially had been a marriage of love. One of Eleanor's conditions for continuing the marriage was that she and her husband would desist from sexual relations. Another was that Roosevelt never see Lucy again. The first condition apparently was met. The second was met for two decades.

During 1919 and 1920 the Roosevelts in public put on an appearance of amiability, but in private their relations were still jagged. Eleanor wrote in her diary one evening a description of many hard evenings: "Dined alone. Franklin nervous and overwrought and I very stupid and trying. Result a dreadful fracas." Franklin did attend church more often than before—Eleanor had complained about his spending Sunday mornings on the golf course—but the messages he heard were more social gospel than the life-changing gospel of man's sin and Christ's grace. Because of his name Roosevelt received the nomination for vice president in 1920 on a Democratic ticket that was obviously going nowhere.

Republicans did not bring up the Lucy Mercer affair during the campaign that year, although it had been gossiped about in Washington, probably because their winning candidate, Warren Harding, was an adulterer himself. Politicians who do not get burned in sexual scandals are rarely twice shy; they are more likely to believe they have charmed lives. Roosevelt was a superstitious man, with lucky numbers, lucky days, lucky hats, lucky shoes, and a fear of Friday the thirteenth. He also saw himself as a man capable of outrunning those who might chase him. Campaigning kept him out of adulterous trouble for a while, but by the end of 1920, after the Democrats were routed, that restraint was gone.

Turner Catledge of the *New York Times* later told friends that Roosevelt's first instinct was always to lie; sometimes in midsentence, according to Catledge, Roosevelt would realize that he could get away with the truth in this instance, and he would switch to accuracy. That tendency already was apparent in 1920, and there was nothing in the Roosevelts' loveless, sexless marriage to indicate that the Lucy Mercer affair would not be repeated when opportunity knocked. Elliott Roosevelt wrote about his parents' "partnership arrangement," and noted that "they never enjoyed *anything* in the way of light-heartedness in their lives."

Biblical teaching about long-term rather than immediate gratification could not be expected to have much of an effect because Roosevelt relied on his own feelings rather than Scripture. His trips to church produced not faith in God's judgment but, as Eleanor Roosevelt wrote, "confidence in himself. . . . He could pray for help and guidance and have faith in his own judgment as a result." Something else was needed to save Roosevelt from destroying himself.

PROVIDENTIAL POLIO

Polio, which Roosevelt came down with in 1921, removed him from politics for several years, but saved his political career, although not in the way conventionally described. Looking back after his father's death, Elliott Roosevelt summarized well the conventional story: FDR as "a restless, flighty young man who learned to concentrate only when he lost the use of his legs, thereby acquiring fresh stability of mind and compassion through suffering." Elliott said that analysis was wrong: "Throughout his adult life, his was the same, consistent personality, the mixture . . . of lion and fox. There was just one, purely physical difference: After 1921 he could not walk."

But there was another physical difference: Roosevelt could not run around after other women. For the first several years after he was stricken, physical helplessness ruled his life. Later, although examining physicians specifically noted that polio had not left Roosevelt impotent, he never liked to be seen unable to do what others did, and it seems unlikely that he would have risked being placed in an inadequate position sexually, except with someone to whom he was very attached over a long period of time. Polio kept Roosevelt from heading toward repeated adultery, which likely would have been exposed at some point, ending any presidential aspirations. Polio may have saved his political career.

The first stage of Roosevelt's life with polio lasted from the summer of 1921 through 1924, and brought spiritual as well as physical trauma. Overnight at Campobello, Roosevelt lost all feeling below the waist. For a time he also lost his faith in himself, and believed, he told his future secretary of labor, Frances Perkins, that God had abandoned him. Roosevelt, downsized, had a choice: He could try to enlarge himself once again, or he could enlarge his understanding of God. He chose a secular form of salvation.

During the second stage of Roosevelt's recovery, from 1925 to 1928, he was strongly bulwarked by his private secretary, Missy LeHand. He was forty-three, she twenty-five, when she began traveling with him regularly. Roosevelt spent 116 of the 208 weeks of those four years away from home, often trying to walk again. Eleanor was with him for four of those weeks, Missy LeHand for 110 of them. All observers attested that Roosevelt and his secretary had an extraordinarily close personal relationship. Roosevelt's cousin Laura Delano once insisted that "Missy was the only woman Franklin ever loved." Elliott Roosevelt thought their love was physical, but that is not certain.

Paralysis was very difficult for Roosevelt, but it did convey some political advantages. His misery was great and his determination to walk even greater, but the one bit of silver lining was that a paralyzed man could be in his bedroom alongside a secretary in her nightgown, and no one would take him to task for it. One man, John F. Kennedy's father, Joseph P. Kennedy, tried. When Roosevelt urged him to carry on his adultery with movie star Gloria Swanson more discreetly, Kennedy shot back, "Not until you get rid of Missy LeHand." Roosevelt had his revenge many years later when he recalled Kennedy from his ambassadorship to Great Britain and sent Missy to meet the Kennedy plane.

Pro-Roosevelt reporters milked the paralysis to propose that Roosevelt was not another politician but a man of character, as indeed he was in his battle with polio. He fought daily to go one more step down the driveway, but did that make him heroic in other realms? Journalist-historian Will Durant, reporting the 1928 Democratic convention for the *New York World,* called Roosevelt "beyond comparison the finest man that has appeared at either convention." Durant wrote of

Roosevelt's "figure tall and proud even in suffering" and his "face of classic profile; pale with years of struggle against paralysis." Adversity overcome can build character, but it also built a public image that was far different from Roosevelt's eight years before, when journalists generally thought him to be an affable lightweight who filled a suit well.

By 1928, Roosevelt and Tammany Hall were ready to go to work once again. Durant was uneasy about his hero's alliance with the political bosses: "A man softened and cleansed and illumined with pain. What in the name of Croker and Tweed is he doing here?" Mid-nineteenth-century presidential candidates played up log cabin backgrounds. When Roosevelt ran for governor of New York that year, reporters who respected his war against pain no longer called him the pampered son of mansions and private trains.

RISING ABOVE DEPRESSION

When the stock market crashed in 1929 and the depression followed, many who wanted governmental action thought the right man was in the right place: Herbert Hoover was in the White House. Hoover had built a reputation as a great engineer and a great humanitarian, delivering food to the European poor trying to survive in the wake of world war. Early in 1920, Roosevelt was pleased with talk of a Democratic ticket with Hoover for president and himself for vice president. Soon afterwards Roosevelt wrote to a friend that Hoover "is certainly a wonder, and I wish we could make him President of the United States. There could not be a better one." At the end of the decade, with such a background and reputation, Hoover was not about to let a depression run its course as others had. He wanted to engineer rapid recovery.

Hoover's strategies were traditional Whig/Republican. First, he encouraged states to spend more on internal improvements and public buildings, and step up the federal building program. But since government construction was paid for by taxes removed from private sources, Hoover was really shifting resources from one part of the economy to the other. Second, he followed the Whig/Republican playbook by raising tariffs, with the goal of preserving domestic American jobs. Hoover called a special session of Congress in 1930 to promote protectionist measures. He came out of it with the Smoot-Hawley tariff that raised rates on most goods from 31 to 49 percent, but that approach backfired. Trade tanked.

Meanwhile, Roosevelt was in Albany, working out of the traditional Democratic playbook with calls for power to states and less power in Washington. He used and often abused elements of the nineteenth-century Democratic tradition. He liked to quote Andrew Jackson saying, "The spirit of equity requires that the great interests of agriculture, commerce, and manufactures should be equally treated." Roosevelt did not reveal that Jackson was proposing equity in the courtroom, not equity in terms of increased government regulation and income redistribution. He occasionally brought in suggestions from the new playbook—more federal "oversight"—developed out of Bryan's rhetoric and the Wilson administration's experience.

As the pleas to do something, anything, amid the depression intensified, Roosevelt's few innovations in public policy—more state welfare—did not receive much scrutiny. Neither did his arrangements for private welfare. In the governor's mansion, Roosevelt and Missy had adjoining bedrooms joined by a door with clear glass panels, while Eleanor's bedroom was down the hall. Elliott Roosevelt commented about the education of Roosevelt children in their teens and early twenties: "It was not unusual to enter his sunny corner room and find Missy with him in her nightgown. There was no attempt to conceal their relationship. Everyone within the family had come to accept the fact that Missy was a special part of our family. I would go in at the start of the day, and the three of us would talk with no embarrassment between us."

Gaining nomination and election in 1932 was surprisingly easy. Roosevelt had the name. He was governor of the largest state. He was also developing a new Democratic message. Much of it was what he had broached in 1912 in speaking about the rhetorical importance of using words like "cooperation" rather than "regulation." When Roosevelt spoke of expanding the federal government, his words were "social action for the prevention of poverty." By merging Bryan's ideas of class warfare and Wilson's calls for the administrative state, he was positioning the Democrats to become more Whiggish than the Republicans, with federal power, in theory, on the side of the poor.

Roosevelt had observed much from his train window. He saw that Democrats could tax the minority to give to the majority, and then reap the electoral credit. There is still a myth that Roosevelt was experimenting all the time, and it is clearly true that he did try many experimental programs. But they were pointed in a particular direction, and his claims that they were just self-evident responses to crisis were political poor-mouthing. A consistent religious vision, based in the social gospel of his youth, underlay his response to crisis.

Roosevelt spelled out his vision during the 1932 campaign, most notably in an October speech in Detroit. There he called for government expansion and emphasized that "the ideal of social justice of which I have spoken—an ideal that years ago might have been thought over-advanced—is now accepted by the moral leadership of all the great religious groups of the country." To show that he was not "radical," Roosevelt proceeded to quote from Christian theological liberals, citing with particular relish a complaint from the Federal Council of Churches about how "the wealthy are overpaid in sharp contrast with the underpaid masses."

Not wishing to offend, Roosevelt also quoted an American rabbinical comment: "We talk of the stabilization of business. What we need is the stabilization of human justice and happiness." A leading rabbi, Roosevelt noted, called for "a revamping of the entire method of approach to these problems of the economic order." Normally, however, Roosevelt called himself "a Christian and a Democrat" and implied that those who were not the latter also were not the former. Ironically, Roosevelt was ready to do away with the system of private and church aid to the poor that encouraged church members to follow in Christ's steps. In Detroit he argued, "if we set up a system of justice we shall have small need for the exercise of mere philanthropy."

THE NEW DEAL'S NEW GOSPEL

Since clothing himself in biblical robes proved effective during the election campaign, Roosevelt returned to scriptural themes in his enormously effective first inaugural address. There he argued that American land was bountiful and great productivity possible, but the problem was that sin had entered this garden. The depression had been brought on by the "lure of profit," the stubbornness and incompetence of the "rulers of the exchange of mankind's goods," the "unscrupulous money changers" who lived by "the rules of a generation of self-seekers." Such enemies of the people, he insisted, "have no vision, and when there is no vision the people perish."

Like an effective preacher who brings down his congregation so he can then buoy them up, Roosevelt moved on to the good news: "The money changers have fled from their high seats in the temple of our civilization. We may now restore that temple to the ancient truths. The measure of the restoration lies in the extent to which we apply social values more noble than mere monetary profit." Roosevelt explained afterwards that he had thought of the line about money changers in the temple while sitting in a pew in St. James Episcopal Church in Hyde Park. But he never made clear what temple he was describing. Was it the Bank of the United States of Jackson's day, a public-private partnership? Was it the speculative stock exchange? Or was it the private enterprise system generally?

However nonspecific the metaphor, Roosevelt's intention to follow in Bryan's and Wilson's footsteps was clear. He wanted to increase federal power so as "to put people to work . . . in part by direct recruiting by the Government itself, treating the task as we would treat the emergency of a war." He would do this through "the unifying of relief activities which today are often scattered, uneconomical, and unequal"—through "national planning for and supervision of all forms of transportation and communications and other utilities which have a definitely public character." The era of big government had begun.

But Roosevelt remembered what he had learned in 1912—talk cooperation, not regulation—as if he had a string tied around his finger. He said he was proposing not "government control" but "partnership." Roosevelt also applied his religious understanding that the depression could not be beaten by bread alone: He said he wished to "add to the comfort and happiness of hundreds of thousands of people," yet the greatest problem was "a loss of spiritual values" in America. The Civilian Conservation Corps, Public Works Administration, Civil Works Administration, and other programs were designed not merely to redistribute funds to the poor but to provide work that could restore the spirit.

This difference was more than rhetorical; the work emphasis of New Deal welfare programs was unlike the Great Society redistribution that followed a generation later. The U.S. Conference of Mayors resolved that Americans should "never consent to the abandonment of the work principle. . . . The dole, based on idleness and groceries, has no place in our American scheme of society." Roosevelt aide Harry Hopkins described "the unemployed themselves protesting against the indignity of public charity. . . . They were accustomed to making a return for their livelihood . . . from which they chiefly drew their self-respect."

After some initial experimentation, Roosevelt was right to make Hopkins's Works Progress Administration the centerpiece of his relief efforts from 1935 on. The WPA, called by its critics "We Piddle Around," was the object of some sarcastic stories about digging and filling up holes, but WPA workers did produce by 1940 over half a million miles of roads and over 100,000 bridges and public buildings, along with 18,000 miles of storm and sanitary sewers, 200 aviation landing fields, 200 million garments for poor individuals, and much else. Most important, a typical recipient who had been unemployed could report, "Now I can look my children straight in the eyes. . . . [When] the kids in the house find that you contribute nothing toward their support, very soon they begin to lose respect for you. It's different now. I'm the bread-winner of the house and everybody respects me."

SHIFTING LOYALTY FROM PRIVATE TO GOVERNMENTAL

But spirit-reviving had its complications. During the 1930s contemporary analysts concluded that New Deal publicists were, in the words of James McCamy, a Bennington College professor, deliberately trying to discredit private institutions in order to promote a "shift of loyalty from private to public authority and decision." Families and churches had cared for most orphans and most of the elderly, but Roosevelt in 1934 stated, "There is no reason why everybody in the United States should not be covered. . . . Cradle to the grave—from the cradle to the grave they ought to be in a social insurance system."

Cradle to the grave sovereignty belonged only to God, Theodore Roosevelt had believed, but Franklin Roosevelt's expressed goal in 1936 was "to eliminate . . . chances in life." Concerning the bad old days he orated, "We have had to take our chances about old age in days past. We have had to take our chances with depressions and boom times. We have had to take chances on our jobs. We have had to take chances on buying homes." Now, the possibility of failure could be eliminated. Roosevelt's Groton headmaster, Endicott Peabody, loved such talk, and saw his own hand in it. He wrote to his famed pupil in 1935, "It is a great thing for our country to have before it the leadership of a man who cares primarily for spiritual things."

Others were not so pleased. The Democratic presidential candidate in 1928, Al Smith, broke with the New Deal and attacked the Roosevelt administration by saying, "It is all right with me if they want to disguise themselves as Karl Marx or Lenin or any of the rest of that bunch, but I won't stand for . . . allowing them to march under the banner of Jackson or Cleveland." Jackson and Cleveland had been known for saying "no" with at times dour faces; under Roosevelt, the Democratic song became "Happy days are here again."

In opposition to Roosevelt and in frustration about his success, Republicans became what they had never before been, the party of constitutional restraint. Leaders such as Herbert Hoover began warning about what would happen if Washington appropriations cut into traditions of civic responsibility, church generosity, and mutual self-help: "If we start appropriations of this character we have not only impaired something infinitely valuable in the life of the American people but have struck at the roots of self-government. Once this has happened it is not the cost of a few score million but we are faced with the abyss of reliance in future upon Government charity in some form or another."

Most Americans in 1936 seemed to care more about the present than the future. During his reelection campaign that year Roosevelt brilliantly alternated fiery class warfare speeches with pastorals. The former pitted "economic royalists" against "the organized power of

Government" (Government, like God, was capitalized.) The latter quoted the Twenty-third Psalm—"He makes me lie down in green pastures; He leads me beside still waters"—and contended that declarations about God from three thousand years ago could be replaced by declarations coming from Washington now: If wages were raised, those who "work in the mill or in the office" could have "a life in green pastures and beside still waters." Roosevelt won in a landslide.

His flexible method of reading Scripture carried over to his method of reading the Constitution. Discussing the inaugural ceremonies in 1937, Roosevelt said, "When the Chief Justice read me the oath and came to the words 'support the Constitution of the United States' I felt like saying: 'Yes, but it's the Constitution as I understand it, flexible enough to meet any new problem of democracy—not the kind of Constitution your Court has raised up as a barrier to progress and democracy.'" Roosevelt worked to get the constitutional clerics out of his way by expanding the Court, but the "court-packing" plan prompted charges of executive arrogance, with former FDR speechwriter Raymond Moley referring to Roosevelt's "Messianic complex" and labeling him a "tin Jesus."

Roosevelt, however, was a messiah whose mandate required constant renewal. As Bryan had broken the stay-at-home mold for presidential candidates, so Franklin Roosevelt broke the twentieth-century pattern of campaigning only during campaigns or in extraordinary circumstances like the League of Nations debate. He anticipated Bill Clinton in campaigning all the time—and always for an instant feedback through supportive public opinion, not a laying of groundwork for more citizen involvement.

This was especially necessary for Roosevelt because in 1937 the economy collapsed again, with unemployment in 1938 reaching that of 1933, despite the continuation of programs such as the WPA and the CCC. Some of those programs may even have prolonged the depression by soaking up resources that otherwise would have been used in the private sector, and some programs even created more unemployment. Acreage limitations imposed by the Agricultural Adjustment Administration, for example, forced use of better technology to gain maximum efficiency. Sharecroppers and farm laborers, who were productive as long as acreage remained large enough to tolerate some inefficiency, lost jobs to machines.

What kept Roosevelt going even when the economy dipped downward again were the political alliances he had made with urban bosses. Jackson and Cleveland had opposed on principle taking money from one part of the country to benefit another, but Roosevelt first pushed through the Tennessee Valley Authority project, and then turned to projects desired by urban political bosses. Depression-era property tax revenues were down, so city officials had less money to spend. Demands from constituents for jobs and other favors were up. When Tammany Hall in 1933 had no choice economically but to lay off city employees and reduce services, Republican Fiorello La Guardia was elected mayor of New York City. Democratic city machines across the country needed money, and fast, if they were to avoid similarly unceremonious boots. State governments were often unwilling and sometimes unable to send funds.

Federal welfare expenditures rescued the city Democratic machines. Works Progress Administration and other funds had to be passed out; party workers did the passing. Bosses who had their photos taken with Roosevelt gained credit for new schools, hospitals, water and sewer systems, bridges and roads. He had started out in politics regarding urban machines as his nemesis; he became their savior, and they his.*
In the 1932 election the twelve largest cities gave Roosevelt 25 percent of his popular vote margin, but in Roosevelt's last race, in 1944, those urban party bosses produced 65 percent of his edge. On almost every New Deal policy issue, congressmen grateful for city projects were Roosevelt's most reliable supporters.

*Some examples:
• In Chicago, Roosevelt gave Mayor Edward J. Kelly control of 200,000 WPA jobs in Illinois, and appointed Kelly ally Robert Dunham the WPA director for the state. Between 1933 and 1940 federal funds enabled Kelly to build a subway, airport, new roads and parks, public housing projects, and thirty new schools. Since the federal government paid 88 percent of Chicago's relief and jobs costs, the state government 11 percent, and the city itself only one penny of every dollar, Kelly did not have to raise property taxes to pay for these projects. He received new terms as mayor in 1935, 1939, and 1943, and delivered Illinois to Roosevelt time after time.
• In Jersey City, dominated by Frank Hague, the WPA alone employed between 75,000 and 100,000 New Jersey residents, most of them in the northern part of the

INTO WAR

Despite the economic failure of many of his depression-fighting projects, Roosevelt called his first two terms successful and even stood against George Washington's precedent by seeking and gaining a third. With the sluggish economy making it evident that his presidential reputation could not depend on bread alone, Roosevelt argued in 1941, in his third inaugural address, that "It is not enough to clothe and feed the body of this Nation, and instruct and inform its mind. For there is also the spirit [that] speaks to us in our daily lives in ways often unnoticed, because they seem so obvious. It speaks to us here in the Capitol of the Nation. It speaks to us through the processes of governing."

In his first inaugural address Roosevelt had been Christ driving out the money changers; in his third it seemed that the Holy Spirit was Roosevelt's majority whip for delivering legislation. But the process of governing became both harder and easier for him when Pearl Harbor transformed him into a wartime statesman. On the one hand, he had Germany and Japan to contend with; on the other, wartime economic needs finally broke the depression, and wartime centralization even

---

state. To get those and other New Deal jobs, applicants often had to acquire cards handed out only by Hague's ward leaders and cronies. Federal funds allowed Hague to expand the Jersey City Medical Center into a 2,000-bed operation, creating more patronage jobs and a humanitarian image. Some newspapers criticized Hague's crushing of political dissidents in his region, but Roosevelt during an October 1936 campaign stop praised Hague for his "great service" to constituents. Roosevelt also prevented federal prosecution of Hague for mail tampering, and Hague in turn delivered New Jersey.

• In Kansas City, Roosevelt made Matthew Murray, a crony of Mayor Tom Pendergast, WPA director for Missouri. Missouri governor Guy Park, a Pendergast ally, referred all Missouri residents seeking federal jobs to Pendergast, and about 88,000 joined the WPA rolls. But Pendergast had a falling-out with Park's successor, Lloyd Stark, just as scandals concerning police collusion with criminals and ballot fraud put Pendergast's name in unflattering headlines. Pendergast lost control of the Missouri Democratic Party in 1938, so FDR then threw him overboard, not only giving his federally paid patronage opportunities to a more reliable hack, but supporting a Justice Department investigation of Pendergast's bribe-taking and a Treasury Department investigation of Pendergast's tax returns. In 1939, Pendergast went to prison at Leavenworth.

greater than that of World War I made Washington even more the controller of industry.

Much can still be debated concerning American readiness. Isolationist sentiment held Roosevelt back, but so did his confidence that, even internationally, we had little to fear but fear itself. In December 1937, for example, Roosevelt predicted to his cabinet that in the event of war against Japan, the navy would readily "block" Japanese advances, with the entire nation of Japan "brought to her knees within a year." When the war began, Army Chief of Staff George Marshall was concerned about Roosevelt's subjectivity: "I frankly was fearful of Mr. Roosevelt's introducing political methods of which he was a genius into a military thing which had to be on a fixed basis. . . . You can't treat military factors in the way you do political factors." Marshall always worried about Roosevelt's "tendency to shift and handle things loosely," his "cigarette-holder gestures."

Yet, Marshall came to realize, there was some advantage in having a politician as commander in chief. After the war he said, concerning the generals' dislike for some Roosevelt decisions that produced victories without great strategic significance, "We failed to see that the leader in a democracy has to keep the people entertained." That sentence reflected some exasperation but increasing admiration: American dedication to the war effort started out at high pitch because of Pearl Harbor, but Roosevelt over the subsequent three and a half years kept involvement high by communicating war objectives plainly and persuasively and (helped by all-too-real villains in Germany and Japan) turning the whole effort into a holy war.

In 1942, Roosevelt also did a better job of placing the right military leaders (George Marshall, Douglas MacArthur, Ernest King, Hap Arnold, Dwight Eisenhower) in command than Lincoln had done in 1862. He misjudged the military potential of China and, toward war's end, the peacekeeping potential of the Soviet Union, but he showed good strategic understanding of the importance of winning naval battles in the North Atlantic and going on the offensive in the South Pacific. His friendly relations with Joseph Stalin led to postwar disaster, yet his ability to relate well to Winston Churchill and other Allied governmental heads made that postwar come sooner.

But Roosevelt's most useful trait, during the war as during the depression, was the ability to communicate confidence to his constituents, an ability that arose out of his faith in himself and his progressive reading of history. During World War II the rector of St. James, the Episcopal church at Hyde Park that Roosevelt occasionally attended, put up a sign labeling his building "The Church of the President." Roosevelt laughed one Sunday when he saw that someone had added the words "(Formerly God's)"—and it was faith more in Roosevelt than God that animated some Americans. God, after all, spoke of raising some civilizations and breaking others. Roosevelt, in his inaugural address on March 4, 1945, gave assurances: "I remember that my old schoolmaster, Dr. Peabody, said. . . , 'The great fact to remember is that the trend of civilization itself is forever upward."

Roosevelt sometimes had trouble responding personally to friends whose trend was downward. Early in the war Missy LeHand, his wife-in-effect for sixteen years, had a stroke that paralyzed her left arm and leg, and left her almost entirely unable to speak. Missy eventually moved in with her relatives in Somerville, Massachusetts, and Roosevelt largely abandoned her. The LeHand relatives were so upset when Roosevelt did not even call during the Christmas/New Year's fortnight that one wrote a protest note: "She started crying New Year's Eve about 11:30 and we couldn't stop her, and then she had a heart spell and kept calling 'F.D. come please come, Oh, F.D.'—it really was the saddest thing I ever hope to see. We were all crying. . . . She was especially expecting you to call on Christmas Day. . . .'"

Roosevelt, however, had not forgotten her. He altered his will so that up to half the income from his estate could be used to pay Missy LeHand's medical bills, with the remainder going to Eleanor. (Roosevelt told his son James, "If it embarrasses Mother, I'm sorry. It shouldn't, but it may.") As it turned out, money did not have to substitute for love once again in Roosevelt's life, for Missy died in 1944. She had a cerebral hemorrhage while looking at old photographs of him. He had a navy cargo ship named in her honor.

Meanwhile, Roosevelt had begun seeing Lucy Mercer again, after a parenthesis of more than two decades; she had married an elderly man who had a long illness and eventually died in 1944 also. They dined at the White House when Eleanor was away, spent time together in New Jersey and South Carolina, and spoke frequently on the phone. Switchboard operators had instructions to put her right through to Roosevelt when she called; if others were in the vicinity he would sometimes speak in French. When Roosevelt died in April 1945, the last face he saw, according to Franklin, Jr., was Lucy Mercer's.

And what of Roosevelt's legacy? Especially for a president elected four times, that short question needs more than a simple answer. In some ways Roosevelt's limitations became the nation's strengths. Herbert Hoover, a realist who had observed poverty firsthand, did not help matters by pushing for higher tariffs and some public works in the Whig tradition, but he went no further, knowing that additional government programs in the long term were likely to hurt more than they helped. Roosevelt, however, viewing life from a railway car, did not have a ground-in sense of how bad things were objectively, and therefore was free to emphasize subjectivity. His most famous sound bite, "the only thing we have to fear is fear itself," arose partially out of ignorance; breadwinners unemployed for many months were staring at some cold realities, not phantasms.

Yet, since Roosevelt rushed in where Hoover feared to tread, he did provide additional temporary help that preserved some families, while probably hindering the full recovery of an economy that did not spring back until rising war production lifted all boats. Roosevelt's characteristic impatience with detail also had its immediate pluses but long-term minuses. Concerning social security, he said, "This system ought to be operated through the post offices. Just simple and natural—nothing elaborate or alarming about it." But the system was far more complicated than that, and at the end of the century alarm bells are sounding.

Theologically, Roosevelt was essentially neo-orthodox, choosing to believe without caring much whether the grounds for belief were present. Politically, he also was willing to believe in almost anything that held out hope. But over time, objectivity bit in, for there was more to fear than fear itself. Those who knew that private enterprise worked best could legitimately fear government programs that soaked up otherwise available capital. Those who wanted innovation could fear programs that froze industry in old patterns. Under Roosevelt income redistribution became a Democratic Party staple. The political party that in Cleveland's day was known for saying "no" became the party of "happy days are here again."

Roosevelt's success at glossing over problems and twisting data established a low bar for his successors. He raised expectations in exactly the manner that Jackson and Cleveland feared: The president would be the great bellhop, and citizens could demand that he come to their relief. But as to presidential faith and conduct, Roosevelt continued the trend of lowering expectations to half-mast: He saw utility in Scripture, but certainly wasn't bound by it either in his private life or in his public policy innovations. Yet, harsh judgments of Roosevelt should always be softened by remembrance of the high degrees of difficulty in place in 1933 when he began his high dives in public policy. When a wallowing-in-depression America was sorrowing early in 1933, Roosevelt's confidence—even though it grew out of the view from a train window, the theology of a toothless god, and the ability to escape scandal—did help for a time.

CHAPTER 12

John F. Kennedy

John F. Kennedy provides the ultimate example of both distinct public and private images and the complexities of biography. He spoke in his inaugural address about a willingness to "pay any price, bear any burden, meet any hardship, support any friend, oppose any foe to assure the survival and the success of liberty." Yet, as is now well known, he went to great lengths to assure the survival and extension of his own sexual liberty. The patterns of secrecy and cover-up that he developed while committing rampant adultery leaked into his public policy work, sometimes with dire results. Yet, when his mindset of sexual ruthlessness translated into diplomatic heat during the Cuban missile crisis, he won a crucial cold war victory.

In the light of all the well-sourced sexual revelations that have come out in recent years, recording Kennedy's adultery is like shooting fish in a barrel. The harder task is to make substantive connections between the private and public Kennedy, and to connect his religious beliefs with his sexual practice. Was he just someone given gifts—financial, political, sexual—throughout his life, and finally the gift of a presidency for which he was unprepared? How, then, can we explain a superb performance during the twelve days of October 1962 and achievements in other areas as well?

The Kennedy story begins with the development of his beliefs concerning God and sex. For John Kennedy, born in 1917, attendance at Sunday mass was an obligation as he was growing up. But his father, Joseph, also taught his sons that real men ignored most of God's ten suggestions during the week. Joseph Kennedy modeled a concept of marriage by maintaining his wife, Rose, in homes and clothes, but skipping fidelity or affection. He brought mistresses into the family home (one for several months) and propositioned his sons' girlfriends. He also provided explicit teaching: John Kennedy once recalled, "Dad told all the boys to get laid as often as possible."

Prep school and college were more of the same. John Kennedy was a mediocre student at the Choate School in Connecticut but "very successful with girls," according to roommate Lem Billings: "Very." They were nervous activists, however. After seventeen-year-old Kennedy and Billings visited a Harlem brothel and paid $3 each, they worried about venereal disease and bought salves and creams at a hospital. The panicked Kennedy woke up a doctor in the middle of the night and paid for an examination, with soothing results. Kennedy then went on to Harvard and wrote to Billings, who entered Princeton, "I can now get tail as often and as free as I want."

Like Franklin Roosevelt, John Kennedy had it easy in other ways as well. He graduated from Harvard in 1940, after writing a senior thesis on British appeasement that he finished with the help of a personal secretary and five stenographers. The thesis was marred by poor writing and faulty analysis, according to faculty readers, but Joseph Kennedy thought it important that his son be an author: "You would be surprised how a book that really makes the grade with high-class people stands you in good stead for years to come." Ambassador Kennedy hired *New York Times* columnist Arthur Krock to restructure the senior thesis, and a ghostwriter to knock into shape what the ghost called "a mishmash, ungrammatical . . . sentences without subjects and verbs . . . a very sloppy job, mostly magazine and newspaper clippings stuck together."

Krock then came up with a title, *While England Slept,* and placed it with a major publisher; when the book came out, Joseph Kennedy bought between 30,000 and 40,000 copies to vault it onto best-seller lists. He and Krock then worked contacts to gain favorable reviews about "the surprise bestseller" that was creating such a sensation. John Kennedy was always very proud of how he had written such a popular and highly praised policy book at age twenty-three. When former Harvard roommate Blair Clark recalled years later that he had rewritten two of the chapters, John Kennedy protested, "You never did a goddamn thing on it."

In such ways Kennedy became used to accepting praise for the good deeds of others, while dodging responsibility for his own misfeasance. Early in World War II, while working at the Office of Naval Intelligence, he became sexually involved with a scintillating Danish woman, Inga Arvad, who was thought by the FBI to be a Nazi spy. (Kennedy called her "Inga Binga"; Hitler had called her a "perfect example of Nordic beauty.") Inga Arvad later told her son details of her Kennedy connection, reporting that "If he wanted to make love, you'd make love—now. They'd have fifteen minutes to get to a party and she'd say she didn't want to. He'd look at his watch and say, we've got ten minutes, let's go. . . . an awful lot of self-centeredness."

Relying on others to indulge his self-centeredness, however, did not leave Kennedy much of a center. Owing so much of his advancement to his father's manipulation, he never developed an independent sphere of influence, and later relied heavily on his father's questionable political judgment even in making cabinet appointments. When the FBI placed a microphone in Arvad's apartment and wiretaps on her phone, so that details of the affair became known in Washington and chortled over for years, Kennedy became subject to blackmail. Most naval intelligence officers would have received a dishonorable discharge for cavorting with a suspected enemy agent, but Kennedy's connections allowed him to avoid that blot and move to command *PT 109* in the Pacific. Even so, possession of the Arvad records and others protected FBI director J. Edgar Hoover from any Kennedy White House attempts to reduce his sovereignty.

Always, there was protection. In the Pacific, Kennedy incompetently had his ship sunk, but through heroic swimming saved the life of one crewman and perhaps more. His father's dollars covered up the incompetence and publicized the valor in a way that catapulted Kennedy to Congress and beyond. In Washington in the late forties, Kennedy's sexual rotation was so extensive that he didn't even ask first names, but merely referred to young women as "kiddo." Lem Billings said, "He knew he was using women to prove his masculinity, and sometimes it depressed him."

Kennedy did not feel the consequences of his actions either emotionally or politically. The testimony of coldness is intense. Anthony Gallucio, a family friend, said that promiscuity "was just physical and social activity for him. . . . Kennedy never got emotionally involved." Katharine Stammers, who dated him, said, "He really didn't give a damn. He liked to . . . enjoy himself, but he was quite unreliable. He did as he pleased." Family friend John White said of Kennedy and women, "He was completely driven to dominate them. Once he got them, he lost interest and moved on to the next." He was publicly unaccountable as well because no newspaper would touch the story, fearing instant economic retaliation from Joseph Kennedy. Political opponents, like press editors, had nude pictures of him together with various women—Kennedy liked souvenirs—but none was ever used.

Kennedy's recklessness continued after he entered the Senate and was married to Jacqueline Bouvier in 1953. FBI reports said that his "extracurricular activities" were a standard joke around the Senate Office Building. At one point Kennedy even stuck above his desk a photograph of himself and other men and women posing nude on a yacht. Newspapers and magazines did not pursue Kennedy adultery stories, partly because he did not employ secretaries merely for sexual services, so his activity was seen as not having an impact on the public payroll, and partly because Joseph Kennedy's power could threaten press payrolls.

The Kennedy publicity apparatus was able to accentuate the positive as well as eliminate the negative. Kennedy hired Professor Jules Davids of Georgetown and others to do research and writing of a mid-1950s book on political leaders, and Theodore Sorensen to style it. The result, *Profiles in Courage,* won a Pulitzer Prize when Joseph Kennedy used his contacts to do some jury tampering; *Profiles in Courage* had not made the list of eight recommendations from the Pulitzer judges. When journalists such as Drew Pearson suggested that the book was ghostwritten, Kennedy aggressively denied that and got away with the defense. Only after his death did disclosures show that he was lying.

Some people were offended. A Georgetown couple, Mr. and Mrs. Leonard Kater, both Catholics, rented a room in 1958 to Kennedy's twenty-one-year-old secretary, Pamela Turnure, and then became used to hearing the sounds of sex. Angry that Kennedy was styling himself an observant Catholic, they photographed him coming away from a tryst and then confronted him: "How dare you run for president under the guise of a good Christian? ... You are unfit to be the Catholic standard bearer of this country." The Katers tried to get the *Washington Star* to investigate, but editors evidently believed in the separation of church and extramarital sex.

Kennedy continued to practice adultery even as he began running for president in 1959 and 1960. Kennedy met a San Francisco woman, Joan Hitchcock, at the Santa Monica home of his brother-in-law Peter Lawford, and sometimes spent the night with her in a small motel in Malibu, checking in under the name of John Thompson. He was more discreet as he became more widely known and received the nomination, yet, as Joan Hitchcock related, their "relationship was no big secret to anyone in California."

KENNEDY AND THE FATHER IN HEAVEN

Reporters not only missed the story on Kennedy sex but also misunderstood the story on Kennedy religion. Kennedy consistently spoke about the irrelevance of his Catholicism to his job performance. The Jesuit weekly *America* insisted that "Mr. Kennedy doesn't really believe that. No religious man, be he Catholic, Protestant, or Jew, holds such an opinion." But *America*'s editors did not understand that Kennedy was not a religious man, in terms of either theistic belief or any desire to apply the Bible to public policy issues.

Kennedy's beliefs were clearer to those around him. His speechwriter Theodore Sorensen said Kennedy "cared not a whit for theology. . . . During the eleven years I knew him, I never heard him pray aloud in the presence of others." Sorensen gave Kennedy lots of scriptural language in his inaugural address: "I have sworn before you and Almighty God. . . . the rights of man come not from the generosity of the state, but from the hand of God. . . . the command of Isaiah to 'undo the heavy burdens . . . [and] let the oppressed go free.' . . . asking His blessing and His help, but knowing that here on earth God's work must truly be our own." Only that last line may have been heartfelt; Kennedy, according to historian and aide Arthur Schlesinger, Jr., believed that religion was man-made. That belief freed him from "black-and-white moralism."

Kennedy also believed in the separation of not only church and state but also God (should there be one) and world. Once, when Kennedy answered a question concerning U.S. recognition of Communist China by saying it "was not a moral issue," a priest asked him whether "all law comes from God." Kennedy snapped back, "I'm a Catholic, so of course I believe it—but that has nothing to do with international law." God had nothing to do with government; when the governor of Pennsylvania sent Kennedy a large wooden Bible stand as a present, it made sense for Jacqueline to suggest that it be used as firewood.

In the absence of reporting about Kennedy's true faith, what stood out when Kennedy ran for president in 1960 was his identification as a Catholic. This was great for his campaign because as long as the battle could be waged on that issue, Kennedy was likely to be a winner. He could state repeatedly his confidence that Americans "will vote for what they think is good in the man seeking office, and not for what church he happens to go to on Sunday." Had information about what was bad in the man seeking office come out, his national career would have been over. Instead, with reporting on sex sidelined, the Kennedy campaign was able to focus on a brilliant, four-part strategy to deal with the Catholic issue.

Part one was to insist on something that was easy for Kennedy but looked hard. Protestant ministers led by best-selling author Norman Vincent Peale stated, "It is inconceivable that a Roman Catholic President would not be under pressure by the hierarchy of his church to accede to its policies." Kennedy replied that he would reject the pressure, no matter the cost. That was easy for him to say, since he rejected Catholic teaching regarding virtually everything else in his life, but listeners who saw the hierarchy as extremely heavy-handed and Kennedy as extremely devout heard him saying he would risk personal damnation rather than damn the country.

Part two was to talk repeatedly about separation of church and state, as if that were a part of the Constitution rather than a remark in one of Jefferson's letters. At a well-orchestrated, nationally televised speech to the Greater Houston Ministerial Association, Kennedy (unfaithful in marriage) vowed fidelity to complete separation of church and state. He said he would make decisions according to his own conscience (church not relevant) and in the national interest, which was not something evidently to be viewed in connection with religious concerns.

Theological illiteracy among many reporters contributed to the sense that Kennedy was bucking trends. When he met with the fifty-one-member Council of Methodist Bishops, one Washington reporter said, "that's Daniel going into the lion's den." It would have been if Kennedy were theologically Catholic and the Methodists were theologically biblical Protestants. But Kennedy and most of his questioners had the common denominator of modernism, and it was reported that the bishops applauded him warmly at the end.

Kennedy even became in the eyes of some a new profile in courage as he dramatically explained what he would do. In one televised speech Kennedy said, "When any man stands on the steps of the Capitol and takes the oath of office of President, he is swearing to support the separation of church and state; he puts one hand on the Bible and raises the other hand to God as he takes the oath." Kennedy then looked straight into the camera and raised his hand as if taking an oath to God: He was writing Jefferson's words into the Constitution and making allegiance to them a new sacrament.

The third part of the approach was to state the issue so that anyone who voted against Kennedy would virtually have to classify himself as a bigot. "Nobody asked me if I was a Catholic when I joined the United States Navy," Kennedy told cheering crowds. "Nobody asked my brother if he was a Catholic or a Protestant before he climbed into an American bomber to fly his last mission." One Democratic Party spokesman acknowledged that party workers were instructed to raise the question, "'Do you think they are going to keep Kennedy from being President just because he is Catholic?' It gets a good response. We are winning lots of new votes."

Kennedy supporters played the tolerance card across America. The breakthrough primary victory for Kennedy came in heavily Protestant West Virginia, where voters repeatedly heard that a vote against Kennedy was a vote for prejudice. The *New York Times* reminded readers several times that those who were intolerant concerning Catholics were also likely to turn their ire on Jews, blacks, or other minorities. "I abhor intolerance in any form," the Kennedy campaign had vice presidential candidate Lyndon Johnson declare.

Fourth, and most audaciously, Kennedy became a spokesman for presidential morality. In Columbus, Ohio, in October, Kennedy referred to minor scandals in the Eisenhower administration and promised an atmosphere of "moral leadership" in his White House. While emphasizing the need of the president to "set the moral tone," he committed adultery frequently during the campaign, even on his campaign plane *Caroline* (named after his daughter). Aide Langdon Marvin revealed years later that Kennedy was in a hotel room with a call girl ninety minutes before the first presidential debate. The candidate was so pleased with the results of that debate, Marvin said, that "he insisted we line up a girl for him before each of the debates."

Kennedy arrived at his inauguration with neither his religious nor marital covers blown. In his inaugural day oath he pleased his father and followed tradition by saying, "So help me God." He later told Tip O'Neill that what he was really thinking, as he placed his hand on the family Bible, was how a particular businessman had been able to wrangle a seat behind the Kennedy family, next to O'Neill.

It was politically useful, however, to keep in the public mind the idea that Kennedy worshipped something higher than himself. In addition, the Catholic base could not be offended. Press secretary Pierre Salinger once announced that Kennedy ate bacon and eggs for breakfast one Friday morning. Shortly afterwards he recanted: Salinger told reporters he had erred because Kennedy did not eat meat on Friday. Jacqueline said that if reporters "bought that story, they're dumber than I thought they were," and she used the episode when her husband criticized her for arriving late and leaving early from official appearances. "Why scream at me?" she screamed. "You're the one who got caught eating meat on Friday."

Kennedy did go to mass every Sunday. Secret Service agents reported that once when he was reluctant, Jacqueline said, "Come on now, you son of a bitch. You got yourself into this and you know your public demands it. So get your damned tie and coat on and let's go."

IMMEDIATE GRATIFICATION AS PUBLIC POLICY

Kennedy emphasized fast action, whether sexual or governmental. The liberal *New Republic* was excited in March 1961 because "Washington is crackling, rocking, jumping." Arthur Schlesinger, Jr., the Kennedy staff historian noted for his worship of Franklin Roosevelt's liberal activist presidency, wrote about how Kennedy's energy was "electric in its intensity.... His fingers gave the clue to his impatience. They would suddenly be in constant action, drumming the table, tapping his teeth, slashing impatient pencil lines on a pad, jabbing the air to underscore a point." Columnist Joseph Kraft noted concerning Kennedy, "At all times he was in motion, smoothing his hair, adjusting his tie, fiddling with his belt, clicking a pen against his teeth, slipping his hands in and out of his pocket."

Part of that activity may have been due to drug-taking. During the 1960 campaign Kennedy became the prize client of Dr. Max Jacobson, who had gained a reputation as "Miracle Max" and "Dr. Feel Good" through giving amphetamine injections to celebrities such as Truman Capote and Tennessee Williams. During his presidency Kennedy received ten to fifteen milligrams of amphetamines as often as twice a week, according to Jacobson's son, Dr. Thomas Jacobson. "Speed" in low concentrations makes people feel alert, invigorated, self-confident, and able to concentrate even when they would otherwise be tired, but at a risk of impaired judgment, hyperactivity, and addiction. Kennedy's risks were heightened because he took a type of steroids for Addison's disease, a failure of the adrenal glands that reduces the body's ability to fight infections. The combination of amphetamines and steroids can result in the restlessness that Schlesinger, Kraft, and many others noted.

Drug stimulation went along with Kennedy's lifelong pattern of seeking immediate gratification, which was apparent in both sexual and political campaigns. Kennedy's habit of gaining applause through insincere promise-making became so evident that even *New York Times* columnist James Reston wrote, "Kennedy has got away with murder on his domestic program. His promises to the farmer, to labor, to old people, are all very exciting, but he has not given anybody the slightest idea of how they are to be financed." Nor did Kennedy care. Once in 1960, after giving a promise-laden speech on farm policy to a South Dakota audience, he told aides, "Fuck the farmers after November."

In the White House, while Kennedy spoke publicly about delaying pleasure to build for the future, his private obsession with the immediate continued. One of Kennedy's hundreds of sexual partners said that his practice was, "Up against the wall, Signora, if you have five minutes, that sort of thing." Publicly, Kennedy told his fellow citizens to "ask not what your country can do for you; ask what you can do for your country." Privately, he told Marilyn Monroe to ask not what he could do for her. She told a columnist that the president skipped foreplay, saying he did not have the time.

In the White House, however, Kennedy learned that diplomacy required both foreplay and some delivery of mutual satisfaction. He ducked out of promises of air support made to Cuban émigrés who tried to regain their homeland by going ashore at the Bay of Pigs, and was left with both huge embarrassment and the political need to pay Fidel Castro ransom for the release of the émigrés who survived. Kennedy, intellectually unprepared for his 1961 summit conference with Nikita Khrushchev in Vienna, was unable to charm the blunt survivor of Stalin's palace infighting; Khrushchev came away from the meeting thinking Kennedy a weakling, and proceeded to erect the Berlin wall, calculating correctly that the United States would not respond.

Kennedy tried to learn from his initial fiascoes. His Cuban debacle led to a decision to avoid military action in Laos. Kennedy aide Theodore Sorensen reported the president saying that September, "Thank God the Bay of Pigs happened when it did. Otherwise we'd be in Laos by now—and that would be a hundred times worse." But Kennedy, disregarding the advice of Douglas MacArthur and others who wanted the United States to defend Japan and the Philippines but not countries on the Asian mainland, placed American soldiers in Vietnam. The Geneva accords of 1954 had authorized the United States to have up to 687 advisors in South Vietnam; Kennedy ignored that public agreement as he disregarded private commitments, and an at-first quiet escalation began.

The tendency to concentrate on immediate political gratification rather than long-term consequences became evident when Under Secretary of State George Ball warned that U.S. military action in Vietnam would lead to hundreds of thousands of Americans being sent there, and Kennedy responded, "George, you're crazier than hell. That just isn't going to happen." By fall 1963, the situation in Vietnam was threatening to become a hundred times worse than the Bay of Pigs, and Kennedy was looking for a way out. A lack of foresight, combined with a search for the quick fix and a fondness for secret plots, led Kennedy to approve a Saigon coup that led to the assassination of Vietnam's President Ngo Dinh Diem and a downward political spiral in Saigon.

After Kennedy's assassination both hawks and doves tried to say that he had been one of them, but Robert Kennedy in 1964 gave a true sense of his brother's adhocracy. When asked what John Kennedy would have done had the South Vietnamese military effort disintegrated, he responded, "We'd face that when we came to it."

Many domestic matters also suffered from an emphasis on immediate gratification and a shirking from long-range thinking. In April 1962, executives of U.S. Steel resolved on a crash program of investment in oxygen furnaces and other new technology, which they needed in the long range to battle foreign competition. To raise sufficient capital they increased prices, and other large steel companies followed. Kennedy, with shrewd political sense, leaped at this opportunity to castigate big business, and attacked the increase as "a wholly unjustifiable and irresponsible defiance of the public interest." He had IRS officials dig out the personal income tax returns and expense accounts of steel executives, and used late-night interrogations and other threats to make U.S. Steel and other companies back down.

Afterwards, columnist David Lawrence noted that "a new era in American history—a declaration of war by the government on the profit system as it functions under private capitalism—has been ushered in by President Kennedy." Senator Barry Goldwater, preparing to run for president in 1964, argued that Kennedy's attack was "something you'd expect in a police state." Nevertheless, the episode worked temporarily and gave Kennedy an immediate political boost, but at an eventual cost to the steel industry of hundreds of thousands of jobs lost, and a politicization of business decisions that led to economic difficulties during the 1970s.

The Kennedy style did work, however, when style was more important than substance. The civil rights movement made great progress during the early 1960s, helped along by Kennedy's willingness to federalize the National Guard at crucial moments of integration such as James Meredith's enrollment at the University of Mississippi in 1962. But the crucial need was for Kennedy to use his television eloquence to emphasize morality, not force. He did so in 1963, explaining, "We are confronted primarily with a moral issue. It is as old as the scriptures . . . whether we are going to treat our fellow Americans as we want to be treated. If an American, because his skin is dark, cannot eat lunch in a restaurant open to the public, if he cannot send his children to the best school available . . . if, in short, he cannot enjoy the full and free life which all of us want, then who among us would be content to have the color of his skin changed and stand in his place?"

Kennedy was able to ask such questions movingly and effectively because, in the eyes of the uninformed public, his own moral standing remained high. His rhetoric of idealism and challenge also propelled both low- and high-tech innovations. The Peace Corps begun by

Kennedy sent volunteers to forty-four countries and became a symbol of American altruism. Kennedy's pledge to put an American on the moon by the end of the decade became a symbol of U.S. ability to win a race with the Soviet Union. On the other hand, the Kennedy battle against organized crime was undercut by the debts he owed to mobsters such as Sam Giancana, who had provided money to help Kennedy win the electoral votes of Illinois in 1960, and who shared a girlfriend, Judith Campbell, with Kennedy.

ONE BRIGHT SHINING MOMENT

What occupied most of Kennedy's business time throughout his administration, however, was the continuing cold war with the Soviet Union, with the daily prospect of it turning hot. In the 1960s, Kennedy was the first American statesman since the 1860s to face the prospect of his territory being shelled. But the bombardment of Atlanta in 1864 was minuscule in comparison to the death and destruction that a single missile fired from the Soviet Union or Cuba a century later could create.

Kennedy had to confront the quick terror of nuclear war, but he could not forget the slower strangulation that would result from caving in to Soviet demands. Joseph Kennedy had given his sons not only advice on bedroom behavior but also a bedrock anti-communism, and John Kennedy himself had seen as a young man the folly of appeasing dictators. He was well suited to keep in mind both the disaster of war and the disaster of surrender, and to navigate between those twin rocks throughout his presidency.

The peak of tension came in October 1962 when U.S. planes provided photographic proof that the Soviets were placing offensive nuclear missiles in Cuba. Kennedy had acquiesced in the erection of a Berlin wall the year before, but lack of response this time would lead to increased physical danger to American citizens. Furthermore, Kennedy was concerned about whether the United States would be seen as a pitiful, helpless giant if it could not exert its will in Vietnam; how much more would its reputation fall if the United States was unable to deal with a new threat ninety miles from its border?

Kennedy and his aides quickly realized that they could not ignore the missiles. They first had to decide whether to respond only diplomatically, or to combine soft speech with some use of a big stick. Diplomacy by itself, Kennedy realized, would drag out the matter, with Soviet missiles becoming an active threat. The idea of direct discussions with Fidel Castro came up, but there was distaste about morally authenticating a regime already beginning to establish itself by terror and torture. Besides, Castro's lieutenant Che Guevara, whose face would soon adorn posters in many New York apartments, was talking about using the missiles "against the very heart of the United States, including New York."

Some U.S. military response seemed necessary, but it was not easy to discern which was best and which, with nuclear weapons ready to fly, beckoned disaster. Kennedy's favorite literary line was from Shakespeare's *Henry IV, Part 1*, where Glendower brags, "I can call spirits from the vasty deep," and Hotspur responds, "Why, so can I, or so can any man; But will they come when you do call for them?" Kennedy's nuclear demons would come if he called, and Nikita Khrushchev had similar power. Would a U.S. invasion of Cuba lead to hydrogen bombs bursting in air, or at least a Soviet response in Berlin? Would a quick U.S. air strike on Soviet missile bases in Cuba also liberate the vasty deep?

As newly revealed tapes of the White House crisis meetings show, Kennedy excelled during the "twelve days of October." He realized that a quick attack by air was hazardous technically and politically. Despite talk of "surgical strikes," bombing was not that precise and might have to be followed by invasion. If Kennedy announced an air strike in advance, Cubans and Soviets would have time to prepare countermeasures. But if the air strike came without warning, the United States would be emulating Japan's Pearl Harbor attack. At one point in their deliberations, Robert Kennedy gave a note to his brother, "I now know how Tojo felt when he was planning Pearl Harbor."

While the internal debates continued, most Kennedy advisors began to favor a blockade of Cuba (which they called a quarantine, since according to international law a blockade is considered an act of war). The quarantine, in Kennedy's words, meant that "All ships of any kind bound for Cuba from whatever nation will, if found to contain cargoes of offensive weapons, be turned back." Proponents saw it as a measure that gave the Soviet leaders time to avoid a fight by turning around their ships. A psychological plus but a potential tactical minus was that the quarantine gave the Soviet leaders the next move: They would have to decide whether their ships would ignore U.S. Navy warnings and precipitate war.

The advisors, meeting as a committee of the National Security Council, voted 11–6 for a quarantine. The decision, however, was Kennedy's. He summoned Jacqueline to return with their children to the White House from the rented Glen-Ora farm that she lived at much of the week. In crisis, Kennedy wanted them close at hand both for their safety and his moral support. Then, he used his eloquence to accentuate patriotism without producing panic. In a televised speech on Monday, October 22, Kennedy announced the quarantine. The waiting began. On Wednesday, Soviet ships began to stop and turn back before hitting the quarantine line, so war did not begin on that day.

A secret exchange of messages over the next several days produced a resolution. One message from Nikita Khrushchev offered removal of the missiles already in Cuba in return for a U.S. pledge not to invade Cuba. A second Soviet message asked that the United States remove its missiles (already outmoded) from Turkey. On Saturday, October 27, Kennedy publicly agreed to the terms of the first message and privately agreed to the terms of the second. Kennedy did not have to resort to his fallback position, which was not revealed until over twenty years later. At that time Dean Rusk reported that Kennedy was prepared to use United Nations Secretary-General U Thant as an intermediary in agreeing publicly to a missile swap.

Kennedy received high praise for his action during the crisis. Pundit Richard Rovere gave the typical response from American journalists: "No one who watched developments here failed to be impressed by the forethought, precision, subtlety, and steady nerves of the President and those around him in preparing our bold and ultimately successful initiative." Lyndon Johnson gave a typical politician's response: "He plays a damned good hand of poker, I'll say that for him." Private lives can affect public policy in strange ways; the emotional detachment Kennedy showed in using women as he did made him a fine cold war poker player. He could coldly go to the brink of nuclear war without being unnerved by a normal man's sensitivities.

SETTING THE MORAL TONE

In a time when tense international relations were the norm, Kennedy's combination of intellect and detachment gave him the potential to become one of the greatest of presidents, a statesman superbly suited to his times. But his stature domestically depended on public perception of him as a moral leader; it is amazing that he was able to maintain appearances as long as he did, but it seems likely that had he lived, the cover would have been pulled off.

Kennedy's recklessness as a member of Congress surprised some; his recklessness as president is astounding. It began the evening of the inaugural balls, when he sent Jacqueline home and then committed adultery with a young lady at the home of columnist Joseph Alsop. Alsop was one of Kennedy's many journalistic protectors; when Alsop in 1958 had told Kennedy that he could easily have the next vice presidential nomination, Kennedy had said with a wink, "Let's not talk so much about vice. I'm against vice, in all forms." When asked the day after the inauguration about Kennedy's visit, Alsop covered up the adultery, saying, "the President was hungry, and so I fed him terrapin."

Day after day Kennedy risked wasting his great gifts. Partners in vice have testified to President Kennedy's adultery at brother-in-law Peter Lawford's beach house north of Santa Monica, at parties with friend and campaign supporter Frank Sinatra, and in many other spots outside the White House. Lawford told an interviewer in 1983, "I was Frank's pimp and Frank was Jack's. It sounds terrible now, but then it was lots of fun." Historians have noted Kennedy's on-the-road sexual connections with actresses Marilyn Monroe and Jayne Mansfield, strippers Blaze Starr and Tempest Storm, and other celebrities, acquaintances, and strangers. Kennedy's pal Lem Billings later reminisced, "It never occurred to Jack that some of the women might be considered dangerous. They were never searched, never questioned in depth."

The White House itself was a beehive of adulterous activity when Jacqueline was away—and she was away most of the time, staying four days a week at Glen-Ora and taking foreign trips that lasted up to three weeks. Three groups of women—staffers, regulars, and one-timers—serviced President Kennedy sexually. The staffers included young Pamela Turnure, who after sleeping with Kennedy for three years became in 1961 the first lady's press secretary, on Kennedy's suggestion but with Jacqueline's knowing acquiescence (apparently on the theory that a known mistress was better than an unknown one). Two Kennedy secretaries, labeled "Fiddle" and "Faddle" by Secret Service agents who did not consider them particularly good-looking, reported for duties at unusual hours.

Regulars not on staff included Judith Campbell, who made twenty sexually oriented visits to the White House, according to her book published in 1977; despite her Mafia ties, Kennedy kept seeing her until J. Edgar Hoover in 1962 pressured Kennedy to stop. By that time Mary Pinchot Meyer, *Washington Post* reporter Ben Bradlee's sister-in-law and Robert Kennedy's next-door neighbor, had become a regular. She came for thirty secret trysts between January 1962 and November 1963, according to her personal diary. The Secret Service conducted full background checks of some of the frequent visitors, including several airline stewardesses Kennedy had met. His personal secretary, Evelyn Lincoln, typically called the outside women, who were picked up in White House cars and escorted into the president's quarters by Kennedy pal Dave Powers.

Numerous one-timers also made appearances for nude swimming-and-sex frolics and other events. Judith Campbell was amazed at Kennedy's lack of discretion, but concluded that the president thought "he was above it all." All White House employees had to sign affidavits swearing themselves to secrecy on what they saw or did in relation to the Kennedys, and Kennedy helped out by telling them on many evenings that since he was expecting company, they should leave dinner in the warming oven and he would serve himself and his guest. Still, there were sights such as the one revealed a decade later by employee Traphes Bryant: He came out an elevator door and had trouble averting his eyes as "a naked blonde office girl ran through the hall."

The most extraordinary aspect of all this activity is that it went unreported. Opposing politicians, of course, were the most likely to make use of the evidence, but Democratic opponents in 1960 decided not to tarnish one of their own. In the general election that year Richard Nixon decided not to go after Kennedy's sexual record for several reasons: Nixon liked Kennedy personally, he wanted to argue foreign policy and economic issues, and—despite his reputation—Nixon at that point still did not believe that the office of the presidency should be won through what would be seen as low blows.

Had Kennedy been alive in 1964, Goldwaterites probably would have placed some of Kennedy's sexual activity before the public, since it fit well with their thesis that America was at the beginning of a moral crisis. But during Kennedy's term of office, with the politicians silent, exposure was up to reporters. According to George Reedy, a reporter who became Lyndon Johnson's press spokesman, "We knew. We all knew." When a *New York Times* reporter covering a Kennedy trip to Manhattan told his editor that he had seen a well-known actress repeatedly going in and out of the president's hotel suite, the editor replied, "No story there"—and the matter became one of many deemed not fit to print.

Historian James Giglio's list of reporters who knew or at least were aware of the Kennedy stories includes some of the biggest journalistic names of the 1960s: Ben Bradlee, David Brinkley, Robert Donovan, Rowland Evans, Fletcher Knebel, Mary McGrory, Clark Mollenhoff, Chalmers Roberts, and Tom Wicker. Some of Kennedy's activities were so well known on the Washington social circuit that even strangers sometimes asked Judith Campbell at parties, "Are you the Judy that's going with Jack Kennedy?"

Newspaper readers saw no evil, however, because reporters were enslaved in a peculiar press convention: the theory that private matters have no impact on public performance. Kennedy's secretaries could type and answer the telephone, so they were not on the public payroll purely for sexual purposes. Kennedy's practice of speed sex—his friend Senator George Smathers of Florida said, "Jack was something, almost like a Roto-Rooter"—meant that his pubic matters took away little time from public matters. Kennedy's press conference wit showcased his knowledge of hot issues. Jacqueline Kennedy was able to repress her rage and make the world believe that she lived in Camelot. So a "sex doesn't affect public business" press stayed compressed. John Kennedy survived.

In June 1963, a piece of the story almost broke through. *New York Journal-American* reporter Don Frasca and managing editor James Horan reported that one of the "biggest names in American politics," a man holding "a very high" elective office, had been sexually involved with a model, who in turn was connected to a London pimp involved in a British spy and sex scandal. Within forty-eight hours Robert Kennedy called the two journalists from the Hearst-owned newspaper to his office. They acknowledged that the reference was to John Kennedy, and that they had evidence of Kennedy affairs in New York City in 1960 and 1961 with the model and with Marie Novotny, a nineteen-year-old prostitute from London who shared an apartment with a suspected Soviet agent. Robert Kennedy immediately threatened an anti-trust suit against the Hearst chain unless further stories were spiked. They were. John Kennedy survived.

Most of the press cover-up was by omission, but some aspects arose by commission. Jim Bishop, in his *A Day in the Life of President Kennedy*, described endearing scenes of Kennedy and his small children playing in the White House swimming pool, and did not note the scenes of sexual frolic that occurred on other evenings. Kennedy was known for frequently falling asleep right after nighttime adulterous intercourse, but Bishop, who had been executive editor of *Catholic Digest*, concluded his description of Kennedy's typical day this way: "Beside his bed, he drops to his knees. The last few minutes of the day belong to God."

Vices Have Consequences

Hervé Alphand, French ambassador to the United States, described President Kennedy as a man who "loves pleasure and women. His desires are difficult to satisfy without causing fear of a scandal and its use by his political adversaries. That could happen one day because he does not take sufficient precaution in this puritan country." During his life, amazingly, Kennedy got by, but when the facts trickled out, cynicism grew. In 1960, *Newsweek* reported that the typical American college student "believes in romantic love, yet attaches scant importance to chastity. He is religious, but in a hazy, uncommitted way." Kennedy proposed to make those college students hear the call of trumpets, not strumpets, and for a while they did, but as the real story came out, the belief that presidents should not be believed grew.

Kennedy set a moral tone for the sixties in other ways as well. Judith Campbell once brought six marijuana cigarettes to the White House. When she offered Kennedy one, he said, "Let's try it," and they did. After smoking the first, Kennedy laughed and said, "We're having a White House conference on narcotics here in two weeks." But marijuana use apparently was a rarity; more common was Kennedy's corruption of Secret Service agents who had to lead him through tunnels from the Carlyle Hotel in New York so he could get to nearby hotels and apartments for sexual interludes without attracting attention. Longtime Kennedy friend Charles Spalding, who was in on the arrangements, later explained that it was "a weird sight. Jack and I and two Secret Service men walking in these huge tunnels underneath the city streets alongside those enormous pipes, each of us carrying a flashlight. One of the Secret Service men also had this underground map and every once in a while he would say, 'We turn this way, Mr. President.'"

Journalist Richard Reeves has noted that Kennedy "used the people around him as pimps and worse." Secretary of State Dean Rusk had to make arrangements for Kennedy's foreign affairs. Some officials and military attachés were proud pimps, thinking that Kennedy was confiding in them and bringing them close to him. But Rusk resented having to reserve an Italian villa for Kennedy so he could have privacy and ambiance for a tryst with a prominent, beautiful European woman. All the other members of Kennedy's official party had to be off the grounds that night. The next day Kennedy met with the pope. Rusk went along to get along, but, as Reeves reported, he "never, never got over it." Three decades later he "talked about how much it hurt him."

Who else was hurt by the pressure to pimp? Kennedy showed no signs of caring. He even seemed to enjoy his position of dominance, to the point where he would stage meetings with himself in the bathtub or on the toilet, and advisors in suits sitting around stiffly. One afternoon, two foreign service advisors carrying secret messages knocked on the door of the Lincoln Bedroom on a summer afternoon. Kennedy flung the door open, revealing a woman in bed, then read the dispatches, made his decision, and returned to adultery. We know that sexual activities of the key London officials damaged efforts during the Revolutionary War and led some capable leaders to seek other occupations; President Kennedy inspired many people to enter public service, but what would have happened had the truth of his character come out, and had he been forced to leave office in disgrace?

We will never, never know because of the events of November 22, 1963. There is no indication that Kennedy was changing his ways; he committed adultery on a trip to Miami just before heading to Dallas. Reporters heard the Kennedys arguing on the grand staircase of the White House just before their appearance at a function the evening before their Texas trip. UPI reporter Helen Thomas thought Jacqueline had been crying. According to Evelyn Lincoln, the Kennedys' marriage was no stronger then than it had been three years before.

In a peculiar fashion President Kennedy's sexual practices even contributed to his death. *Time* magazine correspondent Hugh Sidey reported in May 1987 that Kennedy was wearing his back brace while motorcading through Dallas on the fatal day because he had thrown out his back while engaged in energetic adultery several months earlier. Had he not been wearing the brace, the impact of the first bullet that struck him would have pushed him to the floor of the limousine, with his cranium out of the line of fire of a second bullet. The brace, however, kept him up, a sitting duck for the fatal shot. Journalists, had they exposed his extramarital activity and forced him to stop, would have done him a favor.

Kennedy had no opportunity to utter any memorable last words. Arthur Schlesinger, Jr., however, records that someone in the White House once asked Kennedy what he regretted most. He replied, "I wish I had had more good times." He had given the country the opportunity for good times—but, oh, what he could have accomplished! The legacy he actually left was a time bomb. For a time he was remembered for establishing such a high standard of leadership that experienced politicians like Lyndon Johnson and Richard Nixon became despondent over their inability to emulate him. But when it became known years after his death that Kennedy's gods were sex and power, many Americans came to believe that any gold they perceived in politics was fool's gold. The only way not to be fooled was to define deviancy down.

Curtain

CHAPTER 13

Bill Clinton and Beyond

The United States has had seven presidents in the thirty-five years since John F. Kennedy's assassination. All of them quoted the Bible in their inaugural addresses. Two—Jimmy Carter and Bill Clinton—regularly told interviewers about their evangelical faith and church-related activities, such as teaching Sunday school or singing in the choir. Most of the seven were also the subjects of gossip concerning extramarital sexual activities in their past. One, Bill Clinton, became the focus of investigations involving such activities in the White House.

Of the seven post-Kennedy presidents, then, Bill Clinton is more than any other at the intersection of questions involving religious belief and sexual practice. The sex, of course, has been scrutinized, but little attention has been paid to the support he received from up-and-coming evangelical ministers such as Bill Hybels, pastor of an Illinois megachurch; on inauguration day, 1997, Hybels faced the president during a prayer service and lauded "the development of your heart, your increasing desire to know God, and to live for Him." Hybels said he wanted Clinton to know "to the depths of your being that you are loved by God. And, not incidentally, by many, many of us."

With all the attention paid to Clinton-Lewinsky liaisons, the president's frequent meetings with several ministers, including Hybels and author/orator Tony Campolo, have been unreported; from 1995 to 1997 the two combined received guest passes to the White House even more frequently than the celebrated intern. One early meeting designed to show their kind of love came late in November 1994, soon after voters had repudiated Clinton by voting in a Republican Congress. Its dynamics show much about the role of religion in President Clinton's life.

Clinton had called in Hybels, Campolo, and two other ministers, Gordon MacDonald from Massachusetts and Rex Horne from Clinton's church in Little Rock. The evening meeting in the private study on the second floor of the White House centered on a discussion of the problems Clinton was having in gaining acceptance among evangelical Christians. As one meeting participant recalled and another verified, one of the ministers said that members of his congregation were asking "a very simple question: 'Is the president a good man?'" The minister then asked Clinton, "What can you tell us that would convince them that you're a good man?"

According to the participants, Clinton insisted that he was good, and when pressed for specific detail about his personal life responded even more strongly, in blanket terms. One of the ministers then said quietly, "I don't think any of us can say that, that we're good." He had in mind the biblical understanding that "all have sinned and fallen short of the glory of God," and was pleading with Clinton to confess sin and then rely on God's grace rather than his own pride. Clinton would not buy that; he responded by pointing the finger at others, arguing that some unfair and evil Republicans were trying to bring him down. One of the ministers told the president that he tended to worry about "people out to get you," but should instead pay attention to his own actions that created animosity. Clinton responded by again attacking Republicans.

Several hours later, after a break to allow the president to meet visiting governors, the discussion resumed. One minister noted, "the president started up again with they, they, they. We kept saying, 'We're focusing on you.'" But there was no balm at the end of the tunnel. That was one meeting. There have been others: Hybels met with Clinton on a regular monthly schedule during 1995 and 1996, and Campolo about every one and a half months on an irregular schedule. But after three years of meetings, one regular minister to the president merely shook his head when asked if progress was being made in the central issue of having the president stop blaming others and start accepting responsibility himself.

The meetings with ministers, some of which were publicized—one Associated Press photo showed Clinton and Hybels praying outside the White House—could be viewed as political, an attempt to cut into the tendency of evangelicals to vote Republican. That strategy certainly was successful: Pundits predicted that Clinton would win reelection in 1996 if he could garner 20 to 30 percent of the evangelical vote, and he ended up gaining over a third. It would be a mistake, however, to say that the meetings were all public relations and tips on packaging. ABC's Peggy Wehmeyer summarized well Clinton's need to receive "the gratification of knowing some accept him as a man of faith." He evidently needs to view himself as a good man.

GROWING UP TO BE GOOD

Clinton once said he had consistent church attendance as a child because it was important "to try to be a good person." When he was eight, church was a haven from a stepfather who regularly got drunk, beat his wife, and once was arrested for firing a gun into the wall of his house. Church also was an alternative to Virginia Kelley, Clinton's four-time-married mother who lived for clubs, gambling halls, and racetracks. She recalled that "Bill just got up one day and said he wanted to go to church—all by himself." He continued going all by himself: Every Sunday morning he put on a suit and walked to Park Place Baptist Church with a leather Bible tucked under his arm.

Even though his family was nonreligious, other influences also worked on Clinton to make God part of his consciousness. In Arkansas schools during the 1950s, students read Bible passages over the loudspeaker each morning; school assemblies often resembled chapel services. At age ten Clinton made a public profession of faith and was baptized. At age eleven he asked a Sunday school teacher to drive him fifty miles to Little Rock so he could attend a Billy Graham crusade; he later contributed part of his allowance to the crusade. According to Little Rock minister Rex Horne, Clinton "grew up early looking for help and hope—and found it in the church."

Clinton continued to look to the church through Hot Springs High School graduation in 1964 and through the beginning of his under-graduate education at Georgetown University. There, however, he apparently began defining "good" differently. In Campolo's words, the president "was a very serious Christian during his teenage years, but got away from the Lord from the time he was 19 through his gover-norship. . . . He personally screwed up his life pretty hard for a period of time." In his own description Clinton was an "uneven churchgoer for a long time," from his years at Oxford through his time at Yale Law School and through his entry into Arkansas politics.

Some Clinton backers have said his deviation from religiosity con-cluded in 1980, when voters ousted the one-term governor. *Time* in 1993 quoted Betsey Wright, Clinton's longtime chief of staff: "People overlook what a traumatic occurrence that defeat was. Getting himself into a church family was very important in terms of overcoming what he regarded as his own personal failure." Some Clinton-watchers also cite two other changes in the early 1980s: daughter Chelsea's birth, and a tour of Israel that he took under the auspices of the Reverend W. O. Vaught of Immanuel Baptist Church in Little Rock. Clinton derived multiple benefits from joining that "church family." In a fatherly way Vaught prayed with Clinton and discussed with him the Bible and political questions. Clinton joined Vaught's church, one of Little Rock's largest, and started singing in its choir. Since services were televised throughout the state every Sunday, with the choir often on camera, critics said Clinton was finding a new way to campaign.

Politically, Clinton's changes worked. Helped by Hillary Clinton's decision to stop using her maiden name of Rodham and change her way of dressing and acting, Bill Clinton won a new lease on a governor's life in 1982. He stayed on top of Arkansas for a decade. At the end of that period Wayne Ward, who twice served as Immanuel Baptist's temporary pastor, said of Clinton, "there's no reason to question his deep commitment to Christ" during the decade. But questions are inevitable. The Bible stresses not only being "born again" but increasingly living a life without overt, recurring sin—and that, from many reports, is not the life Bill Clinton lived.

If Clinton's supposed return to Christianity during that decade did not change his personal life, did his renewed faith inform his policies? There is no such indication. As Clinton ascended in national Democratic circles, he moved in a way opposite to biblical teaching on issues such as abortion, from opposition to the practice in 1986 to partial opposition in 1989, support in 1991, and support for even partial-birth abortion in 1996. But on this issue as well it is clear that Clinton wanted to consider himself a good man, within the church family, and some of his statements on abortion have reflected (in a funhouse mirror way) a bit of unorthodox speculation in which Clinton's pastor W. O. Vaught once engaged.*

---

*Vaught said, "I do not believe that a fetus in the body of a mother is a human being. I believe it becomes a human being when the *na shamah* [breath of life] hits the fetus, the embryo, and it begins to breathe." But Vaught added, "I do not believe that would give you the right to say that then anybody can have an abortion and you're not committing a sin. . . . This little fetus is sacred in the sight of God." Clinton, aware of the requirements for upward mobility within the Democratic Party, jumped on the speculative notion and ignored the rest. Vaught died in 1989; his son, Carl, has said his father would find it "absurd" to read his sermon as justifying abortion on demand. That very year Clinton moved from an anti-abortion position to one supporting the procedure in some situations; in 1991 he flopped over to support the *Roe* v. *Wade* decision and its establishment of abortion rights at all months of pregnancy. In 1996 he vetoed a bill banning a procedure so hard to defend, partial-birth abortion, that even some stalwart apologists for abortion bailed out on it.

Clinton spiritual advisor Tony Campolo argued (before the Monica Lewinsky revelations) that Clinton's spiritual rebirth took place when he entered the White House. Campolo said of Clinton, "He got through Arkansas on charm and intelligence, and not until he came to the White House did he become aware that he needed far more than that." Clinton, according to Campolo, spoke of "how the turmoil of the Civil War drove Lincoln to his knees, in the realization that the task was beyond him and he needed help from God." Others also traced a Clinton spiritual renewal to this recent period. Rex Horne in 1994 said the president's spiritual life was growing in "direct relation to the size and enormity of the issues that are facing him."

Knee Deep in the Big Muddy

Except perhaps in 1980, when Bill Clinton lost his first reelection campaign, few people have lost bets by overestimating what he will do for political reasons. And yet, the significance of Clinton's theology should not be underestimated. In 1992 he said, "The Bible teaches us that we've all failed. We'll all continue to fail." Clinton told religion reporters in 1993 that he appreciated in Christianity "the idea of continuous coming back. . . ." Once, when asked if he believed in life after death, Clinton replied, "Yeah, I have to. I need a second chance." Missing in those words was any sense of progress. Biblical Christianity is neither pessimistic nor perfectionist, but it does hold out the promise that individuals, while remaining sinners, will more and more receive the grace to think and act in less sinful ways.

"Watch what he does, not what he says" is the advice one of Clinton's conservative evangelical critics, Gary Bauer, has offered. (The president has offered that same advice in regard to Saddam Hussein.) Sadly, it seems perfectly clear that the lies have kept on coming since Clinton supposedly reconnected with God upon entering the White House. The long list by now includes accusations that last surfaced with such power during the Nixon administration: perjury, obstruction of justice, and the like. Certainly, as Clinton said in describing his theology, "we'll all continue to fail," but does repeated failure require at some point self-analysis concerning patterns of sin? Doesn't a blithe acceptance of forgiveness and a return to wrongdoing indicate a lack of grace?

Bill Clinton late in 1997 and early in 1998 faced a dilemma. He could have told the truth about his relationship with Monica Lewinsky and confessed sexual sin. That would have meant taking a chance with the American people, who have often been remarkably accepting. But it also would have meant admitting publicly that he had made little progress in what appears to be one of his besetting sins, and perhaps even saying in public the words that seem to be the most difficult for him to utter: "I am not a good man." Because he was unwilling to confess that he is a sinner stuck in a rut, he apparently was willing to perjure himself, tamper with witnesses, and suppress evidence.

Other adulterous presidents in the twentieth century have not had to lie publicly about their practice because knowledge of it did not become widespread while they were in office. What has become common, ever since Woodrow Wilson, is lying about matters of state. Dwight Eisenhower reduced presidential credibility when he lied to protect the secrecy of U-2 missions; he at least had the excuse of engagement in a cold war that could turn hot at any moment. Lyndon Johnson and Richard Nixon both defined presidential deviancy down by lying about policy matters and, in Nixon's case, obstructing justice to protect his associates in the belief that taints on his administration would reduce his own effectiveness. They both harmed the presidency, but at least they kept saying "they, they, they" only after receiving notice during those cold war years that their paranoia was partly rational.

Bill Clinton does not have the excuse of a cold war setting. He has benefited from prosperity at home, a general peace abroad, and reporters who for years gave him far easier treatment than he deserved. Just as many citizens early in 1998 seemed so satisfied with the state of the Union that they did not want to deal with issues of presidential adultery and perjury, so journalists often insisted that private action has no effect on public policy. Some went even further, arguing that immorality makes for more creative leaders. *Newsweek*'s Joe Klein declared on *Face the Nation* that presidents with "interesting sexual histories" have made better leaders.

Many journalists have bought into compartmentalization, perhaps because many of the history professors they had in college did also. When Robert K. Murray and Tim Blessing surveyed nearly a thousand professional historians and history professors in 1982, most underestimated the connectedness of ideas and consequences by saying that a president should not let his religious beliefs influence his decisions. That is like telling the waves not to influence the beach. Most of those surveyed also showed hostility to religion by saying that a deep faith in God made presidential success less likely. Clearly, success as defined by the school of Richard Hofstadter has a different meaning than success within an ethic that sees the Bible as central.

If more professors looked deeper into either American or biblical history, maybe there would be more awareness of the importance of stately conduct among statesmen. To take just one ancient example, three thousand years ago Israel's King David, the giant slayer, had come to think that he could conquer at will both foreign lands and a married woman. The Bible tells how "in the spring, at the time when kings go off to war," David did not. He stayed in his palace, from his roof saw a beautiful woman bathing, and summoned Bathsheba. She became pregnant and David conspired with his top general to have Bathsheba's soldier-husband, Uriah, die in a staged military blunder. The cover-up seemed to work: David married Bathsheba and their son was born.

Even successfully hidden private action had public consequences, however. David's adultery began a God-given chain of events that led to the death of that son, rebellion by another son, civil war, the loss of 20,000 men in one battle, and further rebellions. It would have been worse, except that David, confronted with his sin, turned back to God, confessing and worshipping. His successor, Solomon, on the other hand, was every inch a sage, but as he aged he "loved many foreign women," one thousand in all, who "turned his heart after other gods." The public result was a rebellion that eventually split Israel in two—and Israel's kings thereafter kept defining deviancy down.

Americans of the eighteenth and nineteenth centuries generally understood that if great Solomon's reign could disintegrate, how much more readily could the tarnished lives of lesser leaders send their lands spiraling downward! Voters at first took into account the religious beliefs and sexual practices of prospective statesmen, generally electing men like Andrew Jackson and turning down those like Henry Clay when they went head-to-head. But the common sense of past generations has become uncommon. Novelist Larry McMurtry wrote in 1975 that "one seldom, nowadays, hears anyone described as 'a person of character.' The concept goes with an ideal of maturity, discipline and integration that strongly implies repression: people of character, after all, cannot do just anything, and an ability to do just about anything with just about anyone—in the name, perhaps, of Human Potential—is certainly one of the most *moderne* abilities."

Compartmentalization Versus Integrity

Neither George nor Booker T. Washington was *moderne*. They from an early age, and leaders like Jackson, Lincoln, and Cleveland as they grew older, showed integrity, which comes from the Latin word *integritas*, "made whole." Students in past years were advised to become men and women of integrity, not compartments. Those who had integrity could be expected to stand up for what was good and right; those who lacked it were suspected of preferring expediency to truth. A lack of integrity would often come out sooner or later and have dire effects; John F. Kennedy's successful compartmentalizing, for instance, preserved his reputation during his administration, but the eventual revelations marred not only his memory but also the reputation of the presidency.

Today's willingness to accept a lack of integrity and truth-telling has accompanied acceptance of a new academic cliché: the inevitability of postmodernism. We are now sometimes said to be living in a post-moral, post-truth, post-decency political culture. Both critics and supporters often see Bill Clinton as the president appropriate for this new age. His willingness to adopt conflicting policies shows that he believes logical coherence to be unimportant and objective truth nonexistent. His tendency to identify with—to feel the pain of—many different groups, even if they disagree with each other, is both praised and parodied. His ability to manipulate unscrupulously words, facts, and beliefs, if manipulation will advance the cause of "victims" and himself, is legendary. The moral ambiguity of Clinton's own life is icing on the postmodernist cake.

Yet all of the descriptions in the preceding paragraph could have been applied equally well to Henry Clay. Postmodernism in politics may not be all that different from premodern and modern unscrupulousness, but there is one big difference: Citizens became aroused over previous scandals and regularly threw the rascals out. Clay was such a political charmer that he went far, but he was still 0–3 in presidential general elections, while President Clinton's record is 2–0. Those records themselves could be merely the result of some specific electoral circumstances, but they point us toward one important truth: Every president sets up expectations for his successors. A president seen as having high moral character raises the bar for his successors, and the reverse is also true. A series of outstanding presidents increases the likelihood of the populace demanding another outstanding leader, and the reverse is also true.

Bill Clinton is the political beneficiary of a recent lowering of expectations. If he were succeeding a George Washington, an Andrew Jackson, or even a Grover Cleveland, expectations concerning truth-telling would sink a ship of state with such a loose-lipped captain. But Clinton's well-known admiration for John Kennedy provides the incumbent with political points both ways; our tendency is to say, the adulterer wasn't such a bad president. Frequent prevarications of presidents since then have accustomed us to falsity. Since George Bush said, "Read my lips, no new taxes," and then made a 180-degree turn, it is hard to classify his successor, who makes carefully nuanced statements and then turns only 170 degrees, as a new species who uniquely endangers truth.

Examining portraits of presidents and statesmen in different periods shows in small ways how one leader's life touches many others. Since Abraham Lincoln grew a beard, each of the next four elected Republican presidents also had a beard. Since George Washington self-consciously attempted to personify virtue, his successors for a time felt the same pressure. Woodrow Wilson, Franklin Roosevelt, and Lyndon Johnson all were elected after they made promises not to send

American soldiers into foreign wars; Bill Clinton found it easy to set a one-year deadline for removing American troops from Bosnia and then break that pledge. Because our moral expectations for presidents are lower than they once were, President Clinton could see himself both as a good man and as an officeholder legitimately aspiring to a spot on the list of great presidents.

However, the Clinton imitation of his predecessors and amplification of some of their predilections does not absolve him. Every president who speeds up the downward slide makes a return to earlier and higher standards more difficult. If the press and public accept Clinton adultery and lies, future presidents will have a lower bar to hop over: Look how Bill Clinton successfully compartmentalized by delivering a State of the Union address amid questions about sordid sex. If he can do that, why does integrity—"made whole"—matter?

Here's why, as it looks in February 1998. Was Monica Lewinsky of no consequence? Clinton gave her the power to bring down his administration. Did the affair have no effect on the workings of government? Tens of thousands of hours have been spent on the cover-up. And just as we know only now what Kennedy's adultery did to the morale of his secretary of state, Dean Rusk, and others, we probably won't know the effects on Clinton cabinet members for many years. No effect on military morale? As Clinton was meeting with and then distancing himself from Monica Lewinsky, air force pilot Kelly Flinn was caught in adultery and lies and kicked out of the service; Sergeant Major Gene McKinney, the top enlisted soldier in the U.S. Army, was acquitted in a court-martial for alleged sexual harassment of female soldiers under his command. Could the success of the commander in chief, Bill Clinton, in holding onto his job have no effect? The armed forces know what a climate of mistrust does to job performance and unit morale. Why don't we?

The enormous consequences of a lack of integrity at the top became evident during the February 1998 debate about whether the United States should go to war with Iraq. Congressional leaders and members of the public expressed serious doubts about the Clinton administration's strategy, but underlying all of that were doubts about whether President Clinton was to be trusted with any life-and-death decisions. Those who viewed his televised speeches before audiences carefully selected for courtesy often had Monica Lewinsky in the back of their minds, and Clinton himself shied away from forays into the town meeting environment at which he is a master. Instead, on one notable occasion he dispatched his secretaries of state and defense and his national security advisor to a CNN-staged meeting for which they were ill-equipped. Why wasn't Clinton himself there? Because he could not venture into a public forum without being asked about sex, lies, and tapes.

Perhaps President Clinton has not failed us, but we him. If we were to follow Joe Klein's proposal to value leaders with "interesting sexual histories," perhaps all would be merry. Or, if Bill Clinton were given the slack John Kennedy received, perhaps we could be ignorantly misty-eyed about Camelot II. After all, while some Americans think the issue of adultery is important in and of itself, others do not want examination of presidential trysts, and almost all are embarrassed; why not just ignore such matters?

The reason is that even a president like Bill Clinton who appears—when giving a State of the Union address—to be so successful at compartmentalization really is not. If the long record of Clinton infidelity before 1992 had been seen as disqualifying him for the presidency, we would have been spared not only a president lying under oath but improper use of the FBI (and 900 of its files), the Secret Service, the Lincoln Bedroom, other White House rooms (for questionable coffees with political donors), and the White House telephones (for fundraising). We would have been spared payments to Webster Hubbell and attempts to extend executive privilege. We would have been spared much that, if allowed to go unpunished, will lower to the floor the bar for future presidents.

By discerning a candidate's views of God and sex, will we be able to predict particular problems? No, but the lives of leaders show how physical or spiritual adultery are warning signs of deep difficulties that emerge in many different ways: Specifics are unforeseeable, but dangerous patterns of behavior are not. Such patterns were overlooked during the Kennedy administration for many reasons, but one was the existence of a greater danger, the threat of external aggression against which national unity was imperative. Today, the larger threat is internal demoralization, and the White House's white noise feeds it.

BACK TO THE FUTURE

Integrity stores up principal for future generations, but compartmentalization always leaves a bill, although one that might not be presented for many years. John F. Kennedy built up the prestige of the presidency during his lifetime, but in recent years those who learned that Camelot was built on a lie have contributed to a bear market in trust. While stock averages soar that bear market is overlooked, but if economies falter confidence becomes key. If we are not to cement cynicism in place for a generation, we desperately need Clinton's successors to be presidents of integrity.

How do we find such persons? Pollsters since 1993 have regularly asked, "Do you approve or disapprove of the way Bill Clinton is handling his job as president?" But what is his job? If the job is defined as presiding over the economy, the president is only a tad more influential than the vice president, whose constitutional role is to preside over the Senate; we have what used to be known as the greatest deliberative body in the world, and we also have the greatest deliberative economy, where billions of pieces of information are digested and spit up so that millions of decisions are made. Neither president nor vice president has all that much influence over the final outcomes.

A more crucial aspect of the president's job concerns his role as commander in chief of the armed forces and chief law enforcement officer for the nation. To perform well in those spheres a president must maintain at least the basic level of personal conduct required from all those he commands; he must also set an example of how to uphold the law, not tiptoe around it. Beyond these obligatory tasks are those that are not spelled out but, from Washington on, have probably been even more important. Throughout American history the president has represented the United States to foreign leaders; he should not have a personal life that allows him to be readily mocked. Throughout American history the president has been a major role model for children, little lower than the angels; he should not bedevil their lives.

The official positions require discernment in particular tasks, but the unofficial roles demand integrity. Before Americans can succeed in placing a moral leader at the top, we must develop a consensus on the importance of integrity; once that is in place, the likelihood of finding a person who can perform all of the presidential functions is increased. How should we pick one? Historical records show that there are no guarantees, but they do provide warning signals telling us what to avoid. Reverence toward God does not confer the ability to have a successful presidency; look at Jimmy Carter. Faithfulness to a wife is no guarantee of faithfulness to the country; look at the last near-impeachee, Richard Nixon. Faithlessness in both areas, however, is a leading indicator of trouble. Small betrayals in marriage generally lead to larger betrayals, and leaders who break a large vow to one person find it easy to break relatively small vows to millions.

It is also vital to scrutinize a candidate's religious beliefs and the way he has demonstrated or undermined those beliefs through his practice. Individual citizens will have varied views on whether allegiance to biblical values is important, but that is a question for voters, not journalists, to determine. What is required here, of course, are journalistic screeners who take seriously the task of examining the character of potential leaders and reporting the truth. If journalists themselves do not believe in the value of their screening task, they will not make enough of an effort to avoid failure.

Some say failure is now inevitable: Now that the bar has been lowered so far, they say, it is too late to make a comeback. Again, however, history belies the cynics. England in the 1770s pushed forward Montagu, Sackville, and the other immoral incompetents who led its effort to suppress America's revolution. England in the 1790s produced statesmen like William Wilberforce, who led a successful effort to suppress slavery. Wilberforce and his successors also led a religious reformation and moral revival that led to higher standards for British political and family life during the nineteenth century. In the U.S., belief in a theistic God and belief in marriage were both under assault in the 1850s as spiritism and "free love" gained sizable followings. Americans sobered by war, however, rejected those doctrines during the 1860s, and the rest of the century became, for most citizens, a time to re-embrace biblical values concerning marriage and family.

Wars or other disasters are not necessary to bring people sadly to their senses, if leaders teach honesty and display integrity while there is still time. President Clinton could still offer America a wonderful legacy by showing how a president who has violated his oath of office should act. On a trip to Africa early in 1998 he confessed to American complicity in slavery and genocide. On other trips abroad he has confessed to a variety of things done by other people at other times. What if, sooner rather than later, Bill Clinton confessed not only to adultery but to perjury and obstruction of justice?

Bill Clinton does not like personal confessions; few of us do. It is much easier to crusade about international justice than to practice justice in our homes and offices. It is much easier for a man to orate about protecting the rights of women than to protect one woman next to him. But if President Clinton were to show that respect for the presidency required confession and resignation, and that raising the bar in that fashion was more important than personal comfort, he would be handing his successors a presidency diminished by many of his actions but augmented by his last one. Here is a portion of what Bill Clinton's last speech should include:

> My fellow Americans, early in 1998 I stood before you and announced that the state of the Union was strong. Many journalists commented on the strength of my performance after a week of turmoil concerning charges of sexual and official misconduct that I denied.
>
> I am here tonight to confess before all of you that the performance was only that: a performance. I had spent the previous five days in agitated thought: Should I confess the truth—that I had violated oaths to my wife and to my country—and then step down from office? Or should I deny, deny, deny? I chose denial, and had my aides claim executive privilege as Richard Nixon's did. On the surface, our strategy worked at that time, and we were even able to convince ourselves that our lies served a higher purpose.
>
> My fellow Americans, for years I carried a big Bible to church, but I have recently read it, meditated on it, prayed over it, with a new seriousness. Before, I could compartmentalize, ignoring action I was privately ashamed of in order to conduct the public business in ways I thought were right. But, as I read the Bible, God pushed me to acknowledge that the charges against me of both adultery and obstruction

of justice are true. My public face has stayed on these many months, but I now realize the truth of what David wrote about in Psalm 32 some three thousand years ago: "When I kept silent, my bones wasted away through my groaning all day long." So here I stand, and I can do no other.

Although some of my actions have not shown sufficient understanding of a leader's responsibilities, through this act of resignation I hope to show future leaders that a public trust does require individual trustworthiness. Now, I expect that the wheels of justice will grind on, and I will take whatever punishment is exacted of me.

Whether President Clinton leaves a legacy of eventual honesty or further sleight of-hand, the need for moral vision remains vital. Richard Hofstadter praised Woodrow Wilson; this book has painted a contrary portrait, but Wilson did write a discerning political essay in the 1890s, "Government Under the Constitution." A form of government is important, Wilson wrote, but it "has no saving efficiency of its own." Whether it lasts and succeeds depends heavily upon "the men who become governors and upon the people over whom they are put in authority." The Constitution has worked because of the "constitutional morality" of American statesmen and citizens: "We are self-restrained."

A century later Americans who do not feel God-restrained often have less self-restraint, but they still look to leaders to show them the distinction between ethical and illicit action. When shepherds take the wrong path, sheep follow. The United States desperately needs honest and discerning shepherds to lead it into the next century.

Bibliography

Under each name I have first listed the autobiographical sources consulted and then the biographical works.

GEORGE WASHINGTON

Washington, George. *Writings,* John C. Fitzpatrick, ed. Washington, DC: Government Printing Office, 1931–44.

———. *The Diaries of George Washington* (6 volumes). Charlottesville: University Press of Virginia, 1976–79.

———. *The Papers of George Washington* (Colonial Series, 6 volumes). Charlottesville: University Press of Virginia, 1983–88.

———. *The Papers of George Washington* (Revolutionary War Series, 7 volumes). Charlottesville: University Press of Virginia, 1985–97.

Anderson, Fred. *A People's Army.* Institute of Early American History and Culture at Williamsburg, VA: University of North Carolina Press, 1984.

Boller, Paul F., Jr. *George Washington & Religion.* Dallas: Southern Methodist University Press, 1963.

Buxbaum, Melvin H. *Benjamin Franklin and the Zealous Presbyterians.* University Park: Pennsylvania State University Press, 1975.

Currey, Cecil B. *Road to Revolution: Benjamin Franklin in England, 1765–1775.* Garden City, NY: Doubleday, 1968.

Davis, Burke. *The Campaign That Won America.* New York: Dial, 1970.

Ferling, John E. *The First of Men: A Life of George Washington.* Knoxville: University of Tennessee Press, 1988.

Fleming, Thomas. *1776: Year of Illusions.* New York: Norton, 1975.

Flexner, James Thomas. *George Washington: Anguish and Farewell.* Boston: Little, Brown, 1972.

———. *George Washington and the New Nation.* Boston: Little, Brown, 1969.

———. *George Washington in the American Revolution.* Boston: Little, Brown, 1967.

Fuller, Ronald. *Hell-Fire Francis.* London: Chatto & Windus, 1939.

Kaminski, John P., and Jill McCaughan, eds. *A Great and Good Man: George Washington in the Eyes of His Contemporaries.* Madison, WI: Madison House, 1989.

Kitman, Marvin. *The Making of the President, 1789.* New York: Harper & Row, 1989.

Lewis, Paul. *The Man Who Lost America: A Biography of Gentleman Johnny Burgoyne.* New York: Dial, 1973.

McDonald, Forrest. *The Presidency of George Washington.* Lawrence: University Press of Kansas, 1974.

Mackesy, Piers. *Could the British Have Won the War of Independence?* Worcester, MA: Clark University Press, 1976.

———. *The Coward of Minden: The Affair of Lord George Sackville.* London: Allen Lane, 1979.

———. *The War for America, 1775–1783.* Cambridge: Harvard University Press, 1964.

Moore, Frank, ed. *The Diary of the American Revolution.* New York: Scribner, 1860.

Nordham, George W. *George Washington's Women.* Philadelphia: Dorrance, 1977.

Phelps, Glenn A. *George Washington and American Constitutionalism.* Lawrence: University Press of Kansas, 1993.

Royster, Charles. *A Revolutionary People at War: The Continental Army and American Character, 1775–1783.* Chapel Hill: University of North Carolina Press, 1979.

Tuchman, Barbara. *The First Salute.* New York: Knopf, 1988.

Valentine, Alan. *Lord George Germain.* London: Oxford University Press, 1962.

Wood, W. J. *Battles of the Revolutionary War.* Chapel Hill, NC: Algonquin, 1990.

Zall, P. M. *George Washington Laughing.* Hamden, CT: Archon, 1989.

THOMAS JEFFERSON

Jefferson, Thomas. *The Works of Thomas Jefferson* (Federal Edition, 12 volumes). New York: Putnam's, 1904–1905.

———. *The Writings of Thomas Jefferson* (20 volumes). Washington, DC: Thomas Jefferson Memorial Association, 1904–1907.

Adams, Henry. *History of the United States of America During the Administrations of Thomas Jefferson.* New York: Scribner's, 1889.

Ambrose, Stephen E. *Undaunted Courage: Meriwether Lewis, Thomas Jefferson, and the Opening of the American West.* New York: Simon & Schuster, 1996.

Bowers, Claude B. *Jefferson and Hamilton.* Boston: Houghton Mifflin, 1925.

———. *Jefferson in Power.* Boston: Houghton Mifflin, 1936.

Brodie, Fawn. *Thomas Jefferson: An Intimate History.* New York: Norton, 1974.

Cunningham, Noble E. *The United States in 1800: Henry Adams Revisited.* Charlottesville: University Press of Virginia, 1988.

Dabney, Virginius. *The Jefferson Scandals: A Rebuttal.* New York: Dodd, Mead, 1981.

Emery, Noemie. *Alexander Hamilton.* New York: Putnam's, 1982.

Foner, Philip S., ed. *The Democratic-Republican Societies, 1790–1800.* Westport, CT: Greenwood, 1976.

Gaustad, Edwin S. *Faith of Our Fathers: Religion and the New Nation.* San Francisco: Harper & Row, 1987.

Gordon-Reed, Annette. *Thomas Jefferson and Sally Hemings: An American Controversy.* Charlottesville: University Press of Virginia, 1997.

Ketcham, Ralph. *James Madison.* New York: Macmillan, 1971.

McColley, Robert. *Slavery and Jeffersonian Virginia.* Urbana: University of Illinois Press, 1973.

Malone, Dumas. *Jefferson the President.* Boston: Little, Brown, 1970.

———. *Jefferson the Virginian.* Boston: Little, Brown, 1948.

Mapp, Alf J., Jr. *Thomas Jefferson: Passionate Pilgrim.* Lanham, MD: Madison, 1991.

O'Brien, Conor Cruise. *The Long Affair: Thomas Jefferson and the French Revolution, 1785–1800.* Chicago: University of Chicago Press, 1996.

Peterson, Merrill D. *Adams and Jefferson.* Athens: University of Georgia Press, 1976.

ANDREW JACKSON

Jackson, Andrew. *Correspondence of Andrew Jackson,* John Spencer Bassett, ed. (7 volumes). Washington, DC: Carnegie Institution, 1926–35.

Bowers, Claude G. *The Party Battles of the Jackson Period.* New York: Octagon, 1963.

Bugg, James L., Jr., ed. *Jacksonian Democracy: Myth or Reality?* New York: Holt, Rinehart and Winston, 1962.

Davis, Burke. *Old Hickory: A Life of Andrew Jackson.* New York: Dial, 1977.

Ellis, Richard, and Aaron Wildavsky. *Dilemmas of Presidential Leadership, from Washington to Lincoln.* New Brunswick, NJ: Transaction, 1989.

James, Marquis. *Andrew Jackson: Portrait of a President.* New York: Grosset & Dunlap, 1937.

Remini, Robert. *Andrew Jackson and the Course of American Freedom.* New York: Harper & Row, 1981.

Schlesinger, Arthur M., Jr. *The Age of Jackson.* Boston: Little, Brown, 1946.

Sellers, Charles, ed. *Andrew Jackson: A Profile.* New York: Hill and Wang, 1971.

Taylor, George Rogers, ed. *Jackson vs. Biddle's Bank.* Lexington, MA: Heath, 1972.

HENRY CLAY

Clay, Henry. *The Papers of Henry Clay* (11 volumes). Lexington: University Press of Kentucky, 1959–92.

Baxter, Maurice G. *Henry Clay and the American System.* Lexington: University Press of Kentucky, 1995.

Bradford, Gamaliel. *As God Made Them: Portraits of Some Nineteenth-Century Americans.* Boston: Houghton Mifflin, 1929.

Colton, Calvin. *The Last Seven Years of the Life of Henry Clay.* New York: Barnes, 1856.

Eaton, Clement. *Henry Clay and the Art of American Politics.* Boston: Little, Brown, 1957.

Mayo, Bernard. *Henry Clay.* Boston: Houghton Mifflin, 1937.

Poage, George R. *Henry Clay and the Whig Party.* Chapel Hill: University of North Carolina Press, 1936.

Remini, Robert V. *Henry Clay: Statesman for the Union.* New York: Norton, 1991.

Sargent, Epes. *Life and Public Services of Henry Clay.* Auburn, NY: Derby & Miller, 1852.

Schurz, Carl. *Henry Clay.* Boston: Houghton Mifflin, 1887.

ABRAHAM LINCOLN

Lincoln, Abraham. *The Writings of Abraham Lincoln* (National Edition, 7 volumes). New York: Lamb, 1905–1906.

————. *The Collected Works of Abraham Lincoln* (8 volumes). New Brunswick, NJ: Rutgers University Press, 1953.

Baker, Jean H. *Mary Todd Lincoln*. New York: Norton, 1987.

Brooks, Noah. *Washington in Lincoln's Time*. New York: Century, 1895.

Carpenter, Francis B. *Six Months at the White House with Abraham Lincoln*. New York: Hurd and Houghton, 1866.

Charnwood, Godfrey. *Abraham Lincoln*. New York: Holt, 1916.

Current, Richard N. *The Lincoln Nobody Knows*. New York: Hill and Wang, 1958.

Donald, David Herbert. *Lincoln*. New York: Simon & Schuster, 1995.

Herndon, William. *Herndon's Lincoln: The True Story of a Great Life*. Springfield: Herndon's Lincoln Publishing Co., 1921.

Jaffa, Harry V. *Crisis of the House Divided*. Chicago: University of Chicago Press, 1959.

Lee, Richard M. *Mr. Lincoln's City*. McLean, VA: EPM, 1981.

Morgenthau, Hans J., and David Hein. *Essays on Lincoln's Faith and Politics*. Lanham, MD: University Press of America, 1983.

Ross, Ishbel. *The President's Wife: Mary Todd Lincoln*. New York: Putnam's, 1973.

Stoddard, William. *Inside the White House in War Time*. New York: Webster, 1890.

Walsh, John Evangelist. *The Shadows Rise: Abraham Lincoln and the Ann Rutledge Legend*. Urbana: University of Illinois Press, 1993.

Walters, John Bennett. *Merchant of Terror: General Sherman and Total War*. Indianapolis: Bobbs-Merrill, 1973.

BOOKER T. WASHINGTON

Washington, Booker T. *The Booker T. Washington Papers* (13 volumes). Urbana: University of Illinois Press, 1984.

————. *Black-Belt Diamonds*. New York: Negro University Press, 1969.

————. *My Larger Education*. Garden City, NY: Doubleday, Page, 1911.

————. *The Story of My Life and Work*. Chicago: J. L. Nichols, 1900.

————. *Up from Slavery*. New York: Doubleday, Page, 1901.

Butler, John Sibley. *Entrepreneurship and Self-Help Among Black Americans*. Albany: State University of New York Press, 1991.

Johnston, Allan. *Surviving Freedom: The Black Community of Washington, 1860–1880.* New York: Garland, 1993.

Mathews, Basil. *Booker T. Washington: Educator and Interracial Interpreter.* Cambridge: Harvard University Press, 1948.

Riley, B. F. *The Life and Times of Booker T. Washington.* New York: Revell, 1916.

Scott, Emmett J., and Lyman Beecher Stowe. *Booker T. Washington: Builder of a Civilization.* Garden City, NY: Doubleday, Page, 1916.

John D. Rockefeller

Rockefeller, John D. *Random Reminiscences of Men and Events.* Garden City, NY: Doubleday, Doran, 1933.

Collier, Peter, and David Horowitz. *The Rockefellers.* New York: Holt, Rinehart and Winston, 1976.

Folsom, Burton W., Jr. *The Myth of the Robber Barons.* Herndon, VA: Young America's Foundation, 1996.

Latham, Earl, ed. *John D. Rockefeller: Robber Baron or Industrial Statesman?* Boston: Heath, 1949.

Lloyd, Henry Demarest. *Wealth Against Commonwealth.* Englewood Cliffs, NJ: Prentice-Hall, 1963.

Nevins, Allan. *John D. Rockefeller: The Heroic Age of American Enterprise.* New York: Scribner's, 1940.

Tarbell, Ida M. *The History of the Standard Oil Company.* New York: Harper & Row, 1966.

Grover Cleveland

Boyd, James P. *Men and Issues of '92.* New York: Publishers Union, 1892.

Carpenter, Frank G. *Carp's Washington.* New York: McGraw-Hill, 1960.

Goodrich, Frederick. *The Life and Public Services of Grover Cleveland.* Hartford: Scranton, 1884.

Lynch, Denis. *Grover Cleveland: A Man Four-Square.* New York: Liveright, 1932.

McElroy, Robert. *Grover Cleveland, the Man and the Statesman.* New York: Harper & Brothers, 1923.

Merrill, Horace. *Bourbon Leader: Grover Cleveland and the Democratic Party.* Boston: Little, Brown, 1957.

Parker, George. *Recollections of Grover Cleveland.* New York: Century, 1909.

Stoddard, William. *Grover Cleveland.* New York: Stokes, 1888.

Welch, Richard E., Jr. *The Presidencies of Grover Cleveland.* Lawrence: University Press of Kansas, 1988.

Williams, Jesse. *Mr. Cleveland, A Personal Impression.* New York: Dodd, Mead, 1909.

THEODORE ROOSEVELT

Roosevelt, Theodore. *The Works of Theodore Roosevelt* (National Edition, 20 volumes). New York: Scribner's, 1926.

Bishop, Joseph Bucklin. *Theodore Roosevelt and His Time, Shown in His Own Letters.* New York: Scribner's, 1926.

Cotton, Edward. *The Ideals of Theodore Roosevelt.* New York: Appleton, 1923.

Fleming, Thomas. *Around the Capital with Uncle Hank.* New York: Nutshell, 1902.

Foster, Genevieve. *Theodore Roosevelt.* New York: Scribner's, 1954.

Friedenberg, Robert V. *Theodore Roosevelt and the Rhetoric of Militant Decency.* Westport, CT: Greenwood, 1990.

Gable, John Allen. *Theodore Roosevelt: The Bull Moose Years.* Port Washington, NY: Kennikat, 1978.

Morris, Edmund. *The Rise of Theodore Roosevelt.* New York: Coward, McCann & Geoghegan, 1979.

Riis, Jacob. *Theodore Roosevelt, The Citizen.* New York: Macmillan, 1904.

Sullivan, Mark. *Our Times.* New York: Scribner's, 1926.

WOODROW WILSON

Wilson, Woodrow. *The Papers of Woodrow Wilson* (69 volumes). Princeton: Princeton University Press, 1958–93.

Blum, John Morton. *Woodrow Wilson and the Politics of Morality.* Boston: Little, Brown, 1956.

Bragdon, Henry Wilkinson. *Woodrow Wilson: The Academic Years.* Cambridge: Harvard University Press, 1967.

Dabney, R. L. *Discussions of Robert Louis Dabney.* Edinburgh: Banner of Truth Trust, 1982.

George, Alexander L., and Juliette L. George. *Woodrow Wilson and Colonel House: A Personality Study.* New York: Day, 1956.

Heckscher, August. *Woodrow Wilson.* New York: Scribner's, 1991.

Lawrence, David. *The True Story of Woodrow Wilson.* New York: Doran, 1924.

Link, Arthur S. *Woodrow Wilson and the Progressive Era, 1910–1917.* New York: Harper & Row, 1954.

Lovell, S. D. *The Presidential Election of 1916.* Carbondale: Southern Illinois University Press, 1980.

Smith, Gene. *When the Cheering Stopped.* New York: Morrow, 1964.

Thorsen, Niels Aage. *The Political Thought of Woodrow Wilson.* Princeton: Princeton University Press, 1988.

Walworth, Arthur. *Woodrow Wilson, American Prophet.* New York: Longman's, Green, 1958.

Weinstein, Edwin A. *Woodrow Wilson: A Medical and Psychological Biography.* Princeton: Princeton University Press, 1981.

Wise, Jennings C. *Woodrow Wilson, Disciple of Revolution.* New York: Paisley, 1938.

FRANKLIN ROOSEVELT

Roosevelt, Franklin. *FDR: His Personal Letters* (4 volumes). New York: Duell, Sloan and Pearce, 1947–50.

———. *The Public Papers and Addresses of Franklin D. Roosevelt* (13 volumes). New York: Russell & Russell, 1969.

Abbott, Philip. *The Exemplary Presidency.* Amherst: University of Massachusetts Press, 1990.

Best, Gary Dean. *The Critical Press and the New Deal.* Westport, CT: Praeger, 1993.

Daniels, Jonathan. *Washington Quadrille.* Garden City, NY: Doubleday, 1968.

Davis, Kenneth S. *FDR: The Beckoning of Destiny, 1882–1928.* New York: Putnam's, 1971.

Freidel, Frank. *Franklin D. Roosevelt: A Rendezvous with Destiny.* Boston: Little, Brown, 1990.

Gallagher, Hugh. *FDR's Splendid Deception.* New York: Dodd, Mead, 1985.

Goldberg, Richard. *The Making of Franklin D. Roosevelt: Triumph Over Disability.* Cambridge: Abt, 1981.

Goodwin, Doris Kearns. *No Ordinary Time.* New York: Simon & Schuster, 1994.

Lash, Joseph P. *Eleanor and Franklin.* New York: Norton, 1971.

Miller, Nathan. *FDR: An Intimate History.* Garden City, NY: Doubleday, 1983.

Rollins, Alfred B. *Franklin D. Roosevelt and the Age of Action.* New York: Dell, 1960.

Roosevelt, Elliott, and James Brough. *An Untold Story: The Roosevelts of Hyde Park.* New York: Putnam's, 1973.

Rothbard, Murray. *America's Great Depression.* Los Angeles: Nash, 1962.

Ryan, Halford R. *Franklin D. Roosevelt's Rhetorical Presidency.* New York: Greenwood, 1988.

Ward, Geoffrey. *Before the Trumpet: Young Franklin Roosevelt, 1882–1905.* New York: Harper & Row, 1985.

————. *Closest Companion: The Unknown Story of the Intimate Friendship Between Franklin Roosevelt and Margaret Suckley.* Boston: Houghton Mifflin, 1995.

————. *A First-Class Temperament: The Emergence of Franklin Roosevelt.* New York: Harper & Row, 1989.

JOHN F. KENNEDY

Kennedy, John F. *Public Papers of the Presidents of the United States, John F. Kennedy, Containing the Public Messages, Speeches, and Statements of the President, 1961–1963* (3 volumes). Washington, DC: Government Printing Office, 1962–64.

Bishop, Jim. *A Day in the Life of President Kennedy.* New York: Random House, 1964.

Blair, Joan, and Clay Blair, Jr. *The Search for JFK.* New York: Berkley, 1976.

Bradlee, Benjamin. *Conversations with Kennedy.* New York: Pocket Books, 1975.

Brogan, Hugh. *Kennedy.* London: Longman, 1996.

Burns, James MacGregor. *John Kennedy: A Political Profile.* New York: Harcourt, Brace, 1960.

Collier, Peter, and David Horowitz. *The Kennedys: An American Drama.* New York: Warner, 1984.

Fay, Paul B., Jr. *The Pleasure of His Company.* New York: Harper & Row, 1966.

Giglio, James N. *The Presidency of John F. Kennedy.* Lawrence: University Press of Kansas, 1991.

Hamilton, Nigel. *JFK: Reckless Youth.* New York: Random House, 1992.

Hersh, Seymour. *The Dark Side of Camelot.* Boston: Little, Brown, 1997.

Kelley, Kitty. *Jackie Oh!* New York: Ballantine, 1978.

Kennedy, Rose Fitzgerald. *Times to Remember.* Garden City, NY: Doubleday, 1974.

Lasky, Victor. *JFK: The Man and the Myth.* New York: Macmillan, 1963.

Martin, Ralph G. *A Hero for Our Time: An Intimate Story of the Kennedy Years.* New York: Macmillan, 1983.

Paper, Lewis J. *The Promise and the Performance: The Leadership of John F. Kennedy.* New York: Crown, 1975.

Parmet, Herbert. *Jack: The Struggles of John F. Kennedy.* New York: Dial, 1980.

Reeves, Thomas C. *A Question of Character: A Life of John F. Kennedy.* New York: Free Press, 1991.

Schlesinger, Arthur M., Jr. *A Thousand Days.* Boston: Houghton Mifflin, 1965.

Sidey, Hugh. *John F. Kennedy, President.* New York: Atheneum, 1964.

Sorensen, Theodore C. *Kennedy.* New York: Harper & Row, 1965.

Wills, Garry. *The Kennedy Imprisonment.* New York: Pocket Books, 1981.

BILL CLINTON

Barkley, Robert, ed. *Whitewater.* New York: Dow Jones, 1994.

Brummett, John. *Highwire.* New York: Hyperion, 1994.

Carpozi, George, Jr. *Clinton Confidential.* Carlsbad, CA: Dalton, 1995.

Drew, Elizabeth. *On the Edge: The Clinton Presidency.* New York: Simon & Schuster, 1994.

Greenberg, Paul. *No Surprises: Two Decades of Clinton-Watching.* Washington: Brassey's, 1996.

Maraniss, David. *First in His Class.* New York: Simon & Schuster, 1995.

Oakley, Meredith. *On the Make: The Rise of Bill Clinton.* Washington, DC: Regnery, 1994.

Smith, Stephen, ed. *Bill Clinton on Stump, State, and Stage.* Fayetteville: University of Arkansas Press, 1994.

Woodward, Bob. *The Choice.* New York: Simon & Schuster, 1996.

OTHER BOOKS ABOUT PRESIDENTS

Bailey, Thomas A. *Presidential Greatness.* New York: Irvington, 1966.

Bonnell, Joan Sutherland. *Presidential Profiles: Religion in the Life of American Presidents.* Philadelphia: Westminister, 1971.

Brennan, Ruth M. Gonchar, and Dan F. Hahn. *Listening for a President.* New York: Praeger, 1989.

Burton, David H. *The Learned Presidency.* Rutherford, NJ: Fairleigh Dickinson University Press, 1988.

Daugherty, Harry M. *The Inside Story of the Harding Tragedy.* New York: Churchill, 1932.

Dulce, Berton, and Edward J. Richter. *Religion and the Presidency.* New York: Macmillan, 1962.

Gross, Edwin K. *Vindication for Mr. Normalcy.* Buffalo: American Society for the Faithful Recording of History, 1965.

Hutcheson, Richard G., Jr. *God in the White House: How Religion Has Changed the Modern Presidency.* New York: Macmillan, 1988.

Langston, Thomas S. *With Reverence and Contempt: How Americans Think About Their Presidents.* Baltimore: Johns Hopkins University Press, 1995.

McDonald, Forrest. *The American Presidency.* Lawrence: University Press of Kansas, 1994.

Murray, Robert K., and Tim H. Blessing. *Greatness in the White House.* University Park: Pennsylvania State University Press, 1988.

Murray, Robert K. *The Harding Era.* Minneapolis: University of Minnesota Press, 1969.

Neustadt, Richard E. *Presidential Power.* New York: Wiley, 1960.

Russell, Francis. *The Shadow of Blooming Grove: Warren G. Harding and His Times.* New York: McGraw-Hill, 1968.

Smith, Craig A., and Kathy B. Smith. *The White House Speaks: Presidential Leadership as Persuasion.* Westport, CT: Praeger, 1984.

Wildavsky, Aaron, ed. *The Presidency.* Boston: Little, Brown, 1969.

Wilson, Robert A., ed. *Character Above All.* New York: Simon & Schuster, 1995.

OTHER BOOKS ABOUT WASHINGTON, D.C.

Freidel, Frank, and William Pencak, eds. *The White House: The First Two Hundred Years.* Boston: Northeastern University Press, 1994.

Furman, Bess. *White House Profile.* Indianapolis: Bobbs-Merrill, 1951.

Gilbert, Ben W. *Ten Blocks from the White House.* New York: Praeger, 1968.

Green, Constance. *Washington, Capital City, 1879–1950.* Princeton: Princeton University Press, 1963.

Hurd, Charles. *Washington Cavalcade.* New York: Dutton, 1948.

Kiplinger, W. M. *Washington Is Like That.* New York: Harper & Bros., 1942.

Lait, Jack, and Lee Mortimer. *Washington Confidential.* New York: Crown, 1951.

Shuster, Alvin, ed. *Washington: The New York Times Guide to the Nation's Capital.* Washington, DC: Luce, 1967.

Singleton, Esther. *The Story of the White House.* New York: McClure, 1907.

Smith, Marie. *Entertaining in the White House.* Washington, DC: Acropolis, 1967.

OTHER BOOKS ABOUT AMERICAN HISTORY

Ahlstrom, Sydney E. *A Religious History of the American People.* New Haven: Yale University Press, 1972.

Boorstin, Daniel J. *The Americans.* New York: Random House, 1958.

Butts, R. Freeman. *The American Tradition in Religion and Education*. Boston: Beacon, 1950.

Carson, Clarence B. *The Growth of America, 1878–1928*. Wadley, AL: American Textbook Committee, 1985.

Cobb, Sanford H. *The Rise of Religious Liberty in America*. New York: Macmillan, 1902.

Fromkin, David. *In the Time of the Americans*. New York: Knopf, 1995.

Higham, John. *The Reconstruction of American History*. New York: Harper & Row, 1962.

Kraus, Michael, and Davis D. Joyce. *The Writing of American History*. Norman: University of Oklahoma Press, 1985.

Marshall, Peter, and David Manuel. *From Sea to Shining Sea*. Old Tappan, NY: Revell, 1986.

Mulder, John M., and John F. Wilson. *Religion in American History: Interpretive Essays*. Englewood Cliffs, NJ: Prentice-Hall, 1978.

Noll, Mark A. *A History of Christianity in the United States and Canada*. Grand Rapids, MI: Eerdmans, 1992.

Smith, Elwyn A., ed. *The Religion of the Republic*. Philadelphia: Fortress, 1971.

Strout, Cushing. *The New Heavens and New Earth: Political Religion in America*. New York: Harper & Row, 1974.

Sweet, William Warren. *Religion in the Development of American Culture, 1765–1840*. New York: Scribner's, 1952.

Photo Credits

George Washington
National Portrait Gallery, Smithsonian Institution; gift of Mrs. Katie Louchheim

Thomas Jefferson
National Portrait Gallery, Smithsonian Institution

Andrew Jackson
National Portrait Gallery, Smithsonian Institution; gift of the Swedish Colonial Society through Mrs. William Hacker

Henry Clay
National Portrait Gallery, Smithsonian Institution

Abraham Lincoln
National Portrait Gallery, Smithsonian Institution

Booker Taliaferro Washington
National Portrait Gallery, Smithsonian Institution

John Davison Rockefeller
National Portrait Gallery, Smithsonian Institution; gift of John D. Rockefeller III

Stephen Grover Cleveland
National Portrait Gallery, Smithsonian Institution; gift of Francis G. Cleveland

Theodore Roosevelt
National Portrait Gallery, Smithsonian Institution

Thomas Woodrow Wilson
National Portrait Gallery, Smithsonian Institution; transfer from the
National Museum of American Art, gift of the city of New York through
the National Art Committee, 1923

Franklin Delano Roosevelt
National Portrait Gallery, Smithsonian Institution; bequest of Edward
Steichen

John Fitzgerald Kennedy
John F. Kennedy Library

Index